IKE'S IRISH LOVER
THE ECHO OF A SIGH

Kieron Wood

Published in 2016 by Kieron Wood
www.irishbarrister.com/book.html

Copyright © Kieron Wood 2016

Cover pictures:
Front cover: Dwight D Eisenhower ©Wiki Commons

Back cover: Kay Summersby (US Army) and
Mamie Eisenhower (White House)

Map (Wikimedia Commons)

ISBN: 978-1-910179-94-9

A Cataloguing in Publication (CIP) record for this book is
available from the British Library and from the Library of
Congress.

Printed by eprint Ltd, 35 Coolmine Industrial Estate,
Blanchardstown, Dublin 15, Ireland

Table of Contents

Thanks

With many thanks to members of the MacCarthy-Morrogh family (particularly Mike), Tim Rives and the staff of the Eisenhower Library in Abilene, Kansas, the research staff of all the other facilities I visited in Ireland, England and the United States, Alan Brodie of the Noel Coward Estate, Frank Fahy of Skibbereen, Mount Anville archivist Eibhlis Connaughton, Deborah Cortese, the Suffolk County Clerk, David Williams of the Malcolm Muggeridge Society, Martin Dunkley of Toll Manor, Rosemary Harden, manager of England's Fashion Museum, Paul Keane of Inish Beg Estate, everyone else who helped with the information in this book and, last but by no means least, my wife Catherine who occupied the children while I wrote.

IKE'S IRISH LOVER
THE ECHO OF A SIGH

INTRODUCTION

"I'll see you again
Whenever spring breaks through again
Time may lie heavy between
But what has been is past forgetting.
This sweet memory across the years
Will come to me.
Though my world may go awry
In my heart will ever lie
Just the echo of a sigh,
Goodbye."[1]

They were all at it.

British wartime leader Winston Churchill was well aware of what was going on. His married daughter, Sarah, was having an affair with the American ambassador to the United Kingdom, 'Gil' Winant. [2] Churchill's daughter-in-law, Pamela, was having a relationship with Averell Harriman, the European envoy of US President Franklin Delano Roosevelt and 28 years older than her.[3]

One of General Dwight D Eisenhower's closest friends, naval Commander Harry C Butcher ("Butch"), divorced his wife in 1946 and married a girl he'd met in Algiers during the war. General George Patton was said to be having an affair with his 'niece'. General Omar Bradley took not one but *two* WAC girls on holiday to the south of France.

---

[1] *I'll See You Again,* from the 1929 Noel Coward musical Bitter Sweet
[2] He shot himself in 1947
[3] Subsequently US ambassador to Moscow

1

Roosevelt (FDR) was continuing his affair with his wife's former social secretary, Lucy Page Mercer Rutherfurd. He also told his daughter Anna that he believed that Eisenhower was sleeping with his driver, Irishwoman Kay Summersby. Even King George VI of Britain's younger brother, the Duke of Kent, was at it – only he liked men *and* women!

Interviewed after the war, Wren (British women's naval officer) Fanny Hughill made the point that people found their happiness "where they could during the war", as they did not know whether they might be alive the next day. "I think people probably got very lonely," she said.[4]

Kay Summersby said in her ghost-written autobiography that, after the war, she met "dozens of men" at Washington cocktail parties who were married but had had wartime relationships, so were wary around her. So it should come as no surprise if she and Eisenhower fell in love and also had a wartime affair. Many married soldiers had affairs while they were separated by long distances and for lengthy periods from their wives. Such relationships were "off the hometown scoreboard", wrote Summersby; it was not wrong if you were thousands of miles from home and started a relationship with someone close to you.

This book is based on a true story, the love affair between General Eisenhower and Kay Summersby, from the time they met in 1942 until the end of World War Two, and what happened afterwards. The personalities and events are based on fact, though there is inevitably an element of speculation. Nobody can say for certain that Ike (as he was popularly called) and Kay were lovers, but all the evidence, during and since the war, points to the conclusion that they were having an affair.

For example, the two are said to have shared a "love nest" at a secluded property in England's East Sussex,[5] yet this house

4 2004 interview, Imperial War Museum, London
5 Eisenhower's 'love nest' goes on the market, Kent News, 12 August 2010

is not recorded by either of them in their later books. Neither is their other "love nest" in Berkshire.[6] Certainly those in the know at the time were convinced that the two were lovers. Kay is referred to as Ike's "mistress",[7] "girl friend", "hostess",[8] "shadow", "most intimate subordinate"[9] and "companion", about whom Ike was "crazy" and with whom he was having "an affair [that] could have left him open to blackmail".[10]

Chicago Tribune war correspondent Jack Thompson told Lieutenant-General 'Slim Jim' Gavin: "You didn't often see a general kissing his chauffeur."[11] In 1993, Stars and Stripes reporter Andy Rooney said: "She was a wonderfully attractive, bright, beautiful woman. I never faulted Eisenhower for whatever happened between him and Kay Summersby."

General Bradley, who was close to Eisenhower throughout the war, referred to Kay as "Ike's shadow". He wrote in his autobiography that the two were in love, and that Kay accurately portrayed their "close relationship" in her autobiography. General Patton – who, according to Red Cross captain Betty South, "teased the girls about their various love affairs" – joked that, while Ike's wife Mamie was apparently Ike's boss, "Man cannot serve two masters" – an apparent reference to Kay.

Stephen Spingarn, an adviser to President Truman, agreed in a 1967 interview: "General Eisenhower had girl friends: Kay Summersby, for example...What do you expect from human beings?"[12] Ike's chief map-maker, Armenian Technical Sgt Barkev 'Barky' Sagatelian, saw Kay "quite often" and recalled: "High-ranking officers had their own lives. Probably they had love affairs, but we didn't know about

---

6 Eisenhower 'love nest' for sale, Financial Times, 27 October 2001
7 p 11 Irish Press 27 January 1977
8 Burke's Irish Family Records, p 865
9 Holmes Alexander, Rome News-Tribune, 16 December 1976
10 p 73, Fighting Them on the Beaches
11 LA Times, 28 May 1995
12 Jerry Hess interview in Washington DC

those things."[13] Hughill, who worked with Ike and Kay at Southwick House, said in 2004: "I am sure that General Eisenhower was not the only one having some sort of relationship."[14]

Red Cross worker Mollie Ford said in 1977: "There's no denying Ike [Eisenhower] was infatuated with her. He was really crazy about her." Eisenhower's naval aide, Butch, had married Ford straight after the war after divorcing his wife of 23 years. (Butch's first wife, Ruth, shared a Washington hotel apartment with Mamie during the war.)

Butcher's book 'My Three Years with Eisenhower' makes scant mention of Kay – he refers to her just five times in more than 900 pages.[15] Her name does not appear in the index to the important book Bodyguard of Lies, despite the fact that she occupies a full two pages in one chapter.[16] Similarly, a 1946 book by Ike's orderly, Sgt Mickey McKeogh, mentions Kay only once[17] – but that in itself may be evidence that she played a greater role in Eisenhower's life than some historians would suggest.

Butcher does not refer to Kay's constant presence in Ike's life, to the torpedoing of her ship on her way to join Ike in North Africa, to her holidays with Ike in Palestine, Austria or the south of France. He does not explain why Eisenhower called his dog Telek, for example. (Kay herself maintains that the pet was named after the first part of 'Telegraph Cottage' and her initial 'K', two parts of Ike's life which he reportedly said made him "very happy".) Butcher also does not explain why Ike handed over his adored pet to Kay at the end of the war, nor why the Supreme Commander made Kay his "official aide", with her own special insignia.

[13] Los Angeles Times, 28 May 1995
[14] Imperial War Museum, London
[15] My Three Years With Eisenhower, pp 115, 123, 332, 619 and 821
[16] pp 536-537, Bodyguard of Lies
[17] Sgt Mickey and General Ike, p 37

Why did Eisenhower – a "martinet about orthography"[18] – appoint her his secretary when she could neither spell[19] nor type,[20] and had "impossible handwriting"?[21] Why was Kay – an Irishwoman – the only foreigner to be commissioned as an officer in the US Women's Army Corps, over the objections of the head of the WACs?

Nobody has explained why Kay was edited out of the official photograph taken after the signing of the German surrender in Reims. Even the photographer doesn't know. Why should 15 "publishers and editors" put up $1,000 each after the war to bug Kay's phone line in the belief that she sometimes talked to Ike and that they still met occasionally in New York?[22] Why should Kay send Ike a copy of an 'interview' with Telek in a military newspaper which included the message, allegedly from the dog: "In case you ever see anyone who can get word to Ike, tell him I miss him a lot..."?[23]

Pictures and fond personal notes and letters from Ike sold at auction in the past few years also seem to bear out Kay's claim of an affair with Ike. Yet Eisenhower's own published account of the war years, Crusade in Europe, simply said that Kay acted as "corresponding secretary and doubled as a driver".[24] He does not mention her at all in his very personal autobiography At Ease: Stories I tell to Friends.

"During the war," she said, "I was accused over and over again of being more to General Eisenhower than a member of his inner circle."[25] However, it's unlikely that anyone will

---

[18] at ease, p 95
[19] Her handwritten diaries include misspellings such as "cheif of staff", "laison" and "court marshall", and confuse "principle" with "principal", an error which Ike considered "beyond redemption"
[20] Letter from Kay to Ike's secretary 30 September 1945: "As you know, I am no typist"
[21] Letter from Kay to Ike 31 May 1948 and see diaries
[22] Butch 'personal' letter from Radio Kist, 16 October 1950
[23] May 1947
[24] p 133
[25] The Bakersfield Californian, 10 February 1974, p 65

ever know whether the widely-accepted rumours were true, as all of the main characters are now dead.

Eisenhower died after a stroke in 1969 at the age of 78. Kay Summersby (she always used the name of her first husband) died from liver cancer in New York in 1975 aged just 66. Mamie died in 1979 and Butch in 1985. The political and military leaders are all dead too – FDR in 1945, just before the end of the war, Stalin in 1953 and Churchill at the age of 90 in 1965. General Patton, a friend of Kay's, died after a relatively minor car crash in 1945. His 'niece' Jean Gordon was found dead in her gas-filled New York apartment weeks later.

Even Telegraph Cottage burned down in 1987. So now we can never be certain.

KAY

Kathleen (known as Kay) Helen Mary MacCarthy-Morrogh first saw the light of day on 23 November 1908 in Schull, West Cork.[1] Her father registered her birth in Skibbereen 23 days later.[2] Kay took great pride in her Irishness. In her application for a US immigration visa, Kay described herself as of the 'Irish race'.[3] "I was born in County Cork and am not an 'Englishwoman', as President Truman described me,"[4] said Kay in her autobiography.

One of Kay's ancestors, James Morrogh,[5] took the Mac-Carthy name when he inherited the MacCarthy lands, and the family name became MacCarthy-Morrogh.[6] Kay was the eldest in a family of three girls and a boy: Elizabeth Evelyn ('Evie'), 14 months younger, James Clement, known as Seamus (born January 1912 in Kinsale and a wartime commando)[7] and Mary Sheila (known as Sheila or 'Pick', who was born in 1915 and died of cancer in May 1948). Initially, Kay lived at Dereenatra near Schull, but by January 1912 she had moved to Ardbrack, a Georgian house about a mile outside Kinsale. In 1916, when Kay's grandfather James died, Kay's father inherited Inish Beg (a corruption of 'Little Island' in Irish). While the West Cork island had been in Kay's family since at least 1827, the house itself was completed only in 1899.

The history of Inish Beg goes back to ancient times; the remains of a cromlech were found in a nearby field and

---

[1] Group registration ID 627810, US Dept of Justice naturalisation file 7775 322
[2] Copy birth certificate, 2 October 1944
[3] 23 August 1945
[4] Kay's US immigration file of 23 November 1945 shows her "quota nationality" as "Irish (Eire)"
[5] Morrogh motto: *Virtus invicta* (Unconquered virtue)
[6] With or without the hyphen, and variously Mac or Mc
[7] Royal Engineers (British Army) 1936-1956

priests' tunnels were discovered under the house. Today the "somewhat run-down estate" on the Ilen estuary halfway between Baltimore and Skibbereen (but slightly closer to Baltimore) is a 97-acre organic farm with self-catering properties to rent. The "overgrown and neglected" estate was acquired by Paul and Georgiana Keane in September 1997 after the death of Seamus. Today, 42 acres are in pasture with cattle, sheep and ponies, 42 remain woodlands, while buildings and gardens comprise the remaining 13 acres. Surveys in the 1990s found a mixture of native and exotic trees on the island (to which the current owners have added some 20 new species), 62 types of bird and seven types of animal. From this "small but lovely emerald island", the children – accompanied by their Scotty dog, McTavish – would spend sunny summer days drifting on a raft the four miles down the estuary to the Atlantic Ocean.

Although Sheila attended Mount Anville school in Dublin as a boarder from Easter 1929 until Christmas 1930, her older and younger sisters were educated at home. (Seamus was a boarder at Stonyhurst College in England.) So Kay grew up with "a succession of governesses, hunts, riding in the fields and along the long avenue fringed with old trees". As she grew older, Kay used to play bridge in the first-floor schoolroom while the governess was away. She enjoyed tennis and après-hunt parties, sailed and shot (on one occasion taking one of her father's prized Purdey guns without asking and cracking the stock when she accidentally dropped it).

Kay's father, Donal Florence, ten years older than her mother, came from a large family. Donal's father had originally owned around 16 estates in Cork but, under the 1903 Land (Purchase) Act, many Munster tenant farmers were able to buy their farms from the landlords, leaving Donal with little more than Inish Beg, including its rambling gardens. He became "quite a noted gardener", according to Kay.

Donal had formerly served in Ashanti, West Africa, with the Nigerian Frontier Force. Later he became a major in the Royal Munster Fusiliers. (Based in Tralee in nearby Kerry, the Munsters were one of eight Irish regiments in the British Army and won three Victoria Crosses in the First World War, which began when Kay was just six years old.) Donal, then a Lieutenant-Colonel, was mentioned in dispatches for "distinguished and gallant services" during the evacuation of Gallipoli.[8] While there, he "liberated" the binnacle from the SS River Clyde, a collier used as a landing ship, and brought it back to Inish Beg.

Kay's mother, Vera Mary, née Hutchinson (known as "Kul"), was from Caernarvonshire, Wales, one of five sisters educated in convents in France and Belgium. Donal married her in 1906 in Sussex.[9] But the couple often argued, and gradually grew apart. Eventually, in 1924, Kul took Kay, 16, and Evie, 15, to London after another blazing row with Donal. The visit was ostensibly for the 'season', when girls of good breeding were introduced to the King, but they never came back. Kay's father died in May 1932, when he was 62 and she was just 23.

Kul and her two daughters moved into a flat (which was later bombed) in Warwick Court in west London.[10] The slim and pretty[11] Kay – 5 feet 9 inches tall and weighing 130 pounds, with dark brown hair and blue-grey eyes[12] – decided not to do the 'season' which most debutantes did, but instead to travel around European capitals for six months, to Helsinki, Oslo, Brussels and Paris, sometimes accompanied by her mother.

---

[8] 13 July 1916, London Gazette, p 6943 (12 days after Ike married Mamie!)
[9] Volume 2B, page 829, line 373
[10] She moved to 25 Holland Villas Road, Kensington, London W14
[11] Life magazine, 9 November 1942. The Cork Examiner described her as "tall and vivacious" (p 3, 13 June 1945) and "extremely personable and pretty" (p 5, 21 January 1977). Cork's Southern Star called her "beauteous" (3 January 1953)
[12] US Dept of Justice naturalisation file, 10 March 1950, and Alien Registration form 15 July 1944

Ike's Irish Lover

When she returned to London, Kay couldn't make up her mind what to do next. She briefly attended business college and art school, worked for a spell as a photographer, then as a stage actress in The Miracle, a play about a nun who ran away with a knight. She also worked as film extra before meeting 26-year-old publisher Gordon Thomas Summersby at a party in St James's Square in London in 1936. Gordon, who was also an accountant, boxer and skilled poker player, was a couple of years younger than Kay. They hit it off straight away, and he even taught her to drive. They married in June 1936[13] in Kensington,[14] but the marriage was "a dismal failure". At the outbreak of the Second World War, Summersby joined the Royal Artillery and then the Indian Army, in which he rose to the rank of Lieutenant-Colonel.

After Kay and Gordon separated, Kay became a model (or "mannequin") for the London branch of Worth of Paris in Hanover Square. She occupied her spare time by going to polo matches, spending long weekends with friends in Scotland and attending formal balls in the latest Worth gowns.

In September 1939, like most people in Britain, Kay was listening to the radio as British Prime Minister Neville Chamberlain declared war on Germany. The following day, Kay and Evie joined the Mechanised Transport Corps (MTC), a civilian women's uniformed organisation founded earlier that year. Although it was not officially recognised, the MTC's 1,000 vehicles and 2,000 drivers were regularly used by every British government department, senior police officers and even the Home Guard. In the House of Commons, the Secretary of State for War declined to answer a Parliamentary colleague who asked whether the cars were just used by "elderly military men who might more usefully go by omnibus or train"!

---

[13] The date of marriage is given in Kay's US naturalisation form as 24 April 1936
[14] Volume 1A, p 949 of register

MTC drivers earned no salary but received a mileage allowance for the use of their vehicles, so initially the job was open only to those who had money. As one newspaper noted at the time, only two qualifications seemed necessary for women to join the organisation: the ability to drive a car and the capacity to drape themselves in a chic manner across the bars at the Dorchester or the Ritz hotels. In the words of another commentator: "The MTC was composed of socially well connected and generally well-to-do women who volunteered their driving services, and sometimes also their very upmarket vehicles, including Bentleys and Rolls-Royces."[15] Eventually the MTC was formally recognised by the British government, and the uniformed drivers were paid £2.10.0d (£2.50) a week. Although Kay remained – strictly speaking – a civilian, she wore an MTC uniform which cost her nearly £50, a sizeable sum in those days. Like all the women drivers, Kay was obliged to carry a gasmask bag, in which she used to keep her lipstick and powder compact.

Many members of the MTC drove staff cars or ambulances during the Blitz, the sustained Axis bombing of major British cities between September 1940 and May 1941. It was a period when the British newspapers used to publish "black-out times" for various cities, and drivers had to find their way round at night by a very dim beam from the headlamps. London drivers came to know the city intimately and could almost find their way around blindfolded. This skill came in useful during the many London 'peasouper' fogs, so thick you literally couldn't see your hand in front of your face.

Kay drove an ambulance from Post No 1 in the Lambeth docks in the east end of London during the Blitz. It was exhausting work, often dangerous, and demanded a readiness to deal with death and the sometimes strange effects of bombs. "The men would bring the bodies out. Usually they were burned, all black and twisted," said Kay in

---

[15] Geoffrey Dudley, The outer cabinet. A history of the government car service (Cabinet Office, 2011)

her autobiography. "Sometimes there was no body. Just bits and pieces." At one cinema, the lights were still on and the front seats were full of people – but all of them were headless. Sometimes Kay's ambulance full of dead bombing victims was turned away because the mortuaries were already full. She used to swig whisky to get the taste of dead flesh out of her mouth. When she confided in a US colonel at a cocktail party during the summer of 1941 that she was tired of driving an ambulance, he suggested that she volunteer instead to chauffeur one of the 17 American "officer-observers".

The United States was not officially involved in the war at that time,[16] so the American soldier-advisers still wore civilian clothes, but their style was very different from that of their British counterparts. For example, at meal times British army officers would leave their drivers sitting in their cars, while the Americans invited their drivers in to eat, according to Kay's mother, "and I think the Americans got better work from theirs".[17] One of the officer-observers Kay drove was Major Dick Arnold, a married man from Florida with whom she began an affair. When his wife found out, she decided to divorce him. Kay's husband, Gordon Summersby, divorced her for adultery with Dick Arnold in June 1943 in London.[18] (He later remarried twice – writer Dylan Thomas's sister Jane and a Belgian woman – and died in the west of England at the age of 84 in October 1994.)

Colonel Arnold, as he had by then become, formally applied for permission to marry Kay on 22 March 1943. Generals Eisenhower and Patton gave him permission to marry Kay in three months' time "or at the conclusion of the Tunisian campaign" if that came later. But on 6 June 1943, while clearing mines in North Africa, he was killed.

---

[16] American President Franklin D Roosevelt had promised not to involve America in foreign wars
[17] Chicago Tribune, 20 December 1948, p 25
[18] US Dept of Justice naturalisation form, 16 January 1951

D. DWIGHT EISENHOWER

David Dwight Eisenhower (generally known as 'Ike') was born in Denison, Texas, on 14 October 1890. Although born in Texas, Ike grew up in (almost neighbouring) Kansas. Whenever Texas used to claim him as one of its own, Ike would maintain: "A chicken may hatch her eggs in the oven, but they're still not biscuits." When Ike was aged two, the family moved back to Abilene, Kansas – the Cow Capital of the World – where he later followed his father into the Belle Springs Creamery.

He was the third of six sons of David Jacob Eisenhower and Ida Elizabeth Stover. Ida called the boy Dwight to distinguish him from his father, whose name was also David. The family's German surname "Eisenhower" meant "iron hewer" or "the man who strikes iron blows".

Dwight came from a religious family, and the boys and their parents would pray every night and take it in turns to read the Bible. Ike himself insisted "Dammit, I am a religious man." He didn't see how anyone could be an atheist; he considered that a man without religion was "lost from the start", although the kind of religion he professed wasn't so important.[1] The family lived in a Mennonite part of Kansas where his mother was a member of the breakaway Mennonite River Brethren Church, and later a Jehovah's Witness.[2] During Ike's upbringing, the Mennonite virtues of "austerity in dress and humility in behaviour"[3] were encouraged. Ida – who somewhat resembled Kay[4] – had "an inflexible loyalty to her religious convictions", particularly despising adultery. She also had a "hatred of war" and

---

[1] Sgt Mickey and General Ike, p 91. Ike was baptised a Presbyterian after becoming US President
[2] Jehovah's Witnesses were particularly targeted by the Nazis because of their pacifist views
[3] Eisenhower, p 56
[4] at ease, p 305

thought Ike's decision to attend West Point was "wicked". Like all members of her Church – and like Ike's father who "never used alcohol or tobacco"[5] – Ida didn't smoke or drink. Ike, on the other hand, was a chain smoker who enjoyed a regular drink – he used to get through a case of Director's Reserve whisky every three months. His wife, Mamie, also drank, though her unsteadiness at public functions in later life was put down to an ear infection.[6]

In 1915, Ike graduated from West Point military academy[7], where his graduation yearbook described him as the "terrible Swedish-Jew". Eisenhower later claimed that the 'Swede' appellation was because of his fair hair.[8] Eisenhower was athletic – weighing 180 pounds – and quite tall, at 5'10", with fast-disappearing hair, blue eyes and a wide grin. But if his appearance was attractive, his behaviour wasn't. His disciplinary record was poor; he came 125th out of 162 graduates in his year. At West Point, "I was, in matters of discipline, far from a good cadet," he admitted.

On 1 July 1916, the day he was promoted to first lieutenant at the age of 25, he was married to Mary "Mamie" Doud at her home in Denver by a British Presbyterian minister. Mamie, who was only 19, was the second eldest of four girls, the daughters of a retired businessman who spent his winters in San Antonio in Texas, where the young infantry officer and Mamie first met.

Ten months after their marriage, the month after the entry of the United States into the First World War, on 6 April 1917, Eisenhower was promoted to captain, but he wasn't sent to Europe to fight. Instead, he was assigned to train tank crews.[9] At the time, armies still relied on horses, and the tank was a new invention. It had first been produced

---

[5] at ease, p 304
[6] But Mamie admitted in a 1973 television interview that she had been called a "dipsomaniac"
[7] 61st out of 164 in his class
[8] at ease, p 34
[9] The British used the word 'tank' to mislead the enemy

only a couple of years earlier as a self-propelled gun platform which could slowly cross shell-pitted ground and trenches, and break through enemy lines while protecting infantrymen with its armour plating. But Ike believed that, some time in the future, tanks would have "sufficient power to run cross-country at a speed of 12 miles per hour" and he prophesied that "there is not the slightest doubt that such a tank can and will be built". In an article for an army magazine, Captain Eisenhower wrote: "The clumsy, awkward and snaillike progress of the old tanks must be forgotten, and in their place we must picture this speedy, reliable and efficient engine of destruction." [10]

Ike and Mamie's first son, Doud Dwight Eisenhower, known as "Little Icky", was born 15 months after their marriage, on 24 September 1917. Ike was then promoted to major in April 1918 and subsequently to Lieutenant-Colonel. But what seemed like an idyllic life was about to turn sour.

The post-war reduction in size of the US Army meant that Ike reverted to his permanent rank of captain in June 1920. The following month, he was promoted to the permanent rank of major, at which level he remained for 16 years. But worse was to follow. Around Christmas 1920, "Little Icky" caught scarlet fever from a servant and died on 2 January 1921, at the age of three. [11] "I have never known such a blow," wrote Ike later. "Within a week he was gone. I didn't know what to do...This was the greatest disappointment and disaster in my life."

Despite the death of their firstborn, Ike made a $250 allowance claim for his son which was subsequently queried, leading to disciplinary action. He narrowly avoided being court martialled but, thanks to the intervention of his mentor, Brigadier General Fox Conner, Ike was instead put in command of the second battalion of the 24th Regiment. The unit for black soldiers had such a poor reputation that it

---

[10] Tank Discussion, Infantry Journal, Vol 27 (1920) pp 453-458
[11] Marigold, the young daughter of Winston Churchill and his wife Clemmie, also died in 1921

was known as the "infantry's Siberia".[12] (The regiment was finally disbanded in 1951.) Ike was rescued from command of the 24th by Conner, whom he joined in Panama at the start of 1922.

Ever after, Eisenhower suffered from stomach problems associated with stress, and he was hospitalised several times for stomach pains. This "strange intestinal ailment" was eventually diagnosed as a "partial blockage". In general, Ike did not enjoy very good health, and the stomach pains were only one of his regular illnesses. As well as damaging his knee at West Point, he had an appendectomy in 1923 which led to a number of episodes of abdominal pain over the years.[13] He also suffered from shingles,[14] from bursitis of the shoulder[15] and from ileitis, inflammation of the small intestine, finally undergoing an operation for the complaint.[16]

The year after their elder son's death, on 3 August 1922, the couple's second son, John Sheldon Doud Eisenhower, was born in Denver. He was to be Mamie's last child.

After a year in Paris in 1928/9 as a member of the Battle Monuments Commission (he didn't speak French), Ike was sent to the Philippines in 1935 to advise the government on development of the Filipino army.[17] He was promoted in 1936 to the permanent rank of Lieutenant-Colonel – though he still had no battle experience. Indeed he "never fired a gun in anger, seldom carried a weapon in his long military career, and was rarely within earshot of battle".[18] Back in the US at the end of his stint in the Philippines where he obtained his private pilot's licence,[19] Ike was promoted to

---

[12] Eisenhower in War and Peace
[13] Often described as "food poisoning": Chicago Tribune, 19 April 1953
[14] at ease, p 238
[15] Chicago Tribune, 19 April 1953
[16] 8 June 1956
[17] Ike used to visit "curtained bungalows" while on duty in the Philippines. (Holmes Alexander, Rome News Tribune, 16 December 1976)
[18] Eisenhower, p 4
[19] Ike first flew solo in May 1937 and his private pilot's licence, number 95, was issued on 5 July 1939

brigadier-general in September 1941. He served on the general staff in Washington and was further promoted to two-star major-general in March 1942. US Chief-of-Staff General George Marshall then sent Ike to London where General James Chaney was due to organise a cross-channel invasion in two years' time – the so-called "Second Front", to take the pressure off the Red Army. Ike met the British top brass at a "large dinner party" in the Dorchester,[20] but back in Washington on June 3, he confessed that he had an "uneasy feeling" about Chaney.

Marshall decided that Ike should take over from Chaney and, within three weeks, sent him back to London as commanding general of the European Theatre of Operations (ETO – known as the "Eisenhower Theatre of Operations"). It was just eight months since America had entered the war. One of Ike's main tasks was to establish and maintain unity between the American and British[21] (and later the French) allies, a task he managed quite successfully,[22] despite his antipathy to British officers like Montgomery.[23] The new head of the ETO considered himself "not the traditional 'hero on horseback' but more of a 'chairman of the board'".[24] Thanks to Ike's influence, many of the American officers in Britain adopted a pro-British stance. But General Patton remarked that Ike was "a neuter general, if he is not pro-British",[25] while other Americans complained that Ike was the "best general the British have".

Once again, travelling to Europe meant separation from his wife and son. During the Second World War, Mamie lived at the Wardman Park Hotel in Washington almost contin-

---

[20] Alan Brooke war diaries, 29 May 1944
[21] "[T]he British war machine was far less fractious than the American equivalent" Churchill, p 258
[22] Ike was "adept at managing Anglo-American commanders on the ground" Churchill, p 320
[23] He gave up carrying a swagger stick in case it made him look "too pro-English"
[24] Eisenhower, p 4
[25] The Patton Papers, p 253

uously. (Also living at the hotel was her close friend Ruth, the wife of naval Lieutenant-Commander Harry Butcher.) Ike's son John remained at West Point in the United States for most of the war and saw his father only briefly. This separation of Ike and his family was to be the hallmark of his married life.

LIFE IN ENGLAND

Kay was initially assigned to drive Major-General Eisenhower and Brigadier-General Mark 'Wayne' Clark for ten days in May 1942. She was annoyed that 'her' generals had only one and two stars, whereas other generals had three or four; she felt she was entitled to higher ranking officers! Kay had her hair done and got up at 5am on the day she was to meet Ike and Clark for the first time, but the generals' plane was delayed by fog at Prestwick airport in Scotland. Eventually, after three days of fog, the American party decided to travel to London by train, and Kay got up at dawn again and drove to Paddington station in London to collect them. The train was three hours late, arriving at 8.30am instead of 5.30am, and the six VIPs were then driven off in the car of US ambassador John G Winant, ignoring their waiting drivers. Kay was furious.

Later that day, she waited at lunchtime with other drivers outside the US headquarters, 20 Grosvenor Square (which later became known as 'Eisenhower Platz'). When the generals didn't appear, Kay left for lunch, returning just in time to see the last of her colleagues driving off. She ran up to her two generals, saluting and apologising for her lateness. Ike and Clark asked her to drive them just a half a mile in the khaki Packard to Claridges hotel, where the men were to share an apartment.

The extremely tall and gangly Clark was six years younger than Ike – he was born on 1 May 1896 – and was two years behind him at West Point. His mother was Romanian and Jewish, though he was baptised an Episcopalian at West Point.[1] Clark – whom some considered "one of the finest officers in the [US] army"[2] – had been wounded in France

---

[1] When Ike asked if Clark was a Jew, Patton said "at least one quarter, probably one half" (Diary)
[2] at ease, p 239

during the First World War. He was appointed commanding general of II Corps in June 1942 and made deputy commander of the European Theater of Operations (ETO) the following month. During the Second World War, Clark worked closely with Ike in England and later in Gibraltar and North Africa, before being appointed to command the Allied Fifth Army and then the Fifteenth Army Group, which captured Rome in June 1944 (just before D-Day). But Clark was accused of concentrating so much on Rome that he allowed the German 10th Army to escape, thus prolonging the war in Italy.

Ike didn't like his bedroom at Claridges.[3] It was decorated in "whorehouse pink" and his sitting room in black and gold, "like some fancy funeral parlour". After putting up with the décor for about a week, he moved to a three-room suite in the Dorchester with his naval aide, Lieutenant-Commander (later Captain) Harry Butcher ('Butch') from Iowa.

Soon after meeting her new bosses, Kay drove Clark and Ike to meet English General Bernard Montgomery (known as Monty), who immediately demanded that Ike put out his Camel cigarette. (Like Ike's mother, Monty didn't smoke or drink. He was nothing more than a "son of a bitch", Ike raged on the way back to London in the back of the car.) It was the beginning of a stormy relationship between the two men. Ike later described Montgomery as "a good man to serve under, a difficult man to serve with and an impossible man to serve over".[4] He said Monty was "unable to work as part of a team" and had "a remarkable ability to irritate".[5] General Marshall later expressed his "full dislike and antipathy" for the British soldier[6] and Kay was "caustic" about the man who "gave her boss his greatest headaches in constantly demanding priority on supplies and men, while playing an over cautious game". But the British found it

---

[3] Sgt Mickey and General Ike, p 29

[4] Eventually Ike "just stopped communicating with him" (p 152, Siegfried)

[5] War Diaries 1939-1945, p xli

[6] Alan Brooke war diaries, 1 February 1945

"most distressing" that the Americans so disliked Monty.[7] Kay told Ike that he needed the patience of an angel to deal with Monty, but Ike replied that it was worth it to "keep the team together". This was Ike's overriding concern and, as far as Kay was concerned,[8] Ike "didn't think of himself as an American, he didn't think of himself as British or French or Polish or anything. He just thought what was best for the whole Allied effort".

Another of Kay's tasks was to drive the two generals to visit US military bases in England. As every base seemed to feed the visitors sprouts or cabbage, her two passengers kept breaking wind and had to roll down the car windows all the time! But Ike showed a real interest in how the war was going in England. On one trip to Dover on the southeast coast, he quizzed Kay about women's roles in the Blitz, about female air raid wardens and even about the history of Canterbury Cathedral (which they passed). She wrote later how impressed she was that the two US officers had treated her as a human being, unlike the "dirty wisecracks, wandering hands and childish chatter" of other American officers. Ike appreciated her, on the other hand, because she was "always punctual, didn't show off and didn't talk".[9]

Eventually Ike said: "Kay I think the war can get along without us for a while. Let's take the afternoon off. And as a starter, where's a good place to have lunch?" It was the first time he'd called her "Kay". She began to fall for him when he and Clark took her to lunch at the Connaught Hotel. They had poached salmon and salad, strawberry tarts and white wine. Afterwards the three went sightseeing in Oxford and stopped for gin-and-tonics ("a real summer drink and a real English drink") at a pub in Beaconsfield, Buckinghamshire, twenty miles outside London.

When Ike returned to the US, his flight from London's Northolt to Prestwick was again delayed by fog. Kay offered

---

7 Alan Brooke war diaries, 3 June 1943
8 The World at War, episode 17 (1973)
9 Chicago Tribune, 20 December 1948

to take him sightseeing again, this time to the Guildhall and Fleet Street, crossing the City of London to the Tower, then back to Westminster. During the tour, Kay told Ike all about her ambulance driving through the unlit streets of London, and about the Blitz and wartime rationing of food and clothes. When Ike eventually flew out from Northolt, he gave Kay a "precious, priceless" box of rationed chocolates.

While Ike was away for three weeks, Kay became the personal driver of USAF Major-General Carl "Tooey" Spaatz, the head of the US air force. (The USAF was known as the 'Spaatzwaffe', a play on the German term 'Luftwaffe'.) On 24 June 1942, Spaatz ordered her to drive to Hendon Airport in north London to meet the 51-year-old Eisenhower. She resumed being his driver and accepted a box of oranges and grapefruit from him the next day at his office in Grosvenor Square flats. Fruit was rationed in England at the time, so Kay was especially appreciative.

The war news when Ike returned was not good. The fall of the Libyan city of Tobruk in North Africa had been a "staggering blow" to the Allies.[10] On 2 July 1942, British Prime Minister Winston Churchill[11] told the House of Commons that the British had lost "upwards of 50,000 men" in the "utterly unexpected" German victory.[12] The war was now unlikely to end in 1942, but was "far more likely to be a long war". Despite this pessimistic outlook, Churchill won a parliamentary vote of confidence by 472 votes to 25.[13]

On the same day, Ike had his first formal meeting with the head of the British army, General Alan Brooke, Chief of the Imperial General Staff, at dinner at the Dorchester. But Brooke did not think much of the American. "He certainly made no great impression on me," said Brooke afterwards.[14] "I had little confidence in his having the ability to handle the

---

[10] Alan Brooke war diaries notes, 21 June 1942
[11] An "ageing leviathan" and "political Methuselah" – Churchill, p 248
[12] Hansard, 2 July 1942, vol 381, cc 527-611
[13] "Good for you," responded FDR
[14] Alan Brooke war diaries notes, 2 July 1942

military situation confronting him, and he caused me great anxiety."[15]

On the other hand, the relationship between Kay and Eisenhower, 18 years her senior, quickly became very close. In a pencilled note to 'Irish',[16] Ike asked Kay: "How about lunch, tea & dinner today? If yes: Who else do you want, if any? At which time? How are you?" Eisenhower learned more personal details about Kay by dining regularly with her mother; Ike and Kul spent "many happy hours" in each other's company.

But Kay wasn't liked by everyone. Ike's wife Mamie despised her – as indeed she disliked most of the women with whom Ike was connected, including all his secretaries. One of Ike's secretaries, Sue Sarafian, said: "Mamie resented me and I can't blame her. She resented all of us when we came back because of all the rumours that had gone on about Kay. And we were connected with Kay."

In London, Ike lived a regimented life. "The Boss" arose at 7am, showered (sitting down, with a rubber tube held over his head[17]) and then worked at his office from 8am till after 6pm seven days a week, including Sunday morning conferences. Such a sustained workload was unknown to the British and French, who were more used to working normal office hours with weekends off, even in wartime. But despite having to be diplomatic in his efforts to hold the Allies together, Ike nevertheless believed in being straightforward. Churchill's minister of information, Irishman Brendan Bracken, said the American always gave an immediate 'yes' or 'no' answer to questions.

Once or twice a week, Kay would drive Ike to the British Prime Minister's London residence, 10 Downing Street, to have dinner with Churchill, and more often for conferences

[15] Alan Brooke war diaries notes, 24 November 1942
[16] Mamie referred to Ike being "highly interested in Ireland" in a letter in September 1945
[17] Life magazine, 9 November 1942

at a bomb-proof government building on the edge of nearby St James's Park. "I always held the [car] door open for him and he always said 'Thank you'," recalled Kay. She also "gingerly" helped Ike with paperwork and phone calls. But Ike could show flashes of his "violent temper", particularly if Kay was late. "Once we were 25 minutes late [when visiting troops] and he really blew his stack," said Kay. "You didn't say anything. You just said 'Yes Sir'."[18]

Ike hated lateness. He remarked that General "Black Jack" Pershing, under whom he had served for 18 months in the mid-1920s, "was always late – up to an hour or more – for every engagement".[19] Ike's insistence on timeliness could be traced back to his West Point days where being a "few seconds late for formation" was considered an offence.[20] The habit continued when he was a general, as his orderly confirmed: "He had a real horror of keeping other people waiting. He was especially determined not to keep officers in the field waiting for him, and men he was going to inspect."[21]

In order to be on time, Kay sometimes had to break the speed limit. Once she was driving too fast near the USAAF headquarters and was pulled up by a US military policeman on his motorbike. "I didn't give him a ticket. I knew better than that," said Gene Stephens. "His staff guy came around and said, 'Do you know who's in this car?' He was very cordial. There was no problem, and he went on his way."

Ike's capacity for bad temper was well known and he himself admitted that "every once in a while my bad disposition gets the best of my good nature". When he became involved in military training, he was noted for being "wickedly harsh and abrupt".[22] But Ike believed that his staff could handle his episodes of bad temper and profanity. "[M]y staff, at least,

---

[18] 1972 Thames Television interview
[19] at ease, p 209
[20] at ease, p 9
[21] Sgt Mickey and General Ike, pp 57-8
[22] Eisenhower, p 6

has always held up under these bursts with an attitude of cheerful resignation," he wrote.

Ike's indiscipline extended to formal occasions. At the US ambassador's lengthy lunch on American Independence Day 1942, he was in a receiving line for more than two and a half thousand guests. He left the line to study a report of the first American raid on German airfields in Holland. Two of the six US planes had been shot down. Ike decided to give four crewmen in one plane the Distinguished Service Cross (DSC) for destroying a German flak battery after their plane was hit.

The following month, he was invited to lunch with the exiled King Haakon of Norway. Because of the tradition about not leaving before the king, Ike didn't get away until 3.15pm. So when the American-born Lady Astor invited Ike for dinner with George Bernard Shaw a few days later, Ike excused himself on the grounds that he had other work to do. At another dinner, Ike was told off for lighting up a cigarette before the loyal toast, even though he was a chain smoker[23] to whom "cigarettes were less a habit…than an addiction". He decided that he wouldn't accept any more social invitations, partly because of his workload but also because service clubs did not allow smoking in their dining rooms.

To relax, Ike used to play bridge. In fact, he was said to be "one of the Army's outstanding experts"[24] at both bridge and poker. (His wife, Mamie, didn't play cards with him "because he would yell at her every time she misplayed".) One of the WACs (members of the US Women's Army Corps) was also a very good bridge player and Kay's youthful experience of the game came in handy. Another of Ike's "official family" who enjoyed playing bridge was Butch, "a kind of aide and company, and friend, and personal public relations officer to the Boss". (Butch was also married but began an affair with a friend of Kay's in North Africa. In 1946, Butch divorced his

---

[23] 1972 Thames TV interview
[24] Life magazine, 9 November 1942, p 124

wife of 23 years, Ruth Barton, and married his wartime lover, Mollie Ford, whom he'd met at the information desk at the Red Cross club in Algiers.)

The other members of Ike's "family" were Captain Ernest 'Tex' Lee (so called because he came from Texas) and Irish Sgt Mickey McKeogh, Ike's orderly and a bellhop at the Plaza Hotel in New York until 1941. McKeogh – an Irishman whose mother was from Leitrim and whose father was from Clare – thought Kay very friendly. "She and the general became good friends," he recalled. "I think she was relaxing to him; she didn't talk about the war, or the war's strategy; she was just a friendly person." Mickey wrote to Ike's wife, Mamie, every week telling her what Ike was doing, "though naturally he did not tell her everything".[25]

In July 1942, a fortnight after Ike's arrival in London, he was promoted to Lieutenant-General (temporary). His promotion meant he had leap-frogged over more than 200 more senior officers, even though he had still not seen action – unlike many officers who had been in World War One, which had ended less than 25 years earlier.

A couple of days after visiting General Brooke to be "put into the picture", Ike was sworn in as a three-star general. He had a celebration lunch at Claridge's on 10 July 1942, and demanded that all his guests produce signed dollar bills to prove they were "short snorters". (The signed dollar bill, or pound note in Britain, was originally given to those who'd flown the Atlantic between Europe and the United States. The note, signed by other short snorters, had to be produced on request, or a fine had to be paid. Eventually, the more successful short snorters had to paste several notes together to accommodate all the signatures.) At the lunch, Clark and two others could not produce any signed American dollar bills so Ike fined them £1 each, but admitted them to the "Order of Short Snorters". The Claridge's event was followed

---

[25] Siegfried, p 129

by a War Office dinner at the Ritz with Winant, Harriman, Clark and Brooke.

Three days later, Ike told Kay he was going to have to go to the London Clinic for a series of painful injections in his shoulder. He had been seeing an osteopath though he had not reported the complaint to the Army doctors. It was just another of the regular illnesses that plagued him. The following month, Ike's shoulder started playing up again, so he had another session with the syringe. Although bursitis was Ike's "chief ailment", Ike's doctor said he was also "susceptible to colds and stomach ailments".[26]

At Ike's first staff conference, he found the British war-weary following the fall of Tobruk. But he was determined that the Allies should remain upbeat. "Pessimism and defeatism will not be tolerated. We are going to have peace even if we have to fight for it," he said. "Pessimism never won any battle." He encouraged a spirit of optimism in his staff, communicating "some of his own gregarious and jovial"[27] personality to them.

But despite his joviality, Ike made sure that everyone knew where he stood on discipline. "When you put on a uniform, there are certain inhibitions that you accept," he said. Officers who were drunk were to be "drastically" dealt with, though Ike didn't have a problem with drink *per se*. He enjoyed the company of social drinkers like Churchill and Mountbatten, and the feeling was reciprocated. Churchill used to invite Ike to his country home, Chequers, while "Dickie", as Ike called Mountbatten,[28] often invited him to stay at his home in Hampshire or on his boat in Scotland. Generally, Ike wasn't regarded as a heavy drinker[29] though General Patton remarked in his diary: "Ike is drinking too much but is terribly lonely."[30]

---

[26] Chicago Tribune, 19 April 1953
[27] Eisenhower, p 58
[28] Diary 15 August 1944
[29] Milwaukee Journal, 25 June 1959
[30] 1 March 1944

BLACK TROOPS AND THE SECOND FRONT

Many British people had never seen a black person before US troops started to arrive in Britain in great numbers, and there was "considerable talk about the colour problem".[1]

Generally, black troops were segregated from their white counterparts.[2] Racially-integrated platoons, as featured in John Huston's 1944 documentary 'The Battle of San Pietro', didn't actually exist.[3] However, Adjutant General Major-General James Ulio told the American Red Cross on 16 July 1942 that black troops would expect to use Red Cross clubs in British cities and were to be given the same pass and leave privileges as white soldiers. A policy directive from Ike's office said this was "obviously desirable" – with the proviso that, "wherever possible, separate sleeping accommodations be provided for negro soldiers". Ike's office added: "Whenever that is not possible, negro soldiers properly on pass or furlough should be given accommodations in the Red Cross Clubs on the same basis as other soldiers." But the directive added that, to avoid "friction between white and negro soldiers, care should be taken so that men of the two races are not needlessly intermingled in the same dormitory or at the same table in dining halls".

During the war, although he, Clark and Patton employed what Ike called "darkies"[4] on their personal staffs, Ike remained opposed to racial integration.[5] At a press conference in August 1942, AJ Leibling, the New Yorker correspondent, asked Ike how he dealt with the "coloured problem". Ike said "coloured" troops were given "equality of

---

[1] My Three Years with Eisenhower 1942-1945
[2] The Germans, on the other hand, insisted "Colored people living in Germany can always go to any church they like." (AI-173-12-44)
[3] Caught In The Line Of Fire, Newsweek, 13 July 1998
[4] Letter from North Africa, 1943
[5] Patton joked in a letter about a "nigger prisoner" (26 June 1943)

treatment, with such segregation as the situation permits". He knew of only "one or two incidents" between black and white troops, including a near-riot on 1 July between "white and coloured" US sailors in Derry in Northern Ireland.

But Ike said that news about race relations, whether good or bad, should flow freely. "Don't join the book burners," he told journalists. "Do not think you are going to conceal thoughts by concealing evidence that they ever existed."

On 2 September, Ike went to a private dinner at Claridge's for the new Red Cross chief. Again there was much talk of the coloured question. Later that month, Brigadier-General Benjamin Davis, the highest-ranking black officer in the US Army, arrived in London from America at Ike's specific request. Davis, who had retired in 1941, had been recalled to act as liaison officer between white and black soldiers. Davis's recall was a foretaste of Ike's future policy on the racial issue. By January 1945, he had allowed black soldiers to join formerly segregated infantry divisions[6] and, as army chief-of-staff, he encouraged desegregation of the army.[7] Later, as US President, he was responsible for the 1957 Civil Rights Act, which established a federal Civil Rights Commission to investigate racial discrimination.

But race was not the only issue on Ike's mind. He also had to consider the Allied undertaking to invade mainland Europe to take the pressure off Soviet troops fighting on the eastern front. On Saturday 18 July 1942, Ike and Kay met General Marshall at Euston station. He had flown from the USA to discuss opening a second front on the Cherbourg Peninsula in France by October 1942. The Russians had demanded that the western Allies start an attack against the Germans in Europe, and Marshall and his party discussed the issue with Ike and with other senior Allies. But Churchill was

---

[6] But Patton had "no confidence in the inherent fighting ability of the race". (October 1944)

[7] General John CH Lee made "a fool of himself over the colored question" (Patton diary 2 March 1944) by proposing that black soldiers should fight, albeit in segregated units

furious that the Americans were discussing strategy with British officers, rather than with him. He insisted that they all meet in Downing Street the following Monday.

There the senior British officers said that they felt that the proposal to open a second front on the European mainland in 1942 was "without the slightest hope".[8] Roosevelt reluctantly accepted their view[9] and instead proposed an attack on Axis forces in North Africa, to become known as Operation Torch. On 24 July, the Combined Chiefs of Staff agreed to support the proposal. An American was to lead Operation Torch, as it was considered that the ruling Vichy French would have fewer problems with Americans than with British soldiers.

This enmity had its roots earlier in the war. Many French despised the British because French soldiers were initially excluded from the British Expeditionary Force retreat from Dunkirk and because of the French casualties the British had inflicted in the early part of the war. Almost 1,300 French sailors had been killed at Mers el Kébir in Algeria in July 1940 when the Royal Navy fired on the French fleet to prevent it falling into German hands. The British had also attacked the French destroyer Richelieu in Dakar days afterwards. More recently, 500 French civilians had been killed during a bombing raid on the Renault factory outside Paris in March 1942.

The British had also bombed the Vichy French on the island of Madagascar in May 1942. In a speech to troops defending Madagascar against the British attack,[10] Admiral François Darlan – later appointed by Ike to lead the Vichy French in North Africa – had said: "Make the British pay as dearly as possible for their highwayman's act...Never forget that the English betrayed us in Flanders, that they traitorously

---

[8] Alan Brooke war diaries, 17 July 1942
[9] Churchill told FDR as early as 22 September 1942 that he had been given the impression that the Second Front "was definitely off for 1943". (T1242/2)
[10] Order of the Day, 6 May 1942

attacked us at Mers-el-Kébir, Dakar and in Syria; that they have murdered civilians in Paris; that they have attempted to starve the women and children at Djibouti...One day, England shall pay." (Another 30,000 French civilians died as a result of subsequent Allied attacks, including 1,000 in Lyon, 1,500 in an assault on the port at Nantes in September 1943, 2,000 in Marseille and 5,000 in Le Havre.)

On the last day of July 1942, Ike met US and British commanders to discuss Operation Torch. The Allies' main objectives were to open the Mediterranean to Allied ships, to force the Germans to move troops from the Russian front and to prevent the Italian and French fleets joining forces, possibly at Casablanca or Dakar. If the Italian and Vichy navies had joined forces, Allied ships would have to be stationed off the Shannon estuary in Ireland to protect convoys to Britain.

But Operation Torch had other problems. On 1 August 1942, Ike cut short an inspection of air bases to respond to a cable from Marshall querying whether four divisions could be moved through the Straits of Gibraltar without the Germans or Spanish (who had just ended their own civil war) cutting Allied communications. Marshall also questioned why ten or 12 US divisions were now needed for Operation Torch, instead of the original seven. The questions worried Ike. Later that evening, Kay drove him "somewhere in England" to have a quiet night in the countryside, but she said he couldn't sleep.

Operation Torch was tentatively set for 7 October, Ike told General Harold Alexander, who was due to be ground commander after the landings. Ike was junior in rank to the British soldier, who had been in command of the Dunkirk evacuation and had served in Burma. "Alexander ought to be commander-in-chief instead of me," thought Ike. But the joint chiefs still considered that the overall commander should be American, and the "testy" US Admiral Ernest King suggested that Eisenhower should be given the job.[11] General Marshall confirmed Ike as C-in-C for the operation on Friday 7 August.[12]

However, there were later changes in personnel. Alexander was transferred to the Near East and replaced by General Montgomery, but Monty was subsequently ordered to take the place of Lieutenant-General 'Strafer' Gott as commander of the Eighth Army in North Africa. Gott had been killed when the Bristol Bombay transport plane in which he was returning to Cairo was shot down and strafed on the ground while he was trapped in the burning aircraft.

Secrecy about the Torch targets was paramount. On 3 September, Churchill said in a telegram to FDR that the "Free French have got inkling and are leaky".[13] Ike believed that the enemy should be fooled into thinking that the Allies were going to attack elsewhere, rather than North Africa. United Press reported that the Allies were going to invade Norway, while Torch troops were told their tropical kit was for Suez or the Persian Gulf.[14] Other embarking troops were told they were going to Australia and that is why they had to wear tropical kit. A US invasion of the Greek Dodecanese Islands was also part of the deception plan. Other news reports guessed that the Allied operation would take place in southern Russia or the Middle East, though most suggested Dakar in French West Africa, partly because the landing of black troops in Liberia in June 1942 helped focus attention on West Africa.

Kay left a guide to Finland prominently on her desk. Butch kept heavy shoes in his office, suitable for Arctic wear, and correspondents who dropped into the office while Butch was packing on 9 October couldn't help seeing a large map of

---

[11] at ease, p 252
[12] Roosevelt said in a "most secret" telegram to Churchill on 6 August that the US Chiefs of Staff had accepted the British proposal (CHAR 20/78/132)
[13] T1173/2
[14] p83, Bodyguard of Lies

Norway on his wall. Japanese and German sources told the Vichy government that the US planned to start military operations soon against Dakar, Casablanca or both, and captured Axis spies who became double agents speculated to the Germans that Operation Torch was to take place in northern France or Norway.

ALLIED UNITY

American forces in North Africa were to be commanded by General George ("Georgie") 'Blood and Guts' Patton, who had joined Ike and Kay for supper on Sunday 9 August. Kay noted that Patton's neatly-pressed uniform sported more ribbons than anyone on the Imperial General Staff, and it was complemented by "blindingly polished cavalry boots and tailored jodhpurs". The tanned[1] general had an "unending string of anecdotes", privately referring to Eisenhower (DD) as "Divine Destiny".[2] He regaled Kay with stories about his string of polo ponies in the US, and he assured her that his revolver handles were made of ivory "from an elephant", not from mother-of-pearl (which he insisted would only be used by "a New Orleans pimp").

Before dinner, Kay drove Patton on what she called the "64-dollar tour" of London. Many of the English capital's buildings had been destroyed in the Blitz, including the block of apartments where Kul lived. (Kay later went to have "breakfast at my mother's house and it was not there". After the bombing, the house was just a pile of rubble. Kul's mother "managed to fry sausages on the stove in the old house, and the air raid warden and the mail man each reached into the rubble to take a serving".[3])

On the tour, Patton sat bolt upright beside Kay and twisted his snake ring on his finger as she drove past the sights of the damaged city, but when he saw the destruction caused by the Axis bombs, he lost his temper and swore in his "high-pitched womanish squeak". (Patton's high voice was one of his notable characteristics. "It always surprised you. It was as if you were driving along and heard something behind you go 'Peep! Peep!' and turned around thinking

---

[1] Artificially, with the aid of a sun lamp
[2] Sometimes "Devine Destiny". (Letter to his wife, 16 July 1943)
[3] Chicago Tribune, 20 December 1948, p 25

maybe it was somebody on a bicycle and found that what was behind you was a Greyhound bus or a Mack truck," recalled Ike's orderly.[4])

At dinner later with Kay and Ike, Patton, who was also senior to Ike, insisted that he could exercise "mass hypnotism" on troops and "spur any outfit to a high state of morale" within a week. He claimed to have a sixth sense which helped him to guess the intentions of the enemy better than his intelligence staff.[5] He said he would put this talent to good use in Casablanca where he would give the governor a 30-minute ultimatum. Patton said that he would either "accept his surrender and give him all honours of war and parole his troops, or that I will bombard him from the sea, bomb him from the air and attack him on the ground". (When he eventually got to Casablanca, Patton told the Vichy French governor that, unless the city surrendered within ten minutes, he would order the Allied Navy to "shoot the hell out of 'em". Patton "loved to shock people" with his "famed expletives which he employed with startling originality".[6] At social gatherings, he would use "outrageous profanity...if no one paid any attention, he would quiet down".[7])

One of the topics discussed at dinner was the growing anti-British sentiment in the US.[8] One of Ike's main tasks was to preserve the unity of Allied forces, particularly the Americans and British – and later also the French. He was recognised as having a "genius for managing intractable Allies and for making himself agreeable to all he met".[9] This talent was recognised by the chief of Britain's Imperial

---

[4] Sgt Mickey and General Ike, p 54

[5] Ike later rated Patton "energetic, courageous, well-informed, impulsive; definitely a leader type"

[6] Life magazine, 9 April 1951, The War America Fought by General Omar N Bradley

[7] at ease, p 269

[8] At this stage, Ike thought "every American view was right, every British idea wrong". (The Times of India, 12 December 1948)

[9] War Diaries, p xlviii

General Staff, General Alan Brooke, who wrote in his diaries that Ike was "an able political general with a genius for managing intractable Allies and for making himself agreeable to all he met".[10]

Traditionally America had held itself aloof from any involvement in foreign affairs which they felt did not concern them. Many Americans were against involvement in a European war, and President Roosevelt had promised: "I assure you again and again and again that no American boys will be sacrificed on foreign battlefields."[11] But now that the Americans were committed following the attack on Pearl Harbour, Ike felt that the Allies should stick together. He knew that RAF crews were "practically wet-nursing" American aircrews over France – even though US pilots had damaged 19 Spitfires on the ground while taxiing. But the antagonism between the two main Allies – Britain and the United States – remained.

German propaganda played on these divisions throughout the war. An Axis leaflet aimed at British troops in Italy in 1944 said: "The slogan 'Americans first' applies also to the American soldiers in England. 70 per cent of all American soldiers who came across to Europe are still hanging about at the training camps in England. And while their pals in Italy prefer to stay at the quiet sectors and manage to get withdrawn from the front before offensive operations are started, the Americans in England are proving by all means to be 'quick workers'."[12]

One leaflet showing a US sergeant and a woman getting dressed said: "While you are away, the Yanks are 'lease-lending' your women. Their pockets full of cash and no work to do, the boys from overseas are having the time of their lives in Merry Old England."[13] "England is the cause of all

---

[10] War Diaries 1939-1945 p xlviii
[11] German propaganda leaflet, 31 October 1940
[12] LWP 124 4-44
[13] AI-046-8-44

the trouble," said another German leaflet allegedly from the 'Soldiers Friend Society Inc. Brooklyn'.

The common language helped keep the two main western Allies together, but the different methods of command were causing problems. In the American army, for example, officers were told "what to do, not how to do it". The British, on the other hand, expected that officers should follow detailed orders. At this stage of the war, when the Americans had just joined the struggle, the British War Office was still following the World War I tradition of giving direct orders to generals. But Ike objected to the War Office communicating directly with generals under his command[14] as he felt this undermined the authority of the Combined Chiefs of Staff. He suggested that, if British troops felt they were being put in danger by an order of the Allied commander, their commanding officer should first speak to that commander (who happened to be Ike). Only if the CO wasn't happy with the response should he appeal to the War Office.[15]

In an effort to ensure Allied unity, Ike asked General Clark to develop an Allied staff with all nationalities working side by side. "Where a section was headed by a Briton, his deputy was an American. And where an American bossed the operation, a Briton filled in as his Number Two man," said Bradley.[16] But Ike still didn't fully understand the habits, mannerisms or modes of speech of the British. Ike would ask English officers how they accounted for their pronunciation of "gas mahsk" (with first the short and then the long 'a'), and would say: "Someday I'll take time off and teach you English English."

---

[14] Ike was unhappy when King George VI sent a message direct to Monty (Alan Brooke war diaries, 29 March 1943)

[15] Patton said: "My boisterous method of command would not work with the British no matter how successful with Americans, while [General Alexander's] cold method would never work with Americans." (Diary 22 June 1943)

[16] Life magazine, 9 April 1951, p 84

Ike's Irish Lover

Initially Ike was opposed to US officers using English expressions, and anyone who used a phrase like "Cheerio" or "I say" had to pay a one penny fine. But even Ike was affected. He used to refer to gasoline as "petrol", anti-aircraft fire as "flak" and lunch as "tiffin"[17] – and he even took to wearing suede shoes.[18]

---

[17] "I truly fear that London has conquered Abilene," said Patton in a letter to his wife
[18] "A la British". (Patton diary, 12 July 1943)

OPERATION TORCH
AND THE DIEPPE RAID

Operation Torch was to involve the "greatest armada of all time", with up to 400 naval transports and 200 warships to be used in the invasion of Vichy-controlled North Africa. The navy would also have to protect the harbours at Casablanca and Oran, and maintain supply lines from Britain and the US. Ike believed that the naval authorities should be in charge of troop movements from embarkation to landing in North Africa, including the embarkation of three tank landing craft in Gibraltar and moving anti-aircraft units from the United States.

The British believed that the seizure of Tunisia could also disrupt the supply lines of Rommel, who would eventually be defeated by Monty's Eighth Army at the second battle of El Alamein in October/November 1942. After the initial landings, the first priority was to be the capture of aerodromes. Patton was initially supposed to secure a beachhead at Oran and then take an aerodrome, supported by the US Air Force. The USAF would be backed by two aircraft carriers with 88 fighters and 38 torpedo planes, and possibly a third carrier with 13 aircraft, but would not support the initial British landings. Total Allied carrier-based fighters were estimated at 166. The Vichy French had about 500 planes in Africa; although the land-based fighters were old, they were still faster than the Allies' carrier-based planes.

One officer who had previously been in North Africa recommended launching the attack on a Sunday morning because he said many of the French left their posts on Saturday afternoon and didn't return until late on Sunday. Patton also recalled that Moslems were not allowed to take part in fighting during the eleventh and twelfth months of the Moslem calendar, which began on November 10 in 1942, so suggested that might be the time to strike. But the Allies were careful to avoid profaning sacred Muslim cities, such as Rabat.

The British Foreign Office expected the Vichy authorities to order the French in North Africa to fight, and Ike felt that, if that happened, the forces proposed for Torch were "not sufficiently powerful". The success of the operation depended on the absence of opposition by the "Vichy gang" in North Africa, as Ike called them.[1] Although the Vichy French had only 14 poorly-equipped divisions in North Africa, if they did oppose the landings – as they had done in Madagascar in the six-month campaign there – the Axis forces would have time to move reinforcements to Tunisia before the Allies had seized their main objectives.

After the first airfields had been secured in North Africa, at least 30 Allied fighters a day had to be sent from Gibraltar, though Spanish attacks or bad weather could reduce that number. Gibraltar – less than 25 miles away from Africa at its closest point – was an important staging post for Torch because the wartime shortage of petrol made it impractical to shuttle equipment and men between Britain and North Africa. The British were also concerned at the vulnerability of the airfield in Gibraltar, which was due to play a major role in Operation Torch. The Rock was in range of Spanish artillery, and Spain could fire on Allied aircraft from the frontier. If, as a result of Torch, Spain entered the war against the Allies,[2] both the naval base and the airfield at Gibraltar would be put out of commission at once. The Germans might also transfer some of their air forces to Spain to be nearer to North Africa. The Allies would also have to create a special force to invade Spanish Morocco in northern Africa and the Canary Islands in the Atlantic.

However, the Allies planned to inform the Spanish author-ities that Torch was not meant to threaten Spanish interests

---

[1] Message S-51959 to General Marshall, 16 May 1944
[2] Churchill predicted that "Spain will not go to war with Britain and the United States on account of Torch" (Telegram to FDR, 26 August 1942 CHAR 20/79A/62-64)

in North Africa nor to undermine trade agreements between Spain and the US or Britain. Although Ike "thoroughly disliked" dealing with General Francisco Franco because of the Caudillo's support for the Italian and German leaders, Benito Mussolini and Adolf Hitler, he believed that Spain should be given a chance to recover from its recent civil war and take its place in the "reconstructed Europe of the future".

On 13 August, while planning Operation Torch, Ike received bad news. The converted aircraft carrier Eagle, earmarked for the North African invasion, had been torpedoed and sunk by a U-boat, and two more Italian and two German divisions had reached Rommel in North Africa. "I'm getting damned tired of looking at these four walls," snarled Ike, and decided to go out with Kay for a drive.

(Kay didn't only drive Ike. When Patton occasionally got a car, she would drive him too. Because Patton believed that Kay's father was a Lieutenant-General – which he wasn't – it was "quite embarresing (sic) to have her get out and hold the door open for me", he told his wife.[3])

In the run-up to Torch, Clark accepted an invitation for Ike, himself and two others to stay at the Governor's House in Gibraltar, even if – according to Gibraltar governor Sir Noel Mason-MacFarlane[4] – any unusual activity on the Rock was known to Berlin within 24 hours.

Ike was officially confirmed as Commander-in-Chief of the Allied Expeditionary Force on Friday 14 August. He celebrated with Clark at dinner that night. But it looked like the Americans might recommend that Torch be scrapped. On 15 August, General Marshall confirmed that US Army officials thought that the proposed operation had less than a fifty-fifty chance of success. "The chances of capturing Tunis before Axis reinforcements arrive look considerably less than fifty per cent," he told Ike. For now, however, planning

---

[3] Letter to Beatrice, 11 August 1942
[4] "An old fart in shorts with skinny red legs," according to Patton

went ahead with the combined British and American staff in Norfolk House. Ike believed that, in preparing for battle, "plans are useless, but planning is indispensable". He pointed out that sending nine American and four British divisions to North Africa would cause a delay of at least six months in the preparation for Operation Roundup, then the name for the invasion of mainland Europe planned for 1943.

The American and British navies said they could not simultaneously attack targets in the Mediterranean and Casablanca (code-named 'Dunkirk' by the British Chiefs of Staff at the Prime Minister's request) and decided that Patton's force should land from the Mediterranean and proceed to take Casablanca overland. But on 3 September, the US Joint Chiefs changed their mind again. This time they suggested that, as well as simultaneous landings in Casablanca and Oran, they should also attack Algiers, which Clark thought would be the best place for headquarters. The British were also keen on including Algiers in the landings.

Churchill was anxious to get the expedition under way, believing that Roosevelt would approve his joint chiefs' compromise.[5] But the date of Operation Torch was still uncertain.[6] President Roosevelt (FDR) insisted that the operation should go ahead before 30 October. The Americans suggested 1 October for the start of the operation, but the British said they preferred an even earlier date, 10 September, mainly because of the favourable moon. They also thought that heavy Atlantic swells would make landings more difficult in the late autumn. There was disagreement about the details of Operation Torch, even among the Americans themselves. President Roosevelt wanted Torch to be entirely American, apart from supporting British naval fire and possibly some air cover, because of the difficulties

---

[5] The operation was to be "a springboard, not a sofa" (Churchill to Chiefs of Staff, 18 November 1942)

[6] Churchill suggested in a telegram to FDR that "the only way to put this job through is to fix a date for the party and make everything conform to that". He suggested 14 October (26 August 1942, T1132/2)

between the British and French. In the meantime, Ike said that the British Chiefs' subsequent proposal that the attack on Casablanca should be abandoned and Philippeville and Bône assaulted, so that the French would experience an overwhelming show of strength, left him "in a hell of a pickle". The British and the Americans finally reached agreement at the start of September 1942.[7]

But secrecy was always uppermost in Ike's mind – especially as his headquarters had the reputation of being "conspicuously leaky as regards information and secrets".[8] "Each day that passes is a day of additional risk with regard to secrecy," he said, "and secrecy is vital to success." The British secret service, MI5, had already recorded a conversation between a British admiral and a confidant of the Duke of Windsor which outlined the details of Operation Torch. When a page of the Torch planning diary disappeared on 7 September, Ike was particularly concerned but decided to tell nobody outside the office. In a letter to his wife about a secret conference, written eight days later, Ike said: "The problem is to have 11 men meet clandestinely that no one even knows they've met! Isn't that something? Think I'll wear a false mustache and dark glasses. Possibly a wig would be more effective!"

On 19 September, the War Department intercepted a message in plain language from a United Press news editor in London to Washington, claiming that American forces would be attacking Casablanca, not Dakar. The heads of UP, Associated Press and the International News Service were called in and agreed not to distribute similar speculative stories from England. American censors were instructed not to approve any cable which could focus attention on any named target. Later that month, a letter written by General Clark to the governor of Gibraltar giving details of Operation Torch – which was then to start on November 4 – was found

---

[7] FDR telegraphed Churchill "Hurrah", to which Churchill responded: "Okay full blast" (CHAR 20/79B/137 and CHAR 20/79B/139)
[8] Alan Brooke war diary notes, 22 October 1942

on the body of a British naval officer washed ashore in Cadiz after his Catalina flying boat crashed between Gibraltar and Lisbon. The envelope was sent to Madrid by the local Spanish authorities, but ultimately reached the British unopened.

A breach of secrecy could even affect a person's military career. Colonel Kent Lambert, formerly Patton's operations officer, in a letter to his wife on 16 November 1942 – eight days after Torch had been launched – gave details of the entire North African landing operation and the positions of the Western Task Force. In May the following year, General Marshall turned down Eisenhower's proposal to promote Lambert and said his breach of secrecy did "not indicate a level-headed individual or a disciplined soldier. Discretion and judgment are glaringly lacking". Eisenhower agreed to withdraw his recommendation because of Lambert's "continuing disregard for instructions", even though Lambert had a "brilliant battle record."

As well as the work on Operation Torch, Ike also insisted on military formality and discipline in Britain. He outfitted the US MPs (Military Police) there with white helmet liners, gloves, belts and leggings (which led to them being nicknamed "Snowballs"). On the night of 18 August, Kay drove Ike through London's West End with his three general's stars on the wings of his car and an American flag on the radiator cap. But passing a group of officers outside the officers' mess in Audley Street, only one of them saluted – and he was British! Ike was furious and said that, if there was any more laxity in saluting, he would take the name of the offender and his unit, and would hold the commander responsible.

Meanwhile, the first assault on mainland Europe since Dunkirk took place on 19 August 1942. Four days after Churchill's return from his first meeting with Stalin, 6,000 Canadian troops raided the Channel port of Dieppe in

Operation Sledgehammer[9] – but ran into a German convoy on the French coast.

The operation was a disaster. Lord Louis Mountbatten told Ike that 2,000 troops were lost or captured, but actually 3,623 of the 6,086 men who made it ashore were killed, wounded or captured.[10] The RAF had committed 68 fighter and bomber squadrons to the raid, giving it a superiority of more than three to one over the Luftwaffe. After the raid, Mountbatten's headquarters claimed that more than 100 enemy planes were destroyed or probably destroyed, and 92 damaged. A Combined Ops HQ statement, a little more realistically, said: "From reports so far received, 82 enemy aircraft are known to have been destroyed." But in fact the Luftwaffe lost 48 aircraft while the Allies lost more than twice as many – 106, the biggest single-day Allied air loss in the war.

New York newspapers headlined: 'US and British Invade France!', 'Tanks and US Troops Smash at French Coast!' and 'US Troops Land with Commandos in Biggest Raid!' But the US papers were exaggerating American involvement. Only 50 American Rangers took part – and more than a quarter of those ended up missing or dead. US Brigadier-General Lucien Truscott, founder of the 1st Ranger Battalion, picked up some of the survivors from a destroyer.

Initially, the British newspapers carried headlines like "Big Hun losses in 9 hour Dieppe battle"[11] while the "Nazi version" of the raid said that more than 1,500 prisoners had been taken, including 60 Canadian officers, 83 Allied planes had been shot down and 28 tanks destroyed. That turned out to be more accurate than the Allied version.

---

[9] Ike was the author of Operation Sledgehammer (p 73, Bodyguard of Lies)
[10] Bodyguard of Lies claims that more than two thirds of the Canadian troops at Dieppe were killed, wounded or captured and the RAF lost 106 planes, compared to the Luftwaffe's 46
[11] Daily Mirror, 20 August 1942

During the landings, a Canadian brigadier took ashore a copy of the operational order, directly disobeying orders. The document, which was subsequently found on the beach by the Germans, included an instruction to "bind prisoners". Bodies of shot German prisoners with their hands tied were found after the raid. This resulted in the Germans threatening to shackle Canadian prisoners in future. And it got worse. Six weeks later, on the night of 3-4 October 1942, ten British Commandoes raided the Channel Island of Sark, which had been occupied by the Germans since June 1940. They took five prisoners whose thumbs were tied behind their backs. Three of the prisoners were later shot dead and one was stabbed to death. The fifth was taken back to England.

This action resulted in the *Füehrer Befehl*, under which captured Commandos – even those in uniform – were to be summarily executed, rather than treated as prisoners-of-war. Adolf Hitler's order said:

"1. For a long time now, our opponents have been employing in their conduct of the war, methods which contravene the International Convention of Geneva. The members of the so-called Commandos behave in a particularly brutal and underhanded manner; and it has been established that those units recruit criminals not only from their own country but even former convicts set free in enemy territories.

"From captured orders it emerges that they are instructed not only to tie up prisoners, but also to kill out-of-hand unarmed captives who they think might prove an encumbrance to them, or hinder them in successfully carrying out their aims. Orders have indeed been found in which the killing of prisoners has positively been demanded of them.

"2. In this connection it has already been notified in an Appendix to Army Orders of 7.10.1942 that in future, Germany will adopt the same methods against these sabotage units of the British and their Allies; i.e. that, whenever they appear, they shall be ruthlessly destroyed by the German troops.

"3. I order, therefore:- From now on all men operating against German troops in so-called Commando raids in Europe or in Africa, are to be annihilated to the last man. This is to be carried out whether they be soldiers in uniform, or saboteurs, with or without arms; and whether fighting or seeking to escape; and it is equally immaterial whether they come into action from ships and aircraft, or whether they land by parachute.

"Even if these individuals on discovery make obvious their intention of giving themselves up as prisoners, no pardon is on any account to be given. On this matter a report is to be made on each case to headquarters for the information of higher command...

"5. This order does not apply to the treatment of those enemy soldiers who are taken prisoner or give themselves up in open battle, in the course of normal operations, large-scale attacks or in major assault landings or airborne operations. Neither does it apply to those who fall into our hands after a sea fight, nor to those enemy soldiers who, after air battle, seek to save their lives by parachute."[12]

This policy of treating Allied prisoners-of-war in the same way as German prisoners were treated also applied in North Africa. When the Allies ordered that German prisoners should not be given any food or drink before being interrogated, the Germans did the same.[13]

Ike declined to give medals to American soldiers who survived Dieppe until the Canadian, British and French troops had been decorated. "The tail shouldn't wag the dog," he said. But the real reason, as Ike later admitted to Kay, was that the raid had been "a fiasco".

---

[12] The 'Commando Order', 18 October 1942
[13] Rommel, The Desert Fox, pp 163/4

TELEGRAPH COTTAGE

Because of the danger of bombing raids in London, and for security reasons, Ike and his "family" moved to a secluded cottage in Warren Road, Kingston-upon-Thames, on the outskirts of London. Telegraph Cottage was set behind a high wooden fence in ten acres of woodland, between Coombe Hill and Little Coombe golf courses. The slate-roofed cottage, which Ike codenamed 'Da-de-da', was half an hour's drive from Grosvenor Square but just minutes from the USAAF headquarters at Bushy Park. Initially Ike and the "family" used the cottage only at weekends but, by the end of the summer of 1942, Ike was living there most of the time.

Unfortunately the retreat was also half a mile from a British decoy for enemy aircraft which burst into flame when enemy bombers came within six miles. As a result, aerial attacks on industrial and military targets were frequently diverted to relatively unpopulated areas near the cottage. But generally the cottage was so peaceful the occupants would never know there was a war on if it weren't for the occasional Spitfire practising dogfights overhead or bomb craters on the golf course. Peaceful or not, Churchill nevertheless ordered that a bomb shelter be built in the cottage grounds.

The house had five small bedrooms and one bathroom, plus a small fireplace in the living room. The rent was about $32 a week, but the owner paid for the maintenance of the garden, including a vegetable garden; all Ike had to supply was bed linen and food. Mickey McKeogh, Ike's orderly, ran the house, patrolled the grounds and made sure there was chewing gum, sweets and his reading glasses on Ike's bed-side table – as well as the essential cigarettes. Two "coloured boys" kept house, Private Johnny Hunt of Petersburg, Virginia, the cook, and Corporal (later Master Sergeant) John Moaney of Easton, Maryland, the houseboy and 'handy-andy'. Moaney (and later his wife) stayed with Ike for many years, and he was eventually a pallbearer at Ike's funeral in 1969. (Clark also had a black orderly, Sergeant William Chaney, as did Patton, Sergeant William Meeks, who was one of the pallbearers at *his* funeral.)

Spare sets of shaving equipment, pyjamas and clean clothes were kept in the cottage by Sgt Moaney, who helped guests get settled in. "Of course, it would depend on who it was; some people come, they didn't want no help, but some did." Kay moved from her flat in Kensington Close, which she had shared with five WACs, to a billet in Bushy Park, but spent a lot of her time at the nearby cottage. Ike's secretary Sue Sarafian said later: "In front of us, the general was very official with her, but we do know that she had dinner – ate at his table a lot, played bridge a lot, rode horses with him."

Ike was "devoted" to riding and shooting. He gave Kay a small Beretta pistol to practise her pistol shooting. (He'd given Mamie a .45, which she promptly hid.) "I'd prefer to see you dead than a prisoner of the Germans," Ike told Kay. Members of the "family" spent their leisure hours practising on the piano, playing badminton and American football, sketching or golfing for "a bob (shilling) a hole".

Initially, Ike would stay at the cottage at weekends and occasionally during the week. He would get up between 6am and 7am and enjoy an unrationed breakfast of orange juice, fried egg and bacon, toast and pineapple jam and black coffee. "He does not like to talk at the breakfast table," recalled Kay.[1] Ike only displayed his bad temper when the coffee was cold – and that was usually his own fault, she said.[2]

For lunch, Ike might make himself vegetable soup (with his special ingredient, nasturtium stems) or potato salad. For dinner, he enjoyed baked beans, pies, rare steak, lemon curd, artichokes and fried onions – but never parsnips, which he detested. At the cottage, Ike could relax in front of the fire in his old brown woolly cardigan, his suede and

---

[1] Milwaukee Sentinel, 26 September 1948, p 18
[2] St Petersburg Times, 13 November 1948, p 16

leather jacket and a shabby old pair of straw slippers from the Philippines, sipping Scotch and water and snacking on salted peanuts. Sometimes he'd show off his athletic prowess by standing stiffly erect then slowly falling forward, breaking his fall at the last instant. Most nights, he'd play bridge with Kay, Butch or Clark for 3d per 100 points. If Ike lost, he sometimes couldn't pay the winners as his pay cheque went straight to Mamie. He loved to sit in front of an open fire and just look into it – and it was also handy to throw his cigarette butts into.

On 25 August 1942, Ike received more disturbing news. King George VI's younger brother, the Duke of Kent, aged 39, was one of 15 crew killed when their Sunderland flying boat crashed into a hill in Scotland en route to Iceland. The Duke – or Prince George – had assumed the rank of RAF Air Commodore for the duration of the war. A briefcase handcuffed to his wrist was full of Swedish 100-kroner notes, worth nothing in Iceland but worth a king's ransom in Sweden. The Duke had had an interesting life. A married man with three children, he was also said to have had affairs with Noel Coward, spy Anthony Blunt and singer Jessie Matthews. He was also reported to have been addicted to morphine and cocaine.

But Ike was still concentrating on Operation Torch. During dinner at Telegraph Cottage in early October 1942, Clark said he was sure that the Germans already knew about Torch and the only question was what they were going to do about it. Young French people in North Africa were on the Allies' side, no matter what happened, he insisted. To help Ike coordinate all the elements of the operation, he appointed General Walter Bedell 'Beetle' Smith his Chief-of-Staff in September 1942. Smith, five years younger than Ike, was a Catholic with a reputation as a brusque, no-nonsense officer. He was said to have a "salty vocabulary" and "the charm of a rattlesnake", but Ike found him indispensable.[3] "In contrast

---

[3] In a telegram to Churchill, Ike referred to Smith as "Bulldog" (CHAR 20/83/96)

to the suave and amiable Eisenhower, Smith could be blunt and curt," wrote his colleague General Omar Bradley.[4] Despite his brusqueness, Beetle could be relied on to handle the more sensitive issues.[5] He negotiated the armistice with Italy and, as chief-of-staff at SHAEF in 1944 and 1945, he also organised food and fuel aid for starving Dutch civilians under German occupation. He also signed the German surrender at Reims on behalf of Eisenhower. After World War II, he served as the US ambassador to the Soviet Union until 1948, before becoming the head of the Central Intelligence Agency.

When Smith arrived in London, he expressed the view that, militarily, Operation Torch would be "a pushover", with FDR handling the political angles with the French. Ike suggested going immediately to Telegraph Cottage to discuss the operation. The next morning, 8 September, Beetle was woken at 4am by a pheasant. He left the cottage and wandered through the pine trees and rhododendron bushes, arriving back at 7am, just in time for coffee. Later that day, Beetle lunched with Ike at the cottage, played handball for five minutes and then spent the rest of the day discussing the supplies needed for Operation Torch.

Beetle said that Patton's force alone would need 5,000 tons of .45-calibre ammunition. Ike said he also wanted $500,000-worth of tea, sugar and white cotton cloth to pay native labourers employed on the construction of airfields, for example. (The Arabs used the white cloths to bury their dead.) Ike also wanted medals for soldiers involved in Operation Torch: ten Medals of Honor, 25 DSCs and DSMs, 50 DFCs, 100 Soldiers' Medals and Silver Stars and 250 Purple Hearts for wounded soldiers.

The two men also discussed the vexed question of how to feed prisoners-of-war. Ike proposed to ask the War Department if he could ship all Axis European prisoners

---

[4] Life magazine, 9 April 1951, The War America Fought
[5] In April 1943, he was almost interned when his aircraft crash-landed in neutral Ireland

(mostly Italians and Germans) directly to the US where they would be held until after the war. If the prisoners were kept in Britain, their food needs would simply add to shipping difficulties. Ike felt that the British should turn over any Axis prisoners to the Americans, so they could be treated in the same way as those captured by the American forces, instead of being shipped across the Atlantic to be interned in the British dominion of Canada.

After the discussions, Ike had an early night, while Beetle continued to talk to Butch and Kay about Operation Torch. He said the Allies had not consulted the "supercilious and self satisfied"[6] General de Gaulle and his National French Committee – set up in September 1941 – because North Africa was now under the authority of Vichy France. "Civil wars are the bitterest," said Beetle, "so we are purposely keeping the de Gaullists out of this picture."

Beetle stayed on at the cottage for a rest and a break from his usual diet of "cigarettes, bourbon and Dexadrine".[7] After a week, he was looking forward to soup made out of baked beans and hambone. However, the cook and houseboy had eaten the ham and beans "for fear they would spoil". (The cook had previously been told to cut down on Ike's food because it was making him too fat! This was a continuing worry for Ike. When he put on weight in France, his orderly reassured him that his shirts had shrunk.) Beetle ordered Hunt to write a report headed: "Status of Baked Beans and Bean Soup as of September 14, 1942". Unfortunately, the report was lost.

While Ike and Beetle were discussing the ultimate fate of Axis prisoners, a number of Italian prisoners-of-war were already on their way to the US in the RMS Laconia. In an episode that became known as the "Laconia Incident', the 20,000-ton ship was torpedoed by submarine U-156 off the West African coast on the night of 12 September 1942.

---

[6] Alan Brooke war diaries, 7 August 1942
[7] Eisenhower, p 14

The armed merchant ship was carrying 87 civilian women and children, as well as 463 officers and crew, 286 British soldiers, 1,793 Italian prisoners of war and 103 Polish guards. Because the Laconia was armed, it was regarded as a legitimate target. Italian prisoners tried to scramble into the lifeboats, but described afterwards how the Polish guards hacked at their hands to keep them away. When the U-boat commander realised that there were civilians aboard the sinking ship, he began a rescue operation with two other U-boats and an Italian submarine, broadcasting the details on open radio channels to Allied forces.

Four days later, sailing on the surface to meet Vichy French Red Cross ships, with its decks covered with survivors, U-156 was attacked by a US B-24 Liberator bomber from Ascension Island, forcing the sub to crash-dive. More than half the survivors drowned or were killed by sharks. The American bomber crew wrongly claimed that they had sunk U-156, and were awarded medals. (The U-boat *was* eventually sunk off Barbados six months later, with the loss of all her crew.)

As a result of the attack on the Laconia, Grand Admiral Karl Dönitz issued the so-called "Laconia order" on 17 September, forbidding German ships to go to the rescue of survivors of torpedoed Allied ships. At the Nuremberg Trials, a US attempt to cite the Laconia order as proof of war crimes by Dönitz backfired when the full story emerged. (Coincidentally, the day after the Laconia was sunk, the Allies lost three destroyers, seven motor torpedo boats and almost 600 troops after a disastrous seaborne attack on Tobruk in North Africa.)

Ike was still obsessed with secrecy. Only the need to keep the details of Operation Torch secret could convince him to take guests to the cottage. On 14 September, Irish-American diplomat Robert Murphy (former US *chargé d'affaires* to the Vichy French government) flew into Hendon from the US as "Colonel McGowan" and was taken directly to Telegraph Cottage.

Murphy, a member of the Bilderberg group who was German on his mother's side, had remained in good standing with Vichy. In February 1941, he had signed an agreement with General Maxime Weygand, delegate-general of Vichy France in North Africa, allowing the French to use funds frozen in the US to buy non-strategic goods needed in North Africa. Murphy was also in contact with the Chief-of-Staff of the Vichy French Army in Algeria and believed that the Allied invasion would not be opposed under certain conditions (though the British press said that Vichy would "no doubt do its utmost to urge resistance". [8]) He was confident that the commander of Maison Blanche airfield at Oran would not oppose the American forces. The French Navy, however, was likely to fight, said Murphy, because of its dislike of the British. Ike agreed that the campaign would be "brutally hostile" unless the Vichy territory were occupied swiftly and sea supplies maintained. [9]

Ike and Murphy relaxed in the cottage's sunny garden for a couple of hours, with Murphy describing the situation in Algeria and French Morocco. Murphy wasn't sure whether the Spaniards would fight, especially in Spanish Morocco, whether they would attack Gibraltar's aerodrome and harbour or try to close the narrow entrance to the Mediterranean. However, if the Straits of Gibraltar were closed, he said, the Allies could drive on a tarmac road from Casablanca to Oran in just ten hours.

At sunset, the two men moved into the living room. Ike authorised Murphy to tell his French co-operators that the initial force would comprise 150,000 men, with an increase to half a million soldiers as quickly as port facilities allowed. Murphy said that the strong Allied force was exactly what his French friends in North Africa had been hoping for.

Murphy was anxious to have supplies for the Arabs as soon as possible and he suggested that the goods could be

---

[8] Daily Mirror front page, 9 November 1942
[9] at ease, p 255

transported from the US by French cargo ships. The antiquated railway system in North Africa could move only 1,500 tons a day, though Murphy believed that US engineers could install sidings to permit more frequent trains. The question of French command in North Africa would have to be settled urgently. Admiral François Darlan[10] was apparently willing to join the Allies and to bring the French fleet with him, on the understanding that he would be made commander-in-chief of French forces in North Africa. However, the navy would go along with the army's decision. The army preferred 63-year-old General Henri Giraud, who had escaped from a German prison by climbing 150 feet down an improvised ladder.[11]

Ike decided to appoint Giraud governor of French North Africa, with responsibility for all French civil and military affairs, while Darlan would be left in command of French military and naval forces in North Africa. But Ike insisted that, until the Allies were sure that the French forces in North Africa could defend the territory by themselves, the US should retain command of the Vichy troops there. While French troops could remain under the command of a French general, they would have to co-operate fully with him as Allied Commander-in-Chief.[12] Any Frenchmen who were uncooperative could be dealt with by de Gaulle's Free French, and Ike would limit US 'interference' to preventing personal acts of revenge.

Murphy spent the night at the cottage and went straight back to Hendon airfield the following morning to return to the US. Later in September, Beetle was admitted to hospital for treatment for a recurring stomach ulcer and was given a blood transfusion. Two weeks later, Kay drove Ike to the hospital in Oxford, two hours away, to visit him. But days

---

[10] In Algiers to see his son who had polio
[11] His wife, two daughters and seven grandchildren were detained in Germany.
[12] But, Churchill told FDR in a telegram on 15 November, "Great care must be taken that we are not double-crossed"

later, Beetle discharged himself and returned to his hotel, so Ike scrapped plans to drive to Oxford to see him again.

Kay regularly drove Ike to Chequers, the British Prime Minister's country residence, for long discussions with Winston Churchill and Allied leaders over dinner – and frequently into the early hours of the following morning.[13] Whenever Kay drove to Chequers, "Winston Churchill would always come to talk to me and would always see that I had magazines and books and dinner and drinks."[14] Churchill would welcome them dressed in his trademark siren suit or in a three-piece suit and white shirt, with the collar held closed by a bow tie and a handkerchief sprayed with 'Blenheim Bouquet' cologne rubbed across his balding head.[15] On one visit, Ike's orderly forgot his pyjamas, so he had to wear one of Churchill's old silk vests which rode up and almost strangled him during the night.

Over the front door of Chequers were the Latin words, *Pro Patria Omnia*, which Ike translated as "All for the Fatherland", and written over a gate leading to the gardens were the words "All care abandon ye who enter here". But it was difficult to abandon all cares when the house was a "damned icebox".[16] Modern central heating could not be installed because of the ancient wood panelling, some of which was 500 years old. The hall was full of paintings of Englishmen with bulbous noses and royalty with dirty necks, said Ike.

On one memorable occasion, Kay drove Ike and Clark to Chequers for dinner. During the first course, Churchill "crouched over the plate" with his nose almost in the soup, which "disappeared to the accompaniment of loud gur-glings". When the Prime Minister accidentally knocked a glass off the table, he continued talking, not even looking

---

[13] Churchill's life consisted of mornings "spent working in bed, regular baths, formal dinners and after-dinner games" – Churchill, p 277
[14] 1972 Thames Television interview
[15] Alan Brooke war diaries, 26 March 1943
[16] The house was renowned for its coldness

around to see where the glass had fallen. He smoked a "terrifically long and big" cigar, but played with it more than he smoked. During the evening, he changed his shoes and socks in front of his guests with no sign of embarrassment. Later he scratched his back vigorously against the edge of the open door, a habit which he said he'd picked up in Egypt.

Often Churchill would have second (or third) thoughts after dinner. He would follow his guests down the long hall as they were leaving to discuss the new thoughts that had struck him. Once when Ike went to bed at 10.30pm, Churchill's secretary rang half an hour later, wanting to know if Ike could go to 10 Downing Street "later that evening". Ike agreed but was woken again around midnight when the PM's secretary rang to ask whether it would be more convenient for him to come at 10.30 the next morning. At 5am, the switchboard operator rang Ike to say it was time for him to get up, but the operator had the wrong extension!

After lunch on 23 September, Kay drove Ike to High Wycombe to visit Fighter Command headquarters. Ike was keen to know whether there were any plans to deal with the German fighter aircraft that could fly at 43,000 feet, as Spitfires could not reach that height. The next day Ike visited US Bomber Command in a girls' school. While Ike was at the school, he heard bells ringing in the old administrative offices. It turned out that bomber crews, who occupied rooms where the girls used to sleep, had noticed a sign above the bell pushes saying "If mistress is desired, ring bell"!

At Bomber Command, Ike was told that, in 194 sorties so far, 352 tons of bombs had been dropped and a quarter of a million rounds of ammunition fired. But weather and cloud conditions in Europe were only suitable for daylight bombing for up to a quarter of the year, although daylight bombing by US Flying Fortresses was substantially more accurate than the RAF's night bombing. One example came that month when US Fortresses had attacked a factory near Albert in Belgium. Although the 42 bombers came under continuous attack from enemy fighters on the way to the target, they pushed on and bombed the target "accurately and destructively".

Back at HQ, American photographer Peggy Bourke-White took a photograph of Ike's immediate circle of colleagues, including Kay, for Life magazine. But the picture showed Kay with her tongue "impudently" sticking out and another secretary, Mary Alice Jaqua, "seemingly eye-flirting" with Ike who was "caught in a pose too jovial for these stern times", according to Butch. So Bourke-White was asked to retake the picture, as well as numerous close-ups of Ike standing before his Lieutenant-General's flag and the Stars and Stripes.

On Sunday 4 October, Ike took the day off, lounging around Telegraph Cottage and practising .22 target shooting. "It's far more important to be able to hit the target than it is to haggle over who makes a weapon or who pulls a trigger," said Ike. The following Sunday, Kay drove Ike to the cottage to play golf but, because the golf course was crowded due to the fine weather, he opted instead to continue with his .22 target practice.

Kay missed having animals in London. She used to have a pet Scottie named McTavish (Tavvy) in Ireland. Wouldn't Ike buy a dog before he left for North Africa, she pleaded? Ike agreed and decided on a Scottie, despite efforts to persuade him to choose a Dandie Dinmont.[17] "What counts is not necessarily the size of the dog in the fight – it's the size of the fight in the dog," he said. "I like the independent attitude of a strutting Scottie," insisted Ike. "You can't talk war to a dog and I'd like to have someone – or something – to talk to occasionally that doesn't know what the word means." Kay found a black Scottie, and Ike agreed to pay $60 for him.

---

[17] Hitler's girlfriend, Eva Braun, had two Scotties, Stasi and Negus. The German Füehrer preferred Alsatians

The thoroughbred dog, son of "Davah Queen", was registered as "Braeside Chief" at the Duke Street kennels near Selfridges, where he had been born on 29 June 1942. The dog came of good stock – his grandparents were the champions "Heather Necessity", "Alborne Romance", "Tremont Warrana" and "Dauntless May".

Ike named the dog Telek. He told Kay that the name comprised the first part of TELEgraph Cottage and Kay's first initial– "two parts of my life that make me very happy". But the secret wasn't shared with everyone. McKeogh, who was given the job of "Sergeant Dog Walker", said Telek was "named, in some fashion not altogether clear to me". [18] Although Ike paid for the dog, it really belonged to Kay. Secretary Sue Sarafian said: "His dog, Telek, was more her dog. I mean she had entire care of Telek." Ike gave Kay the puppy – complete with miniature parachute and harness – on his 52nd birthday. Telek soon learned to take the logs out of the fireplace, bury bones in the garden and follow Ike or Kay up the stairs.

The same day, 14 October 1942, Ike received his third star and a cable from the US Chief-of-Staff: "My Prayers, Best Wishes And Complete Confidence To You On Your Birthday. Marshall." Kay, Clark, Beetle, TJ, 'Tex' Lee, Mickey and Butch organised a surprise birthday party, and Mickey arranged for a cake with three stars and three candles to mark Ike's new rank. Kay gave Ike a Western magazine for a present. "It was a toss up between the magazine and a package of chewing gum," she wrote later.

---

[18] Sgt Mickey and General Ike, p 42

NORTH AFRICAN ADVENTURES

Ike, Kay, Beetle and Butch had a goodbye dinner at the cottage for General Clark who was flying to Gibraltar and then going aboard the British submarine HMS Seraph to rendezvous off Algiers with "Colonel McGowan" and his French friends. Clark, who was "as happy as a boy with a new knife", left the cottage before midnight with Beetle, while Ike, Kay and Butch stayed the night.

Clark was particularly concerned with monetary arrangements in North Africa and whether civilians there would be allowed to exchange American dollars for the yellow-seal variety provided to US troops by their government. Regular British and American currency was removed from circulation so that it would not fall into enemy hands. But no decision could be made about currency until the dangers of counterfeiting and black marketeering had been properly assessed.

On Sunday 18 October 1942, Major (later Lt Col) Paul Tibbets flew Clark from England to Gibraltar. (Tibbets was later to drop the first atomic bomb on Japan, a bomb "2,000 times as powerful as any ever made before."[1] He said of that mission: "My edict was as clear as could be. Drop simultaneously in Europe and the Pacific because of the secrecy problem – you couldn't drop it in one part of the world without dropping it in the other."[2] Fortunately there was no need to drop the atom bomb in Europe[3] – but the Allies had been concerned that "the Boche would forestall us with the Atomic Bomb and snatch victory from under our noses".[4])

---

[1] New York Post, 6 August 1945
[2] http://www.theguardian.com/world/2002/aug/06/nuclear.japan
[3] Churchill approved the use of the atom bomb against Japan at the start of July 1945
[4] War Diaries 1939-1945, p xxxii

The same day as Clark flew to Gibraltar, Ike left the cottage early to catch the train for the 16-hour journey to Kentallen in Scotland to watch troops taking part in night exercises in practice for Torch. He travelled aboard his private train carriage, Bayonet, fitted with an office, a dining room which seated up to ten and sleeping accommodation for six. North of Inverary, a caravan of ten cars, led by Ike's, drove 90 miles in the rain, with Ike stopping regularly to talk to soldiers and observe the operation. At 4am, he left to return to London via Edinburgh, depressed that the officers had not dispersed the men as soon as they reached the beaches. The problems were still on his mind when, two days later, he wrote to Marshall: "If a man permitted himself to do so, he could get absolutely frantic about questions of weather, politics, personalities in France and Morocco, and so on. To a certain extent, a man must merely believe in his luck."

On Tuesday night, Ike – suffering from a cold due to his Scottish excursion – and Beetle had their regular dinner with the Prime Minister at 10 Downing Street. They discussed the unsuccessful attack by US Flying Fortresses on the submarine base at Lorient, in which three of the 15 B-17 bombers were shot down and six were hit by enemy fighters. The others returned to base because of the bad weather.

Back at the cottage on Wednesday night, Ike told Kay he was "greatly concerned" about a mix-up regarding the time for Clark's rendezvous in North Africa. Nothing was heard until about midnight on Saturday 24 October, when a message arrived from Clark in Gibraltar saying that he had completed his mission, was flying back to London and would come straight to the cottage. When Clark arrived back, he told Ike and Kay how he'd had to wait in a British submarine for 36 hours off the coast of Algiers until a light was shone from a window to confirm the rendezvous. Unfortunately, as Clark was being ferried through the rough surf, a box containing £100,000 in gold coins to bribe Vichy officials in North Africa (more than £4 million at today's values) was "lost overboard".

During the secret meeting at a farm near the Messelmoun river, local police raided the house following reports of smugglers. Clark hid in a wine cellar but a Commando captain with him had a sudden coughing fit which could have given them away if the police heard. Clark offered him a piece of gum which he'd already been chewing for two hours! Back at the beach, Clark undressed except for his cap but, as they paddled out to the submarine, a large wave overturned the canvas boat and all Clark's clothes fell into the sea. (Fortunately, he managed to hold onto his lucky dice.) He went back to the house and robed himself in a pair of trousers and a French silk tablecloth "like a sheik". Clark then spent a day hiding in nearby woods before setting out again in calmer seas for the submarine, a quarter of a mile offshore.

When Clark had finished telling his story, Ike said he was going to recommend him for the Distinguished Service Medal (DSM) for his adventures. Churchill was so fascinated by the tale that he invited Ike, Clark, Beetle, Brooke and Admiral Dudley Pound for lunch on Monday to hear all the details.

On 29 October, before finally leaving for Gibraltar, Ike paid a farewell visit to King George VI with Kay and Clark (and Telek, who stayed in the car). The Prime Minister then invited Ike to lunch to finalise details of the operation. Ike had a farewell dinner at the cottage on Saturday 31 October with Kay, Clark, Beetle, TJ and Butch. Thereafter Beetle Smith took the cottage until he left for Algiers, when General Russell Hartle occupied it. Ike and Kay spent Sunday evening at a private showing of the latest Henry Fonda film, The Magnificent Dope.

There was a lot of talk about Ike's subsequent disappearance from headquarters in England. It was suggested pretending that he'd been recalled to Washington for consultations, but he was concerned that Mamie might believe the rumour and expect to see him. Eventually Ike decided not to tell Mamie that he was flying to Gibraltar, because he didn't want even the code clerks to know where he was going.

The day before he left England, Ike asked Kay whether she'd accompany him in North Africa, and she agreed.[5] They listened to music on the radio together and, when the song I'll See You Again came on, Kay told Ike that it was her favourite song ever since she'd seen the number performed in the stage production of Bittersweet. The song reminded her that she and Ike wouldn't be apart for long.

The next day, Kay drove Ike and Clark to the station to take the train to Bournemouth. The two generals (and Telek) were due to fly to Gibraltar in Ike's B-17 in a group of seven Flying Fortresses. But bad weather prevented the flight, and the air-raid authorities wouldn't allow the train to remain in sidings in Bournemouth during the day because it would draw attention to the town, so Ike returned to London. He spent the day at the cottage and, in the evening, went with Kay to see The Road to Morocco in Wardour Street in London.

The next day, Kay drove Ike to Addison Road railway station once again. The weather was abominable, with rain, fog and practically zero visibility. In Bournemouth, the pilot of the Red Gremlin – Major Tibbets again – was reluctant to fly, but Ike said to hell with it. Tibbets took off from Hurn Aerodrome on Thursday 5 November, wave-hopped through bad weather and low cloud for three hours, and reached Gibraltar at 4.20pm. After circling for an hour, the planes landed safely. The following day, Brigadier-General Jimmy Doolittle, on his way to Gibraltar too, narrowly escaped death when the co-pilot of his Flying Fortress was hit during an attack by four German Ju-88s over the Bay of Biscay.[6]

The Governor of Gibraltar welcomed the men at Government House, a former convent. A cable from Winston Churchill assured Ike: "I feel the Rock of Gibraltar will be

---

[5] Kay obtained her British passport in November 1942
[6] Daily Herald, 12 November 1942

safe in your hands."[7] Ike was keen to be near the action during Torch and tried to arrange for his headquarters to be aboard a cruiser. But he was unsuccessful and was given an office about a half mile inside the Rock. Since the start of the war, engineers had blasted tunnels deep inside the Rock, and now almost all the hospitals, ammunition stores and military accommodation was underground and safe from bombs. The operations room was 30 feet high, hewn out of solid rock, with a huge map on the wall. Ike and Clark's office was cold and damp which made his cigarettes soggy and left Ike with a long-term cough. Even though Operation Torch was now close to starting, Ike still stressed the need for secrecy. He told the four local press correspondents: "If you violate the faith, I'll shoot you – if I can catch you."

The bridge games continued in Kay's absence. After dinner on 7 November, Torch planner General Alfred Gruenther and Ike beat Clark and Butch. The next day, Ike and Butch borrowed a staff car to visit the apes and Ike patted one for good luck. (There's a tradition that, as long as the Barbary apes are on the Rock, it will remain British.) Then Ike drove Butch around the precipitous roads of the Rock with sheer drops of hundreds of feet on one side. Butch leaned away from the drop, much to Ike's amusement.

Around this time, General Giraud[8] arrived in Gibraltar by submarine from southern France. After dinner hosted by the Royal Navy, Ike and Clark returned to their billets about 10.30pm before starting negotiations with Giraud. The French general (known to the Americans as 'Papa Snooks') insisted that he wouldn't help the Allies unless he was appointed Allied Commander-in-Chief in North Africa. Ike argued for an hour with Giraud and then Clark took over. Giraud was offered the governorship of North Africa, with the cash to build an army, but he insisted that he wanted to lead the existing Vichy forces.

---

[7] Telegram, 7 November 1942 (T.1453/2)
[8] Known to the Allies as "Kingpin" (and to Churchill as a "fellow escapee") (7 November 1942, T.1453/2)

The Allies were aware that Rommel had warned the German General Staff that the Axis forces would be "annihilated" if he did not receive immediate aid. But the outcome of Operation Torch was still uncertain. After all, it would be the first time that untrained American troops had been involved in a battle against the battle-hardened Germans and Italians – and possibly the Vichy French and even the Spanish. In a message to Marshall the day before the landings, Ike said: "We are standing, of course, on the brink and must take the jump – whether the bottom contains a nice feather bed or a pile of brickbats."

The North African landings began at 1am on 8 November. A statement from the White House said the landings aimed to "forestall an invasion" of Africa by Germany and Italy. [9] Further east, in Egypt, the British Eighth Army was pushing back Axis forces in the closing stages of the second Battle of El Alamein. The American newspapers were still speculating that the landings would be at Dakar, in French West Africa, and Algiers. In fact around 31,000 British and American troops landed both sides of Oran, while 33,000 stormed ashore east and west of Algiers. Algiers was the best equipped port in North Africa, except for Tunis and Alexandria, and its facilities were crucial to the build-up of men and equipment vital to consolidate the Allies' hold on North Africa. The Algiers task force included more than 40 ships, two of which tried unsuccessfully to land American infantrymen to seize the port.

Although 98 of the 104 landing craft were lost in the landings (often because the landing ramps were left open and the craft were swamped), other troops managed to seize Maison Blanche and Blida airfields, cut road links with the south and establish a pincer movement round the city of Algiers. Among those liberated by Allied troops were the survivors of RMS Laconia who had been interned at Mediouna camp, awaiting transfer to Germany. Only hours

---

[9] The fact that there had been no formal declaration of war against France was omitted

after the start of Operation Torch, Admiral Andrew Browne Cunningham's Chief-of-Staff, Commodore Roy Dick, reported "Landing successful, A, B, and C beaches, Eastern Task Force". To mark the success of the landings, Marshall cabled Clark that his nomination for promotion to Lieutenant-General had gone to the Senate.

Later that day, Ike cabled the Combined Chiefs saying he had agreed to recognise Giraud as governor of North Africa and Commander-in-Chief of French forces there. As Commander-in-Chief of the Allied forces, Ike would co-operate with him as far as possible, but he still expected Giraud to obey orders from him. However, reports to Ike from North Africa continued to be slow and intermittent, and there was still no word from any Allied ambassador or agent in Spain.

It appeared that defensive actions by the Vichy French, which had seemed half-hearted, had blazed up in many places. No French leader, no matter how sympathetic toward the Allies, seemed able to prevent the fighting. Giraud did not seem inclined to order a ceasefire and was unwilling to go to North Africa as long as the battles continued. The Allied troops were still in the eastern sector when they should be moving toward Bône and Bizerte, and Ike still knew nothing about the whereabouts and condition of the airborne troops.

Ike then received a message from North Africa saying that Vichy French Admiral Jean Darlan wanted to negotiate, but refused to deal with any other Frenchman (including Giraud). Churchill responded: "Kiss Darlan's stern if you have to, but get the French Navy." Ike described Darlan as a "deep-dyed villain" and later recalled: "I wanted nothing to do with him".[10] But the military advantages of an immediate ceasefire were "so overwhelming" that Ike undertook to go

---

[10] at ease, p 255

promptly to Algiers and "immediately recognize Darlan" as the highest French authority in the region.[11]

The British and American press were very opposed to any deal with Darlan, but not everyone was so negative. Ike's orderly, Sgt Mickey McKeogh, later wrote: "Most of the GIs thought that by dealing with Darlan we saved a lot of American lives. The French are no slouches. With a man leading them who really wanted to stop us, they would have taken a lot of beating. The way it was, they didn't and we got where we wanted to go and not as many boys got killed as would have otherwise."[12] And Field Marshal Jan Smuts, after a visit to Gibraltar, sent Churchill a secret telegram asking him to advise FDR of his "strong impression" that "further anti-Darlan statements might be harmful to our cause, and indeed are not called for". He said that Darlan "was not Eisenhower's choice but that of other French leaders, some of whom were his enemies and our strong supporters and who agreed that his leadership [and] cooperation was essential for our operations. It would be [a] great mistake to create impression that he is to be discarded at [an] early date".[13] Even the USSR's Joseph Stalin said that Eisenhower's decision about Darlan was "perfectly correct". "I think it a great achievement that you succeeded in bringing Darlan and others into the waterway of the Allies fighting Hitler," he said.[14]

By the time the Germans realised that the Allies intended to invade North Africa and had started to airlift troops to Tunisia, it was too late. Two days after the Allied invasion, Oran surrendered. Three hundred staff of the German Armistice Commission fled from their "small marble palace", which had belonged to a Jewish newspaper owner in Casablanca,[15] but the Allies seized their records, ciphers

---

[11] at ease, p 256
[12] Sgt Mickey and General Ike, p 63
[13] 20 November 1942
[14] Telegram to FDR, December 1942 (T1726/2)
[15] Alan Brooke war diaries, 16 January 1943

and money, and took eight members of the commission prisoner.

Two French cruisers reportedly left Toulon to join the Allies. At 8am on 11 November, all Vichy French land, air and sea forces in French North Africa, including French Morocco and Casablanca, were ordered to stop fighting and return to barracks. But after Marshal Philippe Pétain, the ruler of Vichy France, declared the admiral "bereft of all public office and military command", Darlan tried to rescind his order. "Damned if you do" said Clark, to which Darlan replied "Then I must consider myself a prisoner." "OK by me," retorted Clark. However, Clark managed to broker a working agreement between Darlan and Giraud, making Darlan the head of civilian affairs and putting Giraud in charge of military matters. As Vichy France broke off diplomatic relations with the US, Darlan set up a "legislative council" to assist him as High Commissioner for French North Africa. [16]

Everything appeared to be going smoothly, and Ike expressed pride in his British-US command. "The final result I don't know, but I do know that every element of my command – all US and British services – are working together beautifully and harmoniously." [17] But newspaper reports in Britain and the US reflected the unpopularity of the deal with Darlan, whom the British Foreign Office regarded as the "antithesis" of "international decency". Some London papers described Darlan's appointment as "revolting" and "disgusting". In a letter to Ike, the Vichy admiral wrote that he felt like "a lemon which the Americans will drop after it is crushed".

Darlan's views about the Jews particularly irked Ike, who had "good friends" in the Jewish community. (While he was still in the Philippines, Ike had been offered $300,000 – worth more than $5 million today – plus expenses for trying

---

[16] Churchill telegraphed Lord Halifax about "certain sections of the Press and public who want to have the advantages of Darlan without Darlan"
[17] Eisenhower diary, 9 November 1942

to obtain refuge for German Jews in Asia and elsewhere. But the offer had "few temptations" and he turned it down.)

From his base in Gibraltar, Ike was keeping in touch with developments in North Africa. On 11 November, Beetle sent a cable reminding Ike that it was Patton's 57th birthday. "Isn't Casablanca enough of a present?" responded Ike. The following day, following an incident in which two American Navy planes shot down a British Hudson bomber in error, Ike said efforts to identify aircraft should be redoubled. But it wasn't the only friendly-fire incident. Later a ship carrying the wives and children of French officers from Dakar was dive-bombed by the US Navy when it tried to leave Casablanca harbour during a battle. "Not sunk, but messy," recorded Butch. Allied anti-aircraft crew also fired 18 rounds at Patton's plane on his way to Algiers.[18]

On 13 November, Clark radioed Ike from Algiers to ask him to come to North Africa. A couple of days later, Ike flew out of Gib's crowded airfield, arriving at Maison Blanche about noon on 15 November. It was the first time Ike had set foot in Africa. He was driven to the Hotel St George,[19] where Murphy told him that Darlan and Giraud had agreed that:

- Darlan was to be the governor of French North Africa;

- the French fleet would surrender to the Allies and Darlan was to try and persuade Dakar's naval commander to cooperate;

- General Auguste Noguès was to remain governor of French Morocco to control the "troublesome Arabs";

---

[18] The Patton Papers, p 137. "It is practically impossible to fly over ones (sic) own troops because they frequently shoot at you thinking you are an enemy." Patton letter to wife, 10 May 1943
[19] Now the Hotel El Djazaïr

- Giraud was to form a French army of volunteers who would start to fight the Germans and Italians in Tunisia within three days;[20] and

- distribution of petrol, sugar, tea and other supplies would start immediately.

Despite their earlier disagreement, Darlan informed Marshal Pétain about the agreement. "Pétain is the living embodiment of France," he said in a radio broadcast. "I am sure I am the true interpreter of the Marshal's thoughts."[21] Ike accepted that the Vichy French in North Africa were coming round to the Allied side. To reflect this, he ordered American soldiers to salute French officers. [22] He then reboarded his Flying Fortress to fly back to Gibraltar. When the pilot arrived in Gibraltar about 7pm, visibility was practically zero and the plane had to circle repeatedly; Ike later said he only started to get scared after about three hours.

Nine days later, Ike flew again from Gibraltar to Algiers, this time to stay. US headquarters had been based at the Hotel St George since 9 November, and the hotel was eventually occupied by British and American staff. Ike and his staff occupied a first-floor corner suite of three bedrooms and a parlour, with Ike in the corner bedroom and Butch in the room next door. Six WACs worked in the office.[23]

Ike had a restless first night in Africa punctuated by Axis bombing. In the office later that day, Ike criticised the city's air defences, particularly the absence of night fighters. Six RAF Beaufighters, equipped with secret gadgets, were quickly flown in from the Middle East. German planes

---

[20] "I have too often listened to your sage advice to be completely handcuffed and blindfolded by all of the slickers with which this part of the world is so thickly populated," said Ike to Churchill in a telegram on 14 November 1942
[21] Daily Herald, 21 November 1942
[22] The French were "much more meticulous" at saluting than the Americans (The Patton Papers, p 161)
[23] New York World Telegram, 8 July 1943

patrolled the skies during the day too. Ike and Clark would be "ducking for the ditches every time we saw a plane in the air (with good reason – almost every plane then flying was an enemy)".[24]

During the day, the beds were cleared out of Ike's new office and replaced by desks and phones, but there was no heat except for a few small fireplaces, and the winter weather in Algiers was surprisingly cold. Allied soldiers bedded down in corridors gritty with mud that was turned to choking dust by the busy brushes of the Arab women cleaners.

To "impress the natives", Ike asked Butch to find villas for him and Beetle Smith in Algiers. Butch found two villas above Algiers that had been owned by a rich pro-German wine merchant. According to FDR's White House secretary, the villas were "finer than anything you have ever looked at before, much less had in your past Army career".[25]

Ike and Clark were installed in the Villa dar el Ouard (Family Villa) overlooking the harbour. The big white house had cold stone and tile floors and no water, gas or heat, but it had "a library, a living room, a music room, a parlor, a dining room, a kitchen, seven bedrooms, and two bath-rooms, and quarters in the basement for some of the staff".[26] A "ping-pong" (table tennis) table was set up in the library to help Ike relax, and movies were shown regularly in the music room, when the piano wasn't being played. Ike's first breakfast of eggs and bacon in the villa was cooked by Clark's orderly over a wood fire in the dining-room.

One of the first issues with which Ike had to deal was the position of the Jews in French North Africa, of whom there were approximately 300,000, compared with 11,000,000 Moslems. The native Arabs had no right to vote or hold public office while the European population of 1,500,000 retained control. As one Frenchman told a US embassy

---

[24] at ease, p 267
[25] Letter from Major Gen Edwin 'Pa' Watson, 21 December 1943
[26] Sgt Mickey and General Ike, p 40

official: "The natives in general wanted citizenship and the vote and at the same time to adhere to their religion. This, France would not countenance."[27] The Jews in French North Africa were subject to the same restrictions as their confreres in mainland France. Darlan had promised to return the Jews' sequestered property, and to restore their right to practise in professions such as medicine and law. But he said that a letter from a Constantine rabbi had called for slowness of reform to avoid Arab reprisals.

Another issue Ike had to handle was the French navy. As Darlan had promised Churchill, the French fleet was scuttled at Toulon to prevent the ships falling into German hands. At 10am on 27 November 1942, Admiral Jean de Laborde reported to Pétain that the fleet "no longer existed".[28] Nevertheless, Ike ordered co-ordinated Allied attacks against shipping (and aerodromes) from French North Africa, the Mediterranean island of Malta and the Middle East.

On Sunday 29 November, Ike and Clark took the semi-armoured Daimler for a visit to the front.[29] Jeeps or scout cars drove in front and behind, with soldiers armed with machine guns in case of aerial attack.[30] They drove well beyond Constantine, but saw nothing. However, the trip was not without incident. A young Arab boy was hit and killed by a scout car, the convoy ran over and killed two dogs and finally another scout car skidded into a ditch, injuring five soldiers. Ike was already feeling ill when he started on the trip and these shocking incidents only made him feel worse. The dispensary doctor prescribed rest and paregoric.

On 1 December, Ike had two VIP visitors: Patton arrived from Casablanca and Tooey Spaatz flew in from London. Ike took the opportunity to pin a DSM on General Clark and told him he was to lead the Fifth Army. Ike had already visited

---

[27] http://algiers.usembassy.gov
[28] Daily Sketch, 28 November 1942
[29] A "Boy Scout trip", according to Clark
[30] Patton letter to his wife, 3 December 1942

most of the 87 American troops who had been wounded in action and presented them with the Purple Heart. The next day, he laid a wreath at the *Monument aux Morts* in Algiers. Afterwards, Darlan entertained him to lunch at the *Palais d'État* and Ike then hosted a reception in honour of Darlan, Giraud and other French leaders. [31]

Ike was still a three-star general, junior to some of those he hosted. Marshall had realised that Ike was in command of four-star generals while still only a Lieutenant-General, and urged Roosevelt to give Ike his fourth star. But Roosevelt replied that, while Eisenhower had done a good job, "he still hasn't knocked the Germans out of Tunisia". While it would be nice to be numbered with Grant, Sherman and Pershing, who were made four-star generals on the battlefield, Ike bet five colleagues $10 each that he wouldn't get his fourth star by Christmas Day.

Rank wasn't Ike's only problem. His British allies also mistrusted him, regarding him as "far too busy with political matters" and "not paying enough attention to the Germans". [32] Ike's bad temper didn't help. When he was about to leave the Hotel St George one rainy night, his car was waiting under a portico so that he wouldn't get wet. When Ike saw that the lobby was packed with officers and men waiting for their own transport in the rain, he shouted: "I'm going to fire an aide". (He didn't carry out the threat.)

A month after the invasion, Ike still thought that the Allies might have to retreat in Tunisia before an Axis force of around 31,000 men who were using dive bombers, tanks and sabotage effectively. The presence of fifth columnists and saboteurs was a constant test of the vigilance of the Allies. Headquarters guards required everyone to show their pass each time they entered or left HQ. But Admiral Cunningham had given his pass to his flag lieutenant for

---

[31] But Ike assured Churchill in a telegram on 5 December that "we are not entering a cabal designed to make Darlan the head of anything except the local organization"

[32] Alan Brooke war diaries, 7 December 1942

safekeeping and, on one occasion when the lieutenant wasn't there, a guard insisted on inspecting the admiral's car. Cunningham thought the guard must have suspected him of trying to steal Ike's rug. On another occasion, when Beetle Smith was walking home after dark, an MP guarding his villa made him place his ID card on the ground, move back ten paces and lie on his stomach until satisfied that Beetle wasn't an enemy paratrooper. But the British were more concerned with the Axis troops that with saboteurs. Churchill said Ike should "go for the swine in front with a blithe heart", while the British Prime Minister remained a "solid fortification" covering Ike's rear.[33]

On 12 December, Ike's brother Milton and Beetle flew in from Gibraltar and stayed at the villa. Butch had to sleep in Mickey's bed in the downstairs cloakroom – and then accidentally stepped in a puddle of Telek's urine on the cold floor in the morning. At dinner, Ike told Milton and Beetle about his fears over the missing page from the Torch diary. He said he was greatly relieved when the landings were successful, as the missing paper must have been burned. Certainly it hadn't fallen into enemy hands, as Operation Torch turned out to be a convincing military surprise for the Axis.[34]

The continued Allied drive eastward into Tunisia was tentatively set for 22 December, with the Allies outnumbering the enemy by three to two. There were about 20,000 British, 11,000 Americans and 30,000 French soldiers, compared to about 20,000 German and 11,000 Italian combat troops, with about 2,500 German Luftwaffe and 5,000 service troops, a total of more than 60,000 Allies against fewer than 40,000 Axis troops. Ike accepted the assistance of a battalion of Japanese-Americans, but

---

[33] My Three Years With Eisenhower
[34] Although "admittedly the political situation is confused and difficult" (Ike telegram to FDR, 16 December 1942)

rejected Giraud's offer of poorly-armed Moroccan troops.[35] "If I could just get command of a battalion and get into a bullet battle, it would all be so simple," said Ike at lunch.

The war was waged just as hard at sea. Admiral Andrew "ABC" Cunningham claimed that 26 enemy subs had been sunk since the start of Torch. In Algiers, Italian frogmen had placed five-pound limpet mines on ships in the harbour, sinking one and damaging two. They had ridden on 'torpedoes' from a sub four miles offshore, with just their heads showing above water. Once in the harbour, they submerged, but one was spotted. He was suspended by his neck over the side of a ship until he confessed where he'd fixed his mine. From then on, ships kept their propellers turning to create a current and make the task of any frogmen more difficult.

On 20 December, the Free French Commissioner of the Interior, General Emmanuel d'Astier de la Vigerie, arrived in Algiers. Darlan wanted to arrest d'Astier as a communist,[36] and turned up at Ike's villa at midnight to urge the commander to expel the commissioner from Africa. Ike arranged for d'Astier to talk unofficially to Darlan, as the administrator of the French territories in Africa. But Darlan still faced opposition. Two days before Christmas, the British war cabinet considered the "continuing unsatisfactory situation" in North Africa and drew attention to the "doubts as to the reliability of some of the Frenchmen who were now occupying controlling positions".[37]

It wasn't just the French allies who were unreliable; so was the weather. An attack on Tunis and Tripoli, which had been set for the night of Christmas Eve, was postponed for 48

---

[35] The division "unfortunately has no A.T. or Flak [anti-tank or anti-aircraft guns] making it of little use in open country" (Ike telegram to Churchill, 16 December 1942)

[36] D'Astier, a "passionate Gaullist" (p 692 Bodyguard of Lies) was associated with the French Communist Party and later became de Gaulle's Minister of the Interior

[37] War cabinet minutes, 23 December 1942

hours because of the deep mud. After consulting locals, General Anderson said that an attack should probably not be attempted for another six weeks. [38]

Kay, who had been in London during the first month of Torch, was preparing to sail to North Africa to be with Ike again. After being inoculated and getting her British passport, Kay packed her two Vuitton suitcases with her diamond earrings from her grandmother, her pearl necklace that had been a 16th birthday present and "a few gold bangles". She left London on 8 December[39] and sailed on the 24,000-ton Strathallan troopship from a rainy Greenock in Scotland three days later. Kay's lover, Dick, did not know that she was coming to Algiers but had written to say that he was in Oran and his divorce had come through.

The troopship, carrying 4,000 souls, set off in a convoy of 12 vessels. Kay shared a cabin with two others. On board too was Life photographer Peg Bourke-White (whom Kay liked, but Ike didn't) and 250 Queen Alexandra nurses on their way to serve in North Africa. Every night (except the last), Kay would pack her 'torpedo bag' with her nylons, jewellery and silk undies in case the ship was attacked.

For days before reaching Africa, the ships battled through gales and 70-mile-an-hour winds, with waves up to 60 feet high. Most of the soldiers were seasick, with the decks covered in vomit. Several passengers were injured by flying sofas, and a piano was smashed as it rolled against a wall. At 2.23am on 21 December 1942, the night before the ship was due to arrive in Oran, a U-boat which had been shadowing the convoy fired a torpedo at the Strathallan. The explosion killed two engineer officers and two Indian crewmen and fractured a boiler room oil tank.

"The torpedo did not make as loud a crash as I had expected, nor did the ship list as much as it does in the movies," said

---

[38] Churchill was "far from happy" about this (Telegram to General Alexander, 28 December 1942)
[39] Diary, 4 January 1945

Peg Bourke-White (who took photographs).[40] But the vessel did quickly develop a 15-degree list to port, and Captain JH Biggs ordered the passengers to abandon ship. All secret books, including the wireless books, were thrown overboard in weighted bags.[41]

Kay went to station 12 on B deck, as she had practised every day in lifeboat drill, and managed to get into a water-filled lifeboat with 63 other people, including Bourke-White and Elspeth Duncan, a Scottish clerk to General Hughes. Seventeen lifeboats, some of them waterlogged, carried up to 100 passengers each. The Strathallan was burning but not sinking, so Kay was not too frightened. Once she was safely in the lifeboat, she joked that, for breakfast that day, she'd like her eggs sunny side up without the yolks being broken. Many of the survivors were seasick – especially the nurses and the Goan dining stewards – as the lifeboats were rocked by a series of depth charges from nearby destroyers to try and destroy any lurking U-boats.

Eight hours after the Strathallan was torpedoed, the British destroyer HMS Verity picked up Kay and another 1,300 survivors and took them the 70 miles to Oran, where they arrived late on the afternoon of 22 December. Another 2,000 people were taken off the burning ship. In all, only six crew members, five nurses and five soldiers lost their lives. Among the survivors was the son of the Earl of Pembroke, a radio officer on the Strathallan, who'd managed to hold onto a pair of enamelled cufflinks which had been a gift from Princess Marina. Ike's American secretary Jeanne Dixon still had her prayer book, while nurse Ethel Westermann had managed to keep her rosary. Kay still had her lipstick and her French-English soldiers' dictionary.

The burning Strathallan was taken in tow by HMS Restive, but eventually capsized and sank 12 miles off Oran at 4am on 22 December.

---

[40] Life magazine 22 February 1943, p 48
[41] Trade Division interview with Captain Biggs, TD/139/1631, January 1943

CASABLANCA AND KASSERINE

As soon as she was safely ashore in Oran, Kay phoned Ike in Algiers. "Thank God you're safe. Are you alright?" he asked. She reassured him that she wasn't hurt. She then met Dick Arnold who took her back to his apartment in Oran and tucked her into bed. The next morning, he gave her a bag with a toothbrush and toothpaste, cold cream, soap, a nail file and a uniform tie, and then drove her to the airfield where she boarded Ike's B-17 to fly to Algiers.

In a freezing Algiers, Kay went to Ike's HQ in the Hotel St George, but he'd left for the front at 6am, and was not expected back for three days, until the evening of Saturday 26 December. She was billeted five minutes away from the hotel, in the *Clinique Glycine* (Wisteria Clinic) maternity hospital. Soon after Ike's return, at his suggestion, she moved into a small house shared by five WAC officers she'd known in London ('the Powerhouse'). Some of them took Kay shopping in Algiers to replace the clothes she'd lost on the Strathallan. She bought two sets of underwear. "The panties were black mesh with a satin vine leaf strategically placed," she said. "The brassières, also black, were cut out at the nipples." The Americans supplied her with a cap and tie, while the British provided gloves, a shirt and raincoat.

The first Kay had seen of Ike for a month was when he returned early to Algiers on Friday, Christmas Day. He came back a day early after Clark phoned him to say there was serious trouble following the assassination of Darlan by a young British-trained royalist. After "30 hours of non-stop driving through rain and sleet", Ike had to deal with the political fallout from the assassination before he and Kay could be together. Clark said Darlan's death was "like the lancing of a troublesome boil", but Ike pointed out that, although it ended one problem, it created many more.[1] The young assassin was promptly executed, shutting his mouth for good. Twelve Frenchmen – including Allied and Axis sympathisers – were arrested after the shooting.[2]

When Ike had dealt with the Darlan fallout, he hurried back to Beetle's villa, to Kay. They hugged and talked "a mile a minute" at Christmas dinner, swapping stories about everything that had happened since they last saw one another. "When the news came through that the Strathallan had been hit, well, I don't mind telling you I never did get to sleep that night," said Ike. Kay told Ike all about the torpedoing, while Ike described his damp Gibraltar HQ, where he'd caught a bad cold. Ike told Kay that the situation in North Africa was worse than expected. "We weren't prepared for these rains, this mud."[3] But Ike's suggestion about deferring attacks on the Germans for two months was described by the British chiefs of staff as "hopeless" and "ridiculous".[4]

The next day, Kay went for breakfast at Ike's villa overlooking the Med, which was surrounded by armed guards and anti-aircraft guns. She shared her bacon with Telek, who'd arrived from Gibraltar on a transport plane a month earlier. After breakfast, Kay drove Ike to his HQ in the St George Hotel. Later that day, Ike attended Darlan's requiem Mass in the Cathedral of *Sainte Marie du Palais d'Este* with Admiral Cunningham and Generals Clark and Spaatz. Giraud, who knelt tearfully at the bier, was elected to succeed Darlan, even though Ike described the French

---

[1] Ike told Churchill's son, Randolph, that the Algiers regime should be liberalised before repression led to further assassinations (CHAR 1/375/7-16)

[2] The chief of police in Algiers, who was among those arrested, later claimed that Ike himself had agreed to pay $38,000 for Darlan's assassination (Alec de Montmorency, http://www.barnesreview.org/)

[3] "Rain and mud are against us" (Ike telegram to Churchill, 28 December 1942)

[4] Alan Brooke war diaries notes, 28 and 31 December 1942

general as "wholly incapable of influencing anyone".[5] Patton, who also attended a requiem for the assassinated admiral, wrote in his diary: "Personally I think [Darlan's] death is a distinct loss."

Although Giraud was now head of the French civil and military authorities,[6] President Roosevelt reiterated that Ike's political and military orders must be strictly obeyed under the "military occupation".[7] However, Ike was reluctant to issue any order that Giraud was likely to refuse to obey, as that would mean the Americans would have to take over the civil administration of the country. Patton warned that, if the French were discredited, 60,000 Allied soldiers would be required in the protectorate of French Morocco "as a starter".

One of Giraud's first actions was to urge Ike to improve the exchange rate of 75 French francs to the dollar in North Africa. He pointed out that the British rate in the former Vichy colony of Madagascar was 38 to the dollar. Giraud also repealed the Nuremberg laws, which barred the Jews from certain professions. The North African courts were ordered to reinstate Jewish lawyers, and Jewish doctors were allowed to reopen their offices. Giraud said that Jewish children could attend school, Jewish property would be restored ten days after an inventory had been taken and Jews could soon re-acquire citizenship. (General de Gaulle had already told Rabbi Dr Stephen Wise, president of the World Jewish Congress, on 4 October 1941 that France would restore the equality of the Jews, once victory was achieved.)

In the evening, Ike and Kay shared supper and then played a game of bridge. At the end of the evening, they strolled out onto the terrace of the villa to watch as German planes bombed the harbour – but they were forced back inside when pieces of shrapnel started to fall nearby. In a bridge

---

[5] at ease, p 258
[6] Approved by FDR on 26 December (T1758/2)
[7] CHAR 20/85/21-22

game which was still going on after midnight on the first day of 1943, Ike bid seven hearts in a bridge game and made a grand slam – a good omen for the coming year, he said. (Harry Butcher later asked Ike for details of his cards so that he could recount the story in his book.[8])

Ike stayed in bed until lunchtime, then went to try out the new two-way teleprinter circuit to the United States. He asked the duty officer in Washington to phone Mamie to ask why she hadn't written recently. Within ten minutes, she replied that she'd been sending regular letters. But already Mamie was fading from Ike's mind as Kay made her presence felt. From then on, she resumed driving Ike. In the glove box of the car, she kept maps, cigarettes, Ike's favourite Zane Grey Western and a bottle of paregoric for his persistent 'Algerian tummy'. Often they would drive the 200 miles to the advance command post in Constantine. General Lucian Truscott had found an empty orphanage in Algeria's third-biggest city with a villa next door, and they served as Ike's quarters from 14 January 1943, the day the Casablanca conference opened.

Ike now had to exercise all his diplomatic skills to keep the alliance together. He believed divisions and their commanders were intimately linked, "how infallibly the commander and unit are almost one and the same thing",[9] so he left Anderson in charge of the First Army in the north, with the French and Americans in the centre and south under Clark. Because of the "very ambitious and unscru-pulous"[10] Clark's efforts to set the Vichy French against the British, Ike later decided that Fredendall, rather than Clark, would command the southern sector in Tunisia, while Clark continued to head the Fifth Army – a mistake Ike came to regret.

The Allies now had almost 15 times as many troops as the Axis in North Africa and the Germans had to bring in

---

[8] Letter of 21 September 1945
[9] at ease, p 253
[10] Alan Brooke war diaries, 4 January 1943

reinforcements. The Allied navies had difficulty stopping the daylight movement of German supplies and men the short distance from Sicily to Tunisia, as the Axis ships sailed through a narrow channel flanked by minefields, with air cover from Italy and North Africa. The nearest British airbase, on the other hand, was over 200 miles away, at Malta. However, on 1 May, the US navy sank three German ammunition ships en route to North Africa. An Axis destroyer bound for Tunisia with 1,600 replacement troops was also sunk and another left burning.

In the middle of all the troubles, Special Services in London cabled to ask if Ike could provide a pianist and drummer for the Kay Francis troupe tour!

Kay did not attend the "spectacularly secret" Casablanca conference from 14 to 24 January. FDR, Churchill, Marshall, Giraud and the "most objectionable"[11] de Gaulle did turn up, but Stalin did not go because he was "too busy" personally directing the Red Army offensives.[12] The conference was centred on the Hotel Anfa.

While Ike was en route to Casablanca, one of the engines on his "battle fatigued" B-17 started to leak oil and stopped. Then another engine began to misfire. Butch shakily helped Ike to put on his parachute and the passengers stood in the doorway of the plane, ready to jump. Fortunately, that wasn't necessary. When the plane landed safely at Casablanca airport about 11.30am, Ike ordered that it be repaired straight away, but the airfield commander reported that the aircraft wasn't repairable and should be scrapped immediately.

At Casablanca (mistranslated by the Germans as the 'White House'– and therefore ignored by the German secret service), the Allies decided they would accept no less than

---

[11] Alan Brooke war diaries notes, 18 January 1943
[12] Daily Mirror, 27 January 1943. In a message to Churchill, Stalin said it was impossible to attend the conference because "front business" was "demanding my constant presence near our troops" (T1726/2)

unconditional surrender from their enemies. But the demand later became a "putrefying albatross" round the Allies' necks, prolonging the war because the Germans realised that unconditional surrender meant there would be no guarantees about the treatment of a conquered enemy.

Another of the issues discussed at the conference was Operation Roundup (later codenamed Overlord), the proposed invasion of mainland Europe. The British Chief-of-Staff, General Alan Brooke, indicated that he had never really supported the idea of an invasion of Normandy – an attitude which reflected the views of Prime Minister Churchill. At a private meeting, Brooke suggested to Ike that the Allies should stay in the Mediterranean, allowing the Allied navies and air forces to attack the Germans while the Russians carried out the land war. He predicted that, at the end of the war, the Soviets would pull back to the Russian border.[13] When discussion at the conference returned to the war in North Africa, Churchill described Rommel as a "fugitive from Libya and Egypt now trying to pass himself off as the liberator of Tunis", but added that Montgomery was on Rommel's trail and "everywhere that Mary went, the lamb was sure to go". Ike returned to Algiers on 16 January, first presenting Patton with his second Distinguished Service Medal (DSM) for the capture of Casablanca.

After the conference, General Marshall and Admiral King came to stay at Ike's villa, with Marshall remarking on the "home-like" atmosphere. Ike was still suffering from a cold and high blood pressure, but gave up his double bed to the Chief-of-Staff. While Ike was telling Marshall how comfortable the bed was, Telek jumped up and urinated on the red silk bed cover and pillow. Ike told his valet: "Mickey, when he does things like that, he's your dog."[14]

Kay didn't like the humourless[15] Marshall, and the feeling was reciprocated. She thought him a "cold fish" and could

---

[13] at ease, pp 263/264
[14] Sgt Mickey and General Ike, p 67
[15] The Patton Papers, Blumenson, vol 2, p 566

never overcome a "touch of fear" of him. "I have always had the distinct impression that General Marshall would have been just as happy if I did not exist," wrote Kay. But Marshall's attitude to Ike was much closer, like that of father and son (though he always called him 'Eisenhower', not Ike, "except on one unwary occasion"[16]). He decided that Ike was trying to do too much and should cut back on his trips to the front, relying more on other people's reports. Ike didn't appreciate this. "He usually blew his top if anyone so much as intimated that he looked tired," said Kay. But Ike eventually proposed that General Omar Bradley be his eyes and ears in North Africa and Marshall agreed.

Before leaving, Marshall told Butch: "You must look after [Eisenhower]. He is too valuable an officer to overwork himself. When an officer isn't fresh, he doesn't add much to my fund of knowledge and, worst of all, doesn't contribute to the ideas and enterprising push that are so essential to winning the war." The Chief-of-Staff told Butch to keep Ike out of the office as much as possible, ensure he came home early, persuade him to take a nap before dinner, organise somewhere he could ride or get other exercise and generally make sure that he was relaxed in mind and body by ensuring, for example, that he had a massage every evening. Butch quickly found a masseur with four years' experience and, when Marshall was back in the United States, sent an urgent secret cable to the assistant secretary of the General Staff saying: "Please advise the big boss that masseur already at work as per instructions."[17] But Ike considered massages "sissy stuff" and said that rubdowns made him feel "more nervous than relaxed".

He was aware, though, that he wasn't getting enough exercise. In a letter to Mamie, he wrote: "I watch my disposition just as I do my diet. Exercise has been out for eight months. I must get started soon."[18] The next day, Ike

---

[16] at ease, p 248
[17] Cable to Col Frank McCarthy, ANFA Casablanca, 26 January 1943
[18] 14 February 1944

enjoyed breakfast in bed and said he'd go to the office about 10am for a couple of hours and deal with important business only, exercise and maybe get a massage before lunch. He'd then take a nap before returning to the office about 3pm, deal with items of world importance, go home around 5pm and then rest. The following day he was up at 7am and, after breakfast with Clark, arrived at the office at 8.15am, complaining that the dust prevented him breathing fresh air.

Admiral King left on 25 January and General Marshall on 26 January, while the war went on. The following day, a German plane dropped a note at an American aerodrome saying: "Why don't the Americans come out and fight?" That night the Americans attacked Maknassy and Sened, taking 80 Axis prisoners and killing 25 of the enemy for US losses of two killed and two tanks lost. Later, in bright moonlight, about 20 German planes bombed three petrol tankers and a transport ship in Algiers harbour. On Sunday 31 January 1943, Ike was delighted to learn that Field Marshal von Paulus had capitulated at Stalingrad. A total of 850,000 Axis troops had been killed, wounded or captured during the battle. The epic encounter was one of the turning points of the war.

On 5 February 1943, Prime Minister Churchill arrived in Algiers after visiting Egypt and Turkey. Ike met him at Maison Blanche airfield and organised for him to go back to the villa in his half-armoured car, with the windows smeared with oil and mud to hide the fact that Churchill was in the car because of reported threats against his life. Back at the villa, Ike told Churchill that Patton was to command the American assault force in Operation Husky (the invasion of Sicily) while Clark was to handle training for the Fifth Army. Churchill said his preferred strategy was to invade Sicily shortly after Tunis was taken, knock Italy out of the war then persuade the Turks to join the Allies (which they eventually did in February 1945).

Ike hosted lunch at his villa for 12: the PM, de Gaulle, Giraud, Boisson, Noguès, Peyrouton, General Alan Brooke,

Anderson, Cunningham, Murphy, Macmillan and Sir Alexander Cadogan. Ike and the PM were co-hosts, with Giraud on Ike's right and de Gaulle on the Prime Minister's right. "I'm militarily and politically outranked by half my guests," Ike joked.

Because of the warm weather, hot baths and comfortable bed, the PM wanted to stay more than the three or four hours allotted. Ike argued that, while the PM was worth an entire army when safe in London, he was just a heavy responsibility in Algiers. However, Churchill insisted on staying. So Butch stood in for the Prime Minister and was driven back to the airport, where Churchill's B-17 took off with only the crew aboard. That evening, the PM was taken by a roundabout route to Maison Blanche airfield, but returned to Admiral Cunningham's villa after one of the two magnetos failed on his plane. (It was later claimed that the magneto wire was removed at Churchill's own suggestion just so he could stay).

In Algiers, he "revelled in long, hot" baths, which were unavailable in England because of fuel rationing.[19] Churchill would smoke his cigars in the overflowing bath and discuss the campaign with Ike, who had nowhere to sit except the toilet seat. Afterwards Ike would have to change into a fresh uniform because the creases had fallen out of the uniform he was wearing in the steamy bathroom.

Kay got on well with Churchill who enjoyed "lolling around". "How do you like driving on the 'wrong' side of the road?" he asked her. At dinner, the Prime Minister would slurp his soup, spill things, pick his nose and unzip his one-piece 'siren suit' to scratch his crotch. He took afternoon naps, so his conferences went on until the early hours of the following morning, leaving Ike and Kay worn out the following day.

---

[19] Churchill had bought "English bath soap and hot water bottles" at the Savoy Pharmacy in Cairo (CHAR 1/378/2)

Churchill was very fond of alcohol[20] and described water as "depressing".[21] On one occasion, he was "very much the worse for wear having evidently consumed several glasses of brandy at lunch".[22] He would frequently consume a whole bottle of champagne, plus port and brandy, at one sitting,[23] with a preference for Pol Roger champagne.[24] His breakfast in Algiers one morning consisted of a bottle of white wine, a bottle of soda water and a dish of ice. He would even drink brandy and smoke his trademark cigars in bed at night.[25] In Cairo, when he was offered a cup of tea at breakfast – just after 7.30am[26] – he swallowed two whiskies and soda then demanded a tumbler of white wine, which he knocked back in one gulp. On an earlier flight to Washington, when fellow travellers asked whether they should have lunch or high tea before arrival, Churchill pronounced that it was time for "high whisky." It was a habit he was known for.[27] On 3 March 1945, Ike told one general in France before a visit by the British Prime Minister: "Churchill likes Scotch. Be sure and have a good supply at hand."[28] Even the night before D-Day, "Churchill spent the evening in his suite at Storey's Gate, drinking brandy".[29]

Just before Churchill took off to return to England, two fighters crashed on the runway at Maison Blanche airfield. One turned over and burst into flames, killing the pilot. But the Prime Minister had no choice; he had to take off and return home. After he'd left, Ike got straight back to the details of the war, complaining to Marshall that the

---

[20] War Diaries 1939-1945, p xviii
[21] Alan Brooke war diaries, 5 August 1943
[22] Alan Brooke war diaries, 20 December 1944
[23] Alan Brooke war diaries, 29 March 1943
[24] Churchill, p 251
[25] Alan Brooke war diaries, 8 January 1945
[26] Alan Brooke war diary notes, 26 January 1943
[27] Professor Warren Kimball of Rutgers University believes that Churchill was not an alcoholic, but "alcohol dependent". But Churchill joked: "I have taken more out of alcohol than alcohol has taken out of me."
[28] The Last HundreD-Days, John Toland, Random House, 1966
[29] p 637 Bodyguard of Lies

Combined Chiefs were issuing commands directly to his subordinates over his head. He insisted that he was the only one who should give orders and he, in turn, was responsible to the Combined Chiefs.

On 12 February, Ike and Kay left his HQ in Algiers on one of their "frequent trips" to the front. Kay would drive Ike on those trips which could take a day or more. But their increasingly intimate relationship was a cause of concern to those close to both of them. The day they left, Kay's friend Elspeth Duncan confided in her boss, General Everett Hughes, that the couple's close relationship could cause a scandal, but Hughes said that maybe Kay could help Ike to win the war.

For the 'combat drive', Kay wore a comfortable Air Corps flying jacket, trousers and boots; Ike said they made her look like Patton, but other military drivers continued to wolf-whistle at Kay, much to Ike's annoyance. "If we're strafed, it's every man for himself," Kay laughed. It took them 26 hours to reach the front, where Kay met her US lover Dick Arnold, but then decided to sleep with Ike in the VIP tent. This incident sparked the initial rumours about their affair, giving Kay her first grey hairs. Many married staff officers had mistresses while overseas, but "Ike had always led a life that was above reproach," said Kay. At the end of the visit, Ike decided not to take a plane back to Algiers but to be driven by Kay, who was then hospitalised for a week with jaundice.

Meanwhile, Rommel was planning to attack. Three hours after Ike had inspected the Faïd and Maizila passes and pinned medals on some of the soldiers, just before dawn on St Valentine's Day, Rommel advanced on Sidi bou Zid in central Tunisia with 140 German tanks, supported by Italian troops and Stuka dive-bombers. It was the first major battle between American and German forces in World War II. The way was clear; the Americans had not laid any defensive mines. The German advance was spotted by the Americans, and the 1st US Armored Division pursued the German tanks, which seemed to be in headlong retreat. But waiting German anti-tank guns opened fire, destroying almost all the American armour. The German tanks then resumed their advance, simply crushing American infantrymen in their shallow slit trenches. The Americans were forced to retreat up to 50 miles from the Kasserine Pass, a two-mile-wide gap in the Atlas Mountains, abandoning much of their equipment, including guns, 20 tanks and 30 half-tracks. The mixture of American, British and French troops added to the confusion, particularly as the French were poorly equipped with World War I artillery and ammunition. Things looked so black for the Allies that General Alexander, who had been appointed Ike's deputy, asked Monty to create a diversion to draw off the Germans. Monty agreed. "We'll soon have Rommel running about between us like a wet hen," he said.

But Rommel quickly realised that any further advance would leave his flanks exposed. At Thala on 22 February, under fire from entrenched Allied positions, the Germans began to withdraw under cover of darkness, leaving behind just nine tanks. The next day, US planes attacked the retreating Germans, and the pass was reoccupied by the Allies late on 24 February. In all, almost 200 American soldiers were killed, more than 2,600 wounded and nearly 2,500 went missing or were taken prisoner, as well as 100 tanks lost.

The Americans claimed that the British had failed to help stop the Axis advance, and had not been active enough after Rommel started his withdrawal. Fredendall later claimed that Anderson had admitted in front of witnesses: "I can't sleep nights for thinking about Kasserine. Mine was the decision to make. I made the wrong decision." But that was untrue, according to Major-General Ernest Harmon, who called Fredendall a "low son-of-a-bitch, and a physical and moral coward".[30] Harmon had been sent to observe the battle on 23 February and had taken temporary command of the Allied forces. Ike told journalists that the failure to hold the pass was mainly due to the incorrect placement of two

---

[30] Omar Bradley diary, 3-2-43

infantry battalions. As a result, Fredendall was posted back to the US to command the Second Army for the rest of the war. He was driven away from his headquarters at 3.30am – the safest time to drive.

One US war correspondent said: "It became fashionable to speak of this as a defeat of 'green' American troops. If there was to be a scapegoat, they believed it should be the army commander."[31] But "Ike was not looking for a goat," said General Bradley, "for the mistakes at Kasserine were too numerous at every echelon of command to be attributed to the dereliction of a single commander."[32] Bradley said the patience and experience of General Alexander had helped the raw and untried United States commanders "mature and eventually come of age".

Ike said he accepted full responsibility for the defeat. "The outstanding fact to me is that the proud and cocky Americans today stand humiliated by one of the greatest defeats in our history," he said. As a result of the Kasserine débâcle, Ike restructured the Allied command, creating a new headquarters under Alexander to strengthen the co-ordination of three of the Allied nations, America, Britain and France.

On March 6, having already asked and been turned down by Clark, Ike asked Patton – "headstrong by nature and fearlessly aggressive" – to "rejuvenate" II Corps, with Bradley as his assistant. Patton noted in his diary: "Well, it is taking over rather a mess but I will make a go of it." Patton arrived with "sirens shrieking"[33] and immediately ordered extra training for the troops of II Corps. Soldiers had to be up early – the mess was closed at 7.30am – and had to wear their helmets all the time.[34] Even doctors using stethoscopes

---

[31] http://archives.chicagotribune.com/1952/08/24/page/207/ article/from-colonel-to-four-star-general
[32] Life magazine, 9 April 1951, p 84
[33] Life magazine, 9 April 1951, The War America Fought, General Omar N Bradley
[34] Patton diary, 6 March

and mechanics working underneath vehicles had to keep their helmets on at all times, on penalty of a $25 fine (the equivalent of a couple of weeks' wages) for a private or for officers.

Patton meant what he said. He recorded in his diary on 13 March – the day after he was made a three-star general – that he had "fined several officers $25.00 a piece for improper uniform. Fined 35 men for same."[35] On one occasion on St Patrick's Day 1943 at the headquarters of II Corps, Patton asked Ike's orderly, Sgt McKeogh: "Do you have $25 to throw away?" McKeogh said he didn't and Patton said that, in that case, he'd better get a helmet. When McKeogh told Ike about the incident, Ike "sort of nodded" and then said McKeogh had better get him one too.[36]

---

[35] Eventually soldiers even saluted Patton in his "bathing suit" (Letter to his wife, 2 July 1943)
[36] Sgt Mickey and General Ike, p 76

SAILOR'S DELIGHT

The day after Rommel attacked, on Monday 15 February, the BBC announced that Ike had been appointed a four-star general, less than two years after he had been elevated to colonel. He'd actually been promoted on Thursday 11 February 1943, though he didn't hear about it until after the BBC broadcast. When Butch told him that he'd heard it on the BBC, Ike swore. "I'm made a full general, the tops of my profession, and I'm not told officially. Well, maybe it isn't true." Then a teletype arrived from Mamie: "Congratulations on your fourth star."

Ike immediately called in Mickey and the four black staff, Hunt, Moaney and two waiters, and promoted each of them one grade. After dinner, Ike and Kay sat around the fire toasting the promotion with Champagne and listening to the phonograph. Ike insisted on replaying 'Roll out the barrel' and his favourite record, 'One dozen roses'. He sang all the words and turned to Kay as he sang "Give me one dozen roses, put my heart in beside them, and send them to the one I love."

But Ike still wasn't taking it easy as Marshall had ordered. To help the relaxation programme, Butch found a farmhouse, Sailor's Delight, ten miles outside Algiers, with tennis courts and stables for the three Arab chestnut stallions which were to arrive shortly. Kay had been an expert horsewoman in Ireland, unlike Mamie who never considered outdoor sports a "worthwhile way to spend her time". Ike and Kay began using Sailors' Delight, riding every afternoon, him in his uniform with high boots and tailored jodhpurs,[1] her dressed in jodhpurs, army shoes, a uniform shirt and kerchief over her hair. On one occasion, Ike told Patton

---

[1] Sgt Mickey and General Ike, p 13

afterwards, he was "speechless with rage"[2] because a soldier had "yahooed" at Kay while she was riding.[3] There was always a security man behind them. "I live in a goldfish bowl. There is never a moment when I don't feel that someone is peering at me," said Ike. They'd ride for a couple of hours then shower, have a drink and supper and head back to Algiers. On a few occasions, they'd spend the weekend together at the farmhouse, watching Westerns, playing bridge, sitting in the sun, practising golf, enjoying a game of table tennis or shooting with a second Beretta Ike had given Kay. (The first was lost when her ship was torpedoed.) Ike and Kay also played tennis until his bad knee – "permanently weakened" playing football against the Carlisle Indians[4] – gave way. The hot wind – the scirocco – meant the giant sand flies were not so troublesome at the farm as in Algiers. Kay's divorce papers from Gordon Summersby arrived in Algiers in the diplomatic pouch, courtesy of Ike. She again met Dick Arnold (now a colonel) and took the day off to go swimming and play tennis with him at Sailor's Delight. Ike laid on a dinner for Arnold with Butch and a few other friends. Also at the dinner was Butch's girlfriend, Mollie Ford, whom Kay had met in Algiers earlier in 1943. "Ike had a tremendous crush on Kay, and Butch knows he did too," Mollie said later. "Butch always tries to cover up for him...But there's no denying Ike was infatuated with her. He was really crazy about her. And jealous too...No matter what Butch says, she was much more than a diversion."[5]

By the end of February, the Allies were increasingly confident about defeating the Axis forces in North Africa. Patton, who had just heard that his son-in-law, Johnnie

---

[2] Ike told Patton he "glared at the man", according to a letter from Patton to his wife (5 May 1943)
[3] Los Angeles Times, 28 May 1995
[4] Life magazine, 9 November 1942
[5] On 2 March, Ike finally wrote to Mamie about Kay, but assured her that he had "no emotional involvements and will have none"

Waters, was missing in action,[6] said with tears in his eyes that he'd personally like to shoot Rommel (who had just lost the battle of Medenine). But at a conference at Maison Blanche on 7 March, Ike cautioned Patton against personal recklessness; he should be a corps commander, not a casualty – and he should be more pro-British. Like many US officers, Patton wasn't too keen on the British way of doing things. But Ike told him that there should be "a feeling of partnership between ourselves and the British". Any American officer spreading anti-British sentiment was to be sent home, and Patton was to be merciless about sacking inefficient officers.

Meanwhile, Kay was keeping in touch with the news from Kul in London, and had just heard how 173 women and children had been crushed to death at Bethnal Green underground station in London on 3 March. People sheltering from German bombs had fallen on a woman who had tripped over. (The local council had called for a crush barrier to be fitted two years before, but was told it would be a waste of money.) News of the disaster was censored at the time because the authorities did not want to give the incident "a disproportionate importance".[7] In fact, it was the largest single loss of civilian life in Britain in the whole war. It wasn't the only bad news. The US Eighth Army Air Force was once again involved in an error of navigation. On 5 April 1943, US bombers attacked an Antwerp factory, but almost all the bombs fell on a residential suburb, killing 936 civilians, including 209 schoolchildren.

On March 8, Archbishop Francis Spellman of New York called on Ike with a letter of introduction from FDR. At lunch with the archbishop, Ike said all Churches and other welfare agencies should provide humanitarian help to everyone, regardless of nationality, race, creed or colour.

---

[6] Subsequently, Patton was in trouble for trying to rescue Waters from Hammelburg POW camp

[7] http://www.bbc.co.uk/history/ww2peopleswar/stories/09/a795909.shtml

(This rather clashed with his views on the Germans!) Meanwhile General Harold Alexander, the army group commander, hoped to open an Allied offensive on March 17. He decided that Monty's Eighth Army should attack the 'impregnable' Mareth line in the east, while Patton's II Corps should create a diversion in the west. II Corps was only expected to regain the ground lost to the Germans at Kasserine, but the three-week offensive ended with a US victory at el Guettar.

Butch took leave in March and flew to the US where he met Marshall who told him that Ike's "rise or fall" depended on the outcome of the Tunisian battle. Butch stayed with his wife at the Wardman Park hotel where a cable from Ike on 19 March said that the "package originally ordered by Skibberene (sic) [Skibbereen – a town in Cork – was one of Ike's pet names for Kay] finally arrived (confidential) but list in your possession is still desired". What exactly Kay ordered from the United States is not mentioned, but Butch had more than 650 pounds of baggage on his return to North Africa, with packages and mail from almost all the "war widows" in Washington. He had even bought a mate for Telek. The dog was named Caacie (pronounced 'khaki'), said to be an abbreviation of "Canine Auxiliary Air Corps". Ike had asked Butch to obtain an automatic bridge-playing machine with advanced lessons while he was in the US. Butch didn't find such a machine, but he did bring back a gold Longines watch engraved with Eisenhower's name and the date. It was one of a number of watches later presented to Ike, including a Patek Philippe wristwatch with ruby hour markers and pocket watch from King Saud of Saudi Arabia, an engraved Leroy pocket watch from French admirers in Paris, an engraved gold Longines watch from the President of Mexico in 1946 and a gold Rolex Oyster Perpetual DateJust presented in 1951 to celebrate the production of the 150,000th Rolex 'official chronometer' watch. Ike told Butch that he had taken up riding seriously and he was "disciplining" himself to stay away from the office as much as possible. However, when things weren't going well with the war, "I catch hell," he said.

On 6 April, the German 15th Panzer and 90th Light Divisions fought "perhaps the best battle of their distinguished careers" at Wadi Akarit, according to General Alexander. Meanwhile the Allies were slowly gaining mastery of the skies. German forces in the Mediterranean town of Sfax (or Sousse, according to General Brooke[8]), 170 miles southeast of Tunis were being targeted by Allied bombers. The previous December, Montgomery had bet Beetle Smith that he could capture Sfax by mid-April 1943. (British newspapers had reported the previous month that the Allied occupation of Sfax was "likely soon".[9]) Beetle jokingly replied that he'd give Monty a Flying Fortress if he did so. When Sfax was taken on 10 April, Monty claimed his "winnings". Beetle protested that the bet had been a joke, but Montgomery insisted on his aeroplane. General Alan Brooke said Monty's demand was just "crass stupidity".[10] However, "being the past master at cementing inter-Allied relations, Eisenhower ordered that Monty should be given the Fortress aircraft, together with the American crew to fly it. Monty had thus gained his aircraft, but in doing so he had annoyed Eisenhower intensely, and laid the foundations of distrust and dislike which remained with Eisenhower during the rest of the war".[11]

Soon after Sfax was taken came news of the German discovery of the bodies of thousands of Poles at Katyn near Smolensk in Russia. In Germany on 13 April, Radio Berlin announced the results of an International Red Cross investigation which suggested that the Russians had killed up to 12,000 Poles while they occupied the area in 1940.[12] The Soviets steadfastly maintained that the Germans were

---

[8] Alan Brooke war diary notes, 3 June 1943
[9] Daily Herald, 21 November 1942
[10] Alan Brooke, war diary notes, 3 June 1943
[11] Alan Brooke war diary notes, 3 June 1943
[12] In fact, the Soviet secret police shot 22,000 Polish officers and intellectuals

responsible for the deaths when *they* had occupied the area in 1941. Defendants at the Nuremberg Trials after the war were refused access to Polish evidence proving Soviet guilt, and the Russians publicly hanged a number of Germans found 'guilty' of the Katyn massacres. On 14 April 1943, Stalin's eldest son, Lieut Yakov Dzhugashvili, who had been captured two years earlier at Smolensk, committed suicide at Sachsenhausen, allegedly overcome by shame at the Russian killings. [13] Ike supported the USSR denial, but British Foreign Office Under-Secretary Sir Alexander Cadogan wrote in his diary at the time: "How can we discuss with the Russians execution of German 'war criminals' when we have condoned this?"

In Africa, the fighting was coming to an end. On 15 April, Ike asked General Alexander to allow the Americans to take Bizerte in the last phase of the battle for Tunisia. He said that, unless the US troops felt they had played a substantial role in the campaign, they would be less interested in the strategy of beating Germany before Japan. Alexander agreed. At this stage, Ike was so confident about the fighting ability of II Corps that he appointed Bradley its commander while Patton went back to Morocco to resume preparing for the landings in Operation Husky. As he left Ike's villa, Patton recalled that, before leaving II Corps headquarters, he'd picked some wild nasturtiums and placed them on the grave of his 27-year-old aide, Dick Jenson, who'd been killed on 1 April by a 500-pound German bomb. "I guess I really am a goddam' old fool," wept Patton.

Kay drove her boss 15 miles north of Beja to see some of the 27 Tiger tanks destroyed by the British on 26 March. They could hear artillery fire about 2,000 yards away, but saw no enemy aircraft, although they spotted bursts of antiaircraft fire. Ike then changed to a jeep driven by Anderson, because Axis planes were known to bomb and strafe the road east. If the vehicles were strafed, Ike was bluntly told that he could

---

[13] Daily Telegraph, 30 July 2000. The Russians finally admitted Soviet guilt in 2010

stay in the jeep or dive into the nearby fields, many of which still had mines left by the Germans. [14]

On the English national day, St George's Day, 23 April, Ike travelled by Flying Fortress and jeep to Alexander's headquarters, where he met Giraud. Then he took a jeep to the headquarters of II Corps' new commander, Omar Bradley, who described the American attack on the remaining Germans which had started the previous night. Rommel, who'd been in command of the German forces in North Africa, had turned over command in Tunisia to Generaloberst Hans-Jürgen von Arnim and had returned to Germany.

After another visit to the front on 30 April, Ike stayed in Constantine overnight. While there, Ike lent Butch his wallet of lucky coins for a poker game. The lucky coins included a silver dollar, a French franc, an English gold five-guinea piece and a Miraculous Medal sent to Ike by a little girl in Detroit – and Butch won. Five days later, Ike and Kay flew to Oujda, the headquarters of General Clark's Fifth Army, and Kay then drove Ike in a car flying a large red flag with four stars. This time, everyone saluted. Ike went to lunch on the battleship HMS Nelson (on which the Italians were to sign their surrender) and discussed the forthcoming attack on Sicily. Marshall had urged Ike to attack immediately, but Ike said the Allies were only "nibbling at the edges" if they picked off Sicily. Besides, they needed more fighting men, rather than headquarters staff. Many US soldiers were being used for purposes other than fighting in North Africa, including 100,000 service troops held in readiness for Operation Anvil, the invasion of southern France. Ike was always being asked to find more clerks, stenographers and secretaries, but it was almost impossible to find office staff among the enlisted men, and he thought more female WACs should be used.

---

[14] "If you see the plane in time, you stop the car and run like hell for 50 yds off the road and lay down. It seems most undignified but all do it." Patton letter to his wife, 11 March 1943

Already Ike's attention was turning to the period after the war. A New York publisher cabled Ike offering him a large sum to write a book about his wartime experiences. Ike turned down the offer, but left the door open in case he wrote a book after the war. [15]

---

[15] He did, asking Kay to type out her diary, which he used as the foundation for Crusade in Europe (1948)

THE END OF TORCH

The capture of Bizerte on 8 May marked the beginning of the end of Mussolini's attempt to turn the Mediterranean into an Italian lake, "Mare Nostrum".[1] The same day, the German High Command ordered its forces finally to abandon Africa. The Americans intercepted goodbye messages from members of the 15th Panzer Division to members of their families, as well as German proposals to evacuate up to 33,000 Germans and 30,000 Italians by sea.

The Germans did not seem short of ammunition, as the Allies had captured huge caches of weapons and ammo, including 1,200 guns, 200 tanks, aircraft and a million rations of food. But the Germans also left mines in munitions dumps, railway cars and storage piles with fuses that could be set to go off any time up to three weeks later, so captured dumps had to be carefully searched.[2] Ike had feared a long-drawn-out battle for the Bon peninsula but he bet Patton $15 that the Allies would have the peninsula cleared by 15 May.[3] Patton lost and "got a new 500 franc bill and presented it to him on a tray with a red rose and the remark 'Hail Caesar'".[4]

In total, Operation Torch lasted 182 days and cost the Allies more than 71,000 casualties, including almost 15,500 killed. The Axis forces had suffered five times as many casualties, including more than quarter of a million men taken prisoner. On 10 May, Bradley, in a brief phone message, told Ike simply: "Mission completed."

---

[1] Latin for 'Our Sea'
[2] The "whole damned country" was full of mines, said Patton in a letter to his wife (15 March 1943)
[3] Patton predicted it would take a month longer
[4] Patton diary, 8 May 1943

Von Arnim, Commander-in-Chief of Army Group Africa –
who was "said to have an English mother"[5] – was captured
by the British Indian Army's 4th Infantry Division on 12 May
when the Germans surrendered to the British in Tunis. Ike
refused to meet him; he really hated the Germans. He was
convinced that the "ruthless desire for domination" was "an
inbred attribute of the German race". He did not try to
understand "finely drawn distinctions between the German
people and the German government" and, in his opinion,
Germany must be "rendered impotent ever to wage war
again".[6] In a short "off the record speech" to 100 members of
the Association of American Correspondents at a lunch in
September 1942, Ike said he would be prepared to "lie, cheat
and steal to beat the Hun", and "good sportsmanship" was
not part of the war. The Allies' "tough and vicious enemies"
would stoop to anything to win, he said.

Von Arnim expected to surrender directly to Ike, but Ike
refused to see him. Ike subsequently wrote in Crusade in
Europe: "When von Arnim was brought through Algiers on
his way to captivity, some members of my staff felt that I
should observe the custom of bygone days and allow him to
call on me...For me, World War II was far too personal a
thing to entertain such feelings. Daily as it progressed, there
grew within me the conviction that, as never before in a war
between many nations, the forces that stood for human good
and men's rights were this time confronted by a completely
evil conspiracy with which no compromise could be
tolerated. Because only by the utter destruction of the Axis
was a decent world possible, the war became for me a
crusade...

"In this specific instance, I told my Intelligence Officer to get
any information he possibly could out of the captured
generals but that, so far as I was concerned, I was interested
only in those who were not yet captured. None would be
allowed to call on me. I pursued the same practice to the end

5 Daily Mirror, 13 May 1943
6 Life magazine, 9 November 1942

of the war. Not until Field-Marshal Jodl signed the surrender terms at Reims in 1945 did I ever speak to a German general, and even then my only words were that he would be held personally and completely responsible for the carrying out of the surrender terms."[7]

According to Butch, Ike's "hatred of the Germans, and particularly of the Nazi ideology" were so strong that he did not trust "his own reactions before a representative of the Prussian and Nazi regime". Ike forgot his own comment that "hating anyone or anything meant that there was little to be gained. The person who had incurred my displeasure probably didn't care".[8] Von Arnim was taken instead before the British commander, General Kenneth Anderson, and then spent the rest of the war as a prisoner-of-war in Mississippi.

The Italians surrendered in droves, and at least one truckload of Italian officers, in smart military uniforms and plumed helmets, rode jauntily into captivity. They had to be kept in separate barbed-wire enclosures from the Germans because of the animosity between the Axis allies. German soldiers also had to be separated from members of the Luftwaffe, whom they accused of providing inadequate air cover in North Africa.

There were so many prisoners that it was to take four months to evacuate them all – though Italians were retained as labourers in North Africa, as relatively few guards were needed for them. The 36th Infantry was stripped to provide guards and escorts, and so much rail transport was needed for moving the prisoners that one armoured division could not be transferred to Morocco to protect the Allies' rear. Ike said he never realised what a headache quarter of a million prisoners-of-war could be, especially when they were evacuated at the rate of only about 30,000 a month. Until that time, the British had not had many prisoners to trade

---

[7] Life magazine 13 December 1948, Crusade in Europe
[8] at ease, p 52

with the Germans but, after 5 May, they had 100,000 Axis prisoners, with 50,000 more to come. II Corps took 33,000 prisoners, of whom fewer than 5,000 were Italians.

By 13 May, the battle was generally over in Tunisia. General Alexander sent Churchill a message: "It is my duty to report that the Tunisian Campaign is over. All enemy resistance has ceased. We are masters of the North African shores" [9] although Algiers was actually bombed again in an early evening raid. Ike and Kay watched the raid from the front porch, the roof of his villa protecting them from falling shrapnel. Smoke-screen devices blanketed the city within minutes.

Now there was time for levity. Ike spent Sunday at the farm composing a cable to Britain's King George VI about the Allied victory. Butch suggested he start it "Dear Kingy." "Or Dear Georgie," Ike proposed. The rearmament of the French was formally agreed by Ike with General Giraud in a military function at the *Foyer Civique*. The transfer had an additional unintended effect. While out riding with Kay after the ceremony, French officers and soldiers who had been passing Ike unnoticed recognised him for the first time and saluted him.

At the North African victory parade on 20 May, Kay – who had driven Ike to Tunis [10] – stood on the reviewing stand near Monty, "a supercilious, woman-hating little martinet" who was still "a thorn in Ike's side". [11] The parade ran an hour over time, and Ike – the only American soldier on the reviewing stand – had to stand at attention almost all the time. The Goums, Moroccan mountain troops who traditionally slit the throats of their enemies, attracted the most applause. [12] The Military Police got some boos from

---

[9] 1.16pm, 13 May 1943
[10] The Patton Papers, p 253
[11] The military correspondent of The Sunday Times says she was wrong; Monty was in London at the time. (The Times of India, 12 December 1948)
[12] An Italian propaganda leaflet on 7 January 1944 said three Moroccan Goums in Castel S Vincenzo "che avevano tagliata la gola ad una madre

other soldiers. The French were allotted a limited number of troops for the parade, but greatly exceeded their allocation in order to impress the native Arabs with their strength. After the parade, the new Bey of Tunis presented Ike with a decoration in a ceremony which featured a gold throne and eunuchs.

Ike told General Marshall that, when the fighting was over he intended to take a "24-hour leave, where no one can find me". But Ike's thoughts were already on the next target – Sicily.

---

italiana e si accingevano ad abusare della figlia quindicenne" (had slit the throat of an Italian mother and were about to abuse her 15-year-old daughter)

OPERATION HUSKY

Washington approved Ike's plans to exploit the Allied success in North Africa in a bid to knock Italy out of the war quickly. To satisfy the Soviets, a second front to gain a foothold on the continent of Europe was to be opened by 1 May 1944, almost a year later.

Ike planned to tackle the 'miniature Gibraltar' of Pantelleria first, as the Mediterranean island had airfields which the Allies could use to provide air cover for landings in Sicily. Pantelleria had no beaches, so it had to be attacked through its small harbour. Intensive air bombardment, supported by naval gunfire, would precede the attempted landing, but the island's heavy fortifications were encased in solid rock. (Later, an Allied aircraft mistook Pantelleria for Malta in the dark and, after running out of fuel, crashed into the sea. Thirteen of the 20 passengers were drowned, including Brooke's aide-de-camp, Colonel Barney Charlesworth.)

After Pantelleria, the next target was the island of Lampedusa, to be followed by the assault on the southern Italian island of Sicily itself. But even as Ike planned the assaults, he had to continue with other engagements. On 28 May, Giraud placed his personal *Grand Cordon* of the *Légion d'Honneur*, the highest military award of France, round Ike's neck (without first consulting de Gaulle, who was consequently furious). Ike said he accepted the decoration as a sign of Allied friendship, but he wouldn't wear it until he and Giraud were both in Metz, on the Franco-German border. Generals Marshall and Brooke had also arrived in North Africa and both stayed at Ike's villa. The first morning they were there, Ike wore his *Légion d'Honneur* medal into Brooke's bedroom, provoking some surprise. Marshall again took Ike's room, inquiring about Telek who was about to sire a litter with Caacie.[1]

Churchill, travelling as an Air Commodore, stayed with Admiral Cunningham ('ABC') next door to Ike while he visited British troops in Tunisia, including his son Randolph, a commando. From ABC's villa, the PM and admiral were driven to Ike's villa for an informal conference with Marshall. The US Chief-of-Staff said he expected to stay a few days, but the Prime Minister intended a longer stay. He planned to swim in the Mediterranean, and wanted to try and persuade Ike to invade mainland Italy and drive the Italians out of the war. But Beetle Smith said an additional 30,000 US troops and 33,000 British soldiers from outside North Africa would be needed for any assault on Italy. Nevertheless, Churchill said he looked forward to eating his 1943 Christmas dinner in Rome. (He would be disappointed!)

On Monday 31 May, Ike and General Marshall were co-hosts at a dinner for the British Prime Minister in Ike's villa. Churchill criticised the practice – followed by Butch – of keeping a daily diary, which could only serve to reflect the writer's changes of mind. He cited the diary of a British general who wrote "There will be no war"; war was actually declared the next day. Ike agreed; he admitted that his early letters showed "a dazzling ignorance of coming events".[2]

At the start of June, as the Prime Minister left for Tunis with Marshall, Cunningham invited Ike to accompany him aboard the admiral's vessel in a week's time during the bombardment of Pantelleria. Allied bombers were already pounding the island's defenders.[3] Ike decided that the marshalling yards on the outskirts of Rome should also be bombed in an effort to destroy Italian communications. Although he believed that the Vatican would be safe from

---

[1] Butch bet Ike $1 for each pup less than four, dead or alive; Ike was to pay Butch $1 each for more than four
[2] at ease, p 135
[3] Alan Brooke war diaries, 1 June 1943

damage, he was concerned about the political repercussions, as Churchill had assured FDR that the Allies would not bomb Rome for the time being. The Allies had bombed Rome for the first time on 16 May, three months before the Germans occupied the city. Pope Pius XII subsequently wrote to FDR asking him to spare Rome "further pain and devastation", and Roosevelt assured him that Allied airmen had been instructed not to drop bombs on the neutral Vatican.4 Ike agreed but he was annoyed at FDR's "autocratic" behaviour.5

Meanwhile, Kay's fiancé, Colonel Dick Arnold, was working on clearing German mines at Sedjenane in Tunisia. He had been appointed commander of the 20th Engineers on 25 May. After studying mine removal for one week, he began work but, on 6 June, a booby trap Teller mine was set off when Second Lieutenant George Lux triggered a hidden wire. Arnold was killed on the spot. Both Lux's legs were broken, but he survived. Arnold was one of seven officers and 19 Allied soldiers killed removing more than 200,000 German mines.6

Ike was planning Operation Husky, the invasion of Sicily due to begin on 10 July, when he heard about Arnold's death. He broke off his planning to tell Kay that Dick had been killed. She burst into hysterical tears, and he hugged her and offered her his handkerchief. Eisenhower's secretary, Sue Sarafian, said that Kay "cried on our shoulder and we cried with her".7 "She threw an Irish tantrum," said Butch. "She had the feeling it was all Ike's fault, that he had

---

4 But while FDR authorised Ike to bomb the San Lorenzo railway junction, he said no bombs must fall on the Vatican. (CHAR 20/113/17) On 9 April 1944, the Allied air forces bombed Rome three times.
5 CHAR 20/113/107
6 After the war, German prisoners were used to clear mines – in breach of the 1929 Geneva Convention. In one three-month period in Norway in 1945, 392 German prisoners were wounded and 275 killed
7 www.ibiblio.org/lia/president/EisenhowerLibrary/oral_histories/ Jehl_Sue-Sarafian.html

set the colonel up. But Ike had nothing to do with Dick Arnold's death."

Mamie referred to Kay's relationship with Dick Arnold in a letter to Ike. He responded on the day Pantelleria was taken: "A very strange coincidence occurred this morning. I had two letters from you (one a V mail written on May 24) and in one of them you mentioned my driver, and a story you'd heard about the former marital difficulties of her fiancé. You said it was a 'not pretty' story. Your letter gave me my first intimation that there was any story whatsoever – I didn't know anything about it. In any event, whatever guilt attached to him has been paid in full. At the same moment that your letter arrived I received a report that he was killed – by a mine! I knew him quite well and I liked him...what young Arnold did, I do not know. But here we considered him a valuable officer and a fine person. I'm saddened by his death."[8]

(Another less newsworthy death occurred the next day – one of Caacie's new puppies. Caacie had the litter under a bed in one of the servant-guest rooms. The largest of the three puppies died, but the remaining male and female prospered.)

After Arnold's death, Ike wrote several letters to Kay's mother. A letter to Kul on 7 August 1943 regretted that he had not met her while he was in London, and apologised that he could not employ her. "Never hesitate to write me frankly and fully. I truly like Kay," he wrote. In another letter 20 days later, Ike again expressed his concern for Kay and his affection for her: "She is quite tired and run down of course, as an inescapable result of her grief and torn emotions... She has been loyal, efficient and a great help for well over a year – so I feel that she is indeed a very dear friend, and one I'd like very much to help." Another letter to Kul from the Advance Command Post in Amilcar on 14

---

[8] http://www.pbs.org/wgbh/americanexperience/features/primary-resources/eisenhower-letters/

September 1943 described Kay's attempts to cope with depression after Arnold's death. "[W]hen some incident or some person suggests poignantly to her all that she has lost, she has spells of complete despair," wrote Ike. Two weeks later, Ike wrote to Kay's mother again saying Kay's health was improving, and commenting on her affection for Telek. A letter on notebook paper on 25 October 1943 asked Kay's mother to send a detailed account of Kay's finances to help Ike settle her income taxes. He set out two pages of financial figures.

Kay threw herself into her work as Ike's chauffeur. She regularly drove Ike between Amilcar, near Carthage on the Bay of Tunis, and Fairfield Rear, Ike's alternative HQ near Sidi Athman. The journey took an hour over roads congested with Arabs, tanks and supply vehicles, many of them ferrying bombs and petrol to the airfields. The heavy traffic made the journey tedious and sometimes quite dangerous, but it helped Kay to come to terms with the death of Dick Arnold.

The bombardment of Pantelleria was due to start on 9 June. The day before, two days after Arnold's death, Kay flew with Ike to Bône and then drove him to HMS Aurora, which set sail during the night. At 5am on 9 June, the ship's loud-speaker announced that there would be 600 aerial sorties that day, including bombs being "skipped" into caves on the island. In between bombings, four cruisers would fire their six-inch guns. Under this salvo, eight destroyers would approach to within 2,500 yards of the shore and fire their smaller guns. Ike, who was suffering from another tummy bug, said his stomach felt like "a clenched fist" – just like before Operation Torch and the final battle in Tunisia. But he believed that the morale of the defenders would be destroyed by the bombardment, so the Allies would subsequently have no difficulty in taking the island.

During the battle, the Allies dropped thousands of copies of a leaflet on the Italians promising them free passage to America if they surrendered. "I hope it wasn't signed," joked

Ike. He said Italian prisoners would be content with "proper food and modest pay" in Africa, but he didn't think he could fulfil a British request for 30,000 Italian prisoners for forced labour.

Reaction to the shelling from the island's defenders was feeble. "If you and I got into a small boat, we could capture the place ourselves," Ike told Cunningham. On Friday 11 June, shortly after noon, Pantelleria surrendered because of a "shortage of water". The Allies estimated there were 11,000 Italian troops on the island, but more than 15,000 were taken prisoner. Churchill had agreed to pay Ike one Italian sou for every Italian over the PM's estimate of 3,000 prisoners. The settlement came to about $1.60.

Air attacks were then switched to Lampedusa, with the larger island being bombed within 90 minutes of Pantelleria's surrender. Lampedusa, which surrendered the next day, had a radar station which the Italians used to report movements of Allied vessels and planes. The islands of Linosa and Lampione, about 90 miles west of Malta, also surrendered.

The day of Lampedusa's surrender, Britain's King George VI [9] flew into Algeria on a secret visit. [10] 'General Lyon' arrived in a converted Lancaster on his first trip out of England during the war. Kay drove Ike to meet him in an armour-plated Cadillac at Maison Blanche airfield and then drove the King to General Gale's villa. After Ike introduced Kay as a "British subject" on loan, the King ignored her. King George had previously expressed concern to the Chief of the Imperial General Staff about the political and military situation in North Africa [11] but, during the drive, he appeared to be up to date on the situation. However, he bombarded Ike with questions about climate, the native Arabs and current Allied operations. He said this was really a holiday

---

[9] "just a grade above a moron. Poor little fellow." Patton diary 13 June 1943
[10] With the King was Sir Alexander Grigg, the Secretary of State for War
[11] Alan Brooke war diaries, 22 February 1943

for him, although it was supposed to be an official inspection trip.

At a press conference that afternoon, Ike confided in more than 100 news correspondents that the next operation would be against Sicily "sometime next month". The Allies might get a "bloody nose" in the battle but he thought the job could be done.[12] Ike then had dinner alone with the King, whose visit was not officially announced for three days. Later, the King invested Ike with the Grand Cross of the Order of the Bath, the highest military honour that the British government could bestow.

Before leaving on his tour of the Med, the King also visited British soldiers in hospital in Tunisia and watched troops training to remove land mines and booby traps. He also saw a display by three artillery batteries, listened as Ike addressed the troops, watched a fly-past by the three Piper Cubs used by Ike, Clark and Butch, inspected the new amphibious Dukw[13] and observed training for Operation Husky. The King then went on to Tripoli and, on Sunday June 20, to Malta before returning to dine with Ike at Admiral Cunningham's villa.

The next day, there were rumours of a French Army revolt against Giraud and of a putsch by Gaullist forces in North Africa. The US newspapers reported that Ike had given de Gaulle an ultimatum that Giraud must continue as commander-in-chief of the French forces, on instructions from the President and British PM. Times were so uncertain that Ike considered carrying a pistol, though this precaution was quickly forgotten.

Later that summer, Butch's girlfriend Mollie Ford rang Ike from Algiers where a French girl had accused an American officer of being the father of her unborn baby. Ford said she had got a job for the girl at the Red Cross, found a doctor to

---

[12] The Star, 10 July 1943
[13] Known as a 'duck', this amphibious vehicle was named by manufacturer GMC

deliver the baby and organised for her to live with a French family who would help care for the child. The officer was eventually traced to a depot near New York. Ike said the man would be brought back to Algiers if the girl would swear an affidavit that he was the father. But the girl said that, although she loved the American, if he didn't choose to return voluntarily, she wouldn't pursue him.

Ike wanted to be closer to the ground and sea commanders for the invasion of Sicily, so he planned to leave North Africa for Malta on 23 June. Before that, Ike and Kay went to see off American troops from Bizerte in Tunisia. However, Ike was taken aback when the soldiers booed him. They felt that, unlike generals such as Patton, he wouldn't be taking part in the actual fighting – just sending ordinary soldiers into battle where they might be wounded or even killed.[14]

Many of the soldiers were among the 150,000 men who would take part in the first assault – 10,000 more than landed in the Casablanca, Oran and Algiers attacks, and they would attack on an 80-mile front. More than 1,000 ocean-going vessels, transport and escorts were to take part in the invasion, 250 more than in the North African landings. Since mid-May, the Allies had flown almost 43,000 sorties, destroying more than 400 German and Italian aircraft for the loss of 250 of their own. Ike wanted to be flown over the beaches soon after the landings, but realised that aerial photographs taken at dawn would be just as good. Patton expected the American landings to be "nasty", yet expected to be able to occupy a beachhead three or four thousand yards long by daylight.

The Germans still weren't sure where the invasion would come, but had moved the Hermann Göering armoured division to Sicily just in case. They were also strengthening their defences on the French island of Sardinia, which the Americans had considered as an alternative target. Allied

---

[14] However, they cheered when he slipped in the mud – twice – at Aachen and Munchen-Gladbach

bombers attacked Sardinia and the Dodecanese, and British commandos landed in Crete to confuse the Germans still further about the ultimate target. In Britain, Major Ewen Montagu[15] disguised the corpse of a down-and-out as "Major William Martin, RM" and put it into the sea near Huelva, Spain.[16] The body carried a briefcase intended to fall into the hands of the Germans, with letters suggesting that the Allies would attack Sardinia and Greece, rather than Sicily. Just in case, Hitler sent Field Marshal Erwin Rommel to Greece to assume command, and the Germans moved minesweepers, minelayers and three Panzer divisions there.

The aerial assault against Sicily started on 3 July and, within a week, only two Sicilian airfields remained usable by Axis planes. The British Chiefs of Staff agreed that a rumour should be broadcast at the same time as the attack on Sicily that Italy had asked for an armistice. Marshall asked Ike to prepare to release a joint message from FDR and the Prime Minister offering the Italians democratic government if they would overthrow Mussolini. But Ike said he didn't want to issue a message to the whole of Italy until the Allies had a stronger foothold.

On 8 July, Ike made the Lascaris Bastion in Malta his HQ for the invasion. The war rooms – a network of tunnels and chambers below the Lascaris Battery in Valletta – were shared with Cunningham, Monty and Tedder. Ike stayed in the Verdala summer palace, built by the Knights of Malta more than four centuries earlier. Ike's office was the reception room upstairs. A huge adjoining bedroom had an ensuite bathroom and stairs leading down to a dungeon. As Kay drove Ike the several miles from the palace to his headquarters, Ike noticed the windmills turning rapidly, an indication of the gales which were to hit the Mediterranean that night.[17] At dinner, Lord Louis Mountbatten predicted

---

[15] Subsequently president of the United Synagogue
[16] This incident was the basis for the 1956 film The Man Who Never Was
[17] A "near-gale" force wind "scattered the aircraft and dispersed the troops". (The Patton Papers, p 275/6)

high waves on the shore where the Americans were to land. Ike gave his lucky coins a rub before going to bed.

The invasion began about 3am on 10 July. Patton's command made all its initial landings by 6am. There was soon a trail of smoke and flame stretching ten miles inland from the coast. Allied bombers attacked the Axis headquarters in the San Dominica hotel and the communications hub in the general post office in Taormina. Ike was delighted to hear that the Americans had taken the target village of Gela,[18] but wondered what had happened at the two other places where Americans were to land in the southwest. The British were to land on four south-eastern beaches, while 20,000 Canadians were to take the Pachino peninsula in the south. But the Allies suffered some reverses. Gliders were to have been turned loose 1,000 feet up, 3,000 yards offshore, but the high wind forced five or six into the sea. During the day, the American destroyer Maddox was also dive-bombed and sunk, with more than 200 sailors killed. Two other US destroyers limped into port at Malta, one towed by a tug.

In the afternoon, Ike slipped down to a Maltese beach for an hour in the sun. The beach was generally barred to soldiers because of the swell and undertow. Ike stayed on the sand, saying he didn't want to swim in "sand mixed with water". Later that night, Ike went to bed straight after dinner – as soon as Maltese governor Field Marshal 'Tiger' Gort stopped talking – but woke at 5.30am the next day.

Allied fighter squadrons from Pantelleria could not take off at dawn because of ground fog, so five fighter squadrons from Malta were assigned to protect the American invaders. But Allied troops in Sicily had itchy fingers, even as the Spitfires flew overhead. Syracuse fell to the Allies at 9pm on the first day. "To think we've done it again!" said Ike. He immediately set sail for Sicily aboard the destroyer HMS

---

[18] Despite an Axis bombing attack in which "no one was hurt, except some civilians". (Patton diary)

Petard to meet Patton aboard the command ship, Monrovia, off Gela. Patton expected to establish his Seventh Army command post ashore during the day.

Ten enemy tanks had been knocked out during an attack the previous day, one of them within 300 yards of Patton, but the general ignored the near-miss. However, command headquarters in Malta couldn't decide whether he needed help, because Patton was not sending back reports to HQ. When Ike left the meeting with Patton aboard the Monrovia, there was tension in the air. Ike went ashore in a Dukw, passing 100 naked soldiers bathing along the beach, and then returned to the Petard. There he had a large gin and then returned to Malta, reaching Valletta harbour at 2.30am.

When Ike got to his advance command post headquarters in Pinto tunnel in the Lascaris Bastion, he was informed that almost 100 Allied paratroopers had been killed the previous night when their planes had been shot down by trigger-happy Americans. US ground and naval forces had fired on 144 C-47 transport planes which flew over Allied lines shortly after a German air raid, shooting down 23 planes and damaging 37, resulting in a total of 318 casualties, including 82 dead. A furious Ike immediately sent Patton a cable ordering him to inquire into this "inexcusable careless-ness and negligence". [19]

On 12 July, Ike flew 300 miles back to Tunisia and the following day, at a news conference in Amilcar, predicted that Sicily would be conquered within a fortnight. How that victory would be achieved was a matter of some controversy. Two days after the news conference, Americans from the 180th Infantry Regiment massacred 79 Italian and German prisoners in two separate incidents at Biscari. [20] Later, at the

---

[19] "Man who have been bombed all day get itchy fingers," said Patton. (Diary, 13 July 1943)
[20] "in cold blood and also in ranks – an even greater error", said Patton (Diary)

Luftwaffe base at Comiso in Sicily, 60 Italians and 50 German prisoners were killed in two further incidents.

Before the invasion, Patton had told officers that, if an enemy soldier shot at the Americans and then tried to surrender as the Allies got within 200 yards, "that bastard will die! You will kill him. Stick him between the third and fourth ribs. You will tell your men that. They must have the killer instinct".[21] Patton wrote in his diary that the dead men should be classed as snipers or else the Allies should claim that the prisoners "had attempted to escape or something, as it would make a stink in the press and also would make the civilians mad. Anyhow, they are dead, so nothing can be done about it". Though Patton promised that the killers would be brought to trial, only two trials went ahead, a captain who captured 43 Germans and had them all shot and a sergeant who killed 36 prisoners at the roadside.[22] One man was convicted, but he was subsequently released to continue serving as an American soldier. Eisenhower decided to give the killers "a chance".

The Allies were now operating out of four aerodromes, and the US Air Force had almost complete domination in the air. Of seven enemy divisions in Sicily, three Italian divisions had already been destroyed or captured. The Americans took 15,000 prisoners, most of them Italians. But Italian and German troops were quarrelling among themselves. At one abandoned Italian battery with a brand new gun, two German artillery instructors were found dead with their throats cut – possibly by their Italian allies.

Back in North Africa, an ammunition ship exploded in Algiers harbour on 17 July and set fire to another ship laden with petrol drums, killing and wounding many people, mostly Arabs. The force of the explosion broke the front

---

[21] http://www.comandosupremo.com/forums/topic/1784-historian-uncovers-new-details-on-sicily-massacre/
[22] "In my opinion, both men were crazy," said Patton, who denied ordering the killing of prisoners

windows of the Hotel St George and even the lamp in Ike's office.

In Rome, Pope Pius XII issued a statement appealing to King Victor Emmanuel to declare Rome an open city, though the Pope said he did not want to become embroiled in politics. [23] But Rome was bombed again on 19 July, regardless of the closeness of the target marshalling yards to the Vatican and important churches, particularly the Basilica of St John Lateran. More than 500 Allied bombers killed around 3,000 Italian civilians during attacks on the airport and freight yards.

Meanwhile in Sicily, one of the difficulties – particularly along the coast road – was demolished roads. On one side was the sea, on the other sheer cliffs. The demolished road would fall into the sea, making the work of Allied army engineers even more difficult. Patton also faced some of "the most ingenious tank traps" he had ever seen. Patton said the Allies were now fighting northern Italians as well, and these were better fighters than the Sicilians. His army had suffered 5,600 casualties, of which 500 soldiers were killed, 1,900 missing and the remainder wounded. This appeared heavy considering that the fighting seemed to have been relatively easy. In western Sicily, the Americans had taken 90,000 of the total of 110,000 prisoners.

The Americans were moving swiftly, and Patton flew to Tunisia to question the order for his Seventh Army to protect the (British) Eighth Army's rear and flank, which meant the Americans would be in a support role. On 23 July, the Seventh Army cleared the western half of the island and entered the Sicilian capital of Palermo. [24] The "very small and quite intelligent" [25] Cardinal Luigi Lavitrano of Palermo said the Americans had treated the Sicilian people with the "utmost courtesy" and that the occupation had been without

---

[23] The Star, 26 July 1943
[24] Patton had bet a bottle of whisky against a bottle of gin that Palermo would be taken by 23 July 1943 (Diary)
[25] Patton diary, 26 July 1943

any "unpleasant incidents". [26] But a sudden explosion in Palermo harbour lifted two 125-foot ships entirely out of the water and onto the quay.

Patton requisitioned the palace of the former king of Sicily. [27] After a Spam lunch in Patton's palace, Ike went to Syracuse to meet General Alexander before returning to the Verdala Palace in Malta. Meanwhile, Montgomery's Eighth Army was stuck at Catania. Monty predicted that victory in Sicily would take another month, but Ike couldn't see why it should take so long, considering the overwhelming strength of the Allied armies, the air support and naval bombardment. Patton claimed that, if Montgomery's Eighth Army had moved as quickly as the American Seventh Army, the Germans at Catania could not have stopped them.

Ike was unable to attend the secret meeting of the Combined Chiefs between 17 and 24 August at the Quadrant Conference in Quebec (where Mamie could have met him). In his absence, the Combined Chiefs rejected his request for four heavy bomber groups from the 8th Air Force to be temporarily assigned to North Africa for bombing targets in northern Italy. The Allied leaders discussed the bombing offensive against Germany and the imminent surrender of Italy, as well as signing a secret agreement for the US and Britain to share nuclear technology. [28] Winston Churchill met FDR in Quebec, and discussed the invasion of Normandy in France the following year. The initial plan was that Marshall would command Overlord (because the Americans were providing most of the troops), and Eisenhower would replace him as US Chief-of-Staff in Washington. But that was not to be.

---

[26] Possibly apart from the deaths of "at least 4,000 civilians" in Caltanissetta due to Allied bombing raids. (Patton diary, 19 July 1943)
[27] The King of Sicily had been overthrown after Garibaldi conquered the island in 1860
[28] Later, "Britain found American unwilling to reciprocate and was brusquely shut out" – Churchill, p 334

THE BATTLE FOR ITALY

Ike recommended to the Combined Chiefs of Staff that, as soon as the Allies took Messina, they should cross the strait to the Italian mainland. This attack would be backed by other landings and perhaps an attack on Naples. Ike said there was little to be gained by getting a toehold on Italy, when a bold kick in the shin might cause Italy to give up the fight. He wanted to offer the Italians a peace deal, including the swift repatriation of Italian prisoners, provided they rejected Fascism and took up arms against the ten German divisions on the Italian mainland. But the Combined Chiefs turned down his armistice terms.[1] In a handwritten memo to "Former Naval Person" Winston Churchill, FDR said the Italian armistice should "come as close as possible to unconditional surrender followed by good treatment of the Italian populace. But I think also that the head devil [Mussolini] should be surrendered together with his chief partners in crime"[2]

General Mark Clark and the Fifth Army were to lead Operation Avalanche, the amphibious landings at Salerno near Naples. On 26 July, Churchill approved the landings but told Eisenhower: "Rome is the bullseye." He now hoped to be in the Italian capital by the end of October 1943[3] (but by then, it was apparent that Allied operations in Italy were "coming to a standstill".[4] Monty did not expect Rome to be taken before March 1944.[5]) However, on 28 July, a planner told Ike that it would be impossible to launch an attack on mainland Italy until 7 September.

The previous day, Mussolini – the "bloated bullfrog of the Pontine Marshes" in the words of Churchill – had been

---

[1] Alan Brooke war diaries, 28 July 1943
[2] 25 July 1943
[3] Alan Brooke war diaries, 29 September 1943
[4] Alan Brooke war diaries, 25 October 1943
[5] Alan Brooke war diaries, 14 December 1943

arrested and martial law imposed throughout Italy. King Victor Emmanuel announced that he was taking direct command of Italian troops, and the prime minister, Field Marshal Pietro Badoglio, was assuming the military government of Italy. Both promised to continue the war, Badoglio warning: "Whoever cherishes illusions of being able to disrupt normal developments or of trying to disturb public order will be inexorably punished."[6] In fact Badoglio, the former viceroy of Ethiopia, was still hoping to arrange an armistice with the Allies but, following his speech, the Allies resumed heavy bombing of Italy, particularly of Naples and of the Rome marshalling yards on 2 August.

Meanwhile the Germans were rushing reinforcements to mainland Italy and the Allies faced some tough fighting. "Penny packet attacks"[7] would not do. Using airfields in Sicily, Spitfires could provide air cover for the Allied troops near Salerno for only 20 minutes and then had to return to Sicily to refuel. What had promised to be a quick Italian collapse had now become uncertain, with the Italians and their German allies strengthening their opposition, perhaps because of the Allies' insistence on unconditional surrender.

While Ike and Kay were at the farm, a message arrived from General Marshall saying that FDR was considering declaring Rome an "open city" (which the British chiefs of staff "strongly opposed"[8]). The Italian government was asking, through the Vatican, what conditions the Allies would impose. Ike said that all military personnel and equipment must be removed from the city, and military movement stopped.

Sicily didn't collapse by 5 August as Ike had predicted, but Patton's 1st Division entered Troina, and Montgomery finally took Catania. Montgomery told war correspondents

---

[6] Tunis Telegraph, 26 July 1943

[7] Alan Brooke war diaries, 16 December 1943

[8] Alan Brooke war diaries, 4 August 1943; US Secretary of State Cordell Hull proposed on 21 November 1943 that the US government recognise Rome's "open city" status

that the Sicilians were "glad to see the last" of the Germans and Italians, who had "taken everything they could".[9] Much to the chagrin of the Americans, the BBC reported that the going was so easy for the US Seventh Army that the troops were eating grapes and swimming, while the British Eighth Army had to confront serious opposition. By mid-August, Ike was exhausted and was ordered to bed for four days after a physical examination for promotion to the rank of colonel in the regular Army.

Ike admitted having made two mistakes so far – the landings at Casablanca and an overcautious approach to Italy. He now thought the Allies should have made simultaneous landings on both sides of the Messina Strait, thus cutting off Sicily. The failure to land Allied troops in mainland Italy and Sicily simultaneously allowed the Germans and Italians to withdraw 120,000 troops. But many remained. By 13 August, the Seventh Army had taken 96,000 prisoners, with more than 10,000 Axis troops dead and wounded, compared to Allied losses estimated at 6,400. The Americans bombed Rome again the same day. The Vatican complained bitterly over the renewed bombing of the Eternal City, when the basilica of San Lorenzo was hit. The Vatican pointed out that the Italians had not bombed Cairo or Athens, yet the Allies had bombed Rome, as well as Catholic churches in other Italian cities.[10] The following day, the Italians declared Rome an open city, though that did not prevent the Allies launching more than 50 more bombing raids against the city in the following 12 months.[11] Allied bomber crews were promised that they could go home after 25 missions but, with losses at nearly 11 per cent, that figure crept up to 30 by the following year.

---

[9] Tunis Telegraph, 26 July 1943

[10] In relation to the Catholic Church, "The British attitude is hostile, almost without exception." (Memo on Anglo-American relations in Italy, 10 April 1944)

[11] Inside Rome with the Germans, by Jane Scrivener (Mother Mary Luke), 1945

When Ike was allowed up again on 14 August, the Surgeon General, Brigadier-General Fred Blesse, showed him a report relating to Patton's visit to two evacuation hospitals in Sicily. The buccaneering general had slapped two patients and thrown them out because he suspected that they were malingering. Ike wrote Patton a "personal and secret letter" [12] on 17 August saying he had heard "shocking" allegations about Patton's personal conduct which he hoped were untrue or represented thoughtlessness, rather than harshness.

"I am well aware of the necessity for hardness and toughness on the battlefield," wrote Ike. "I clearly understand that firm and drastic measures are at times necessary in order to secure the desired objectives. But this does not excuse brutality, abuse of the sick, nor exhibition of uncontrollable temper in front of subordinates." Ike told Patton that he did not intend to begin "any formal investigation", but if the allegations were basically true, "I must so seriously question your good judgment and your self-discipline as to raise serious doubt in my mind as to your future usefulness". (But Ike himself was "irate" later on when he visited Allied soldiers in hospital in Normandy and discovered they were suffering from self-inflicted wounds. [13])

Ike wrote: "No letter that I have been called upon to write in my military career has caused me the mental anguish of this one, not only because of my long and deep personal friendship for you but because of my admiration for your military qualities, but I assure you that conduct such as described in the accompanying report will not be tolerated in this theater no matter who the offender may be." [14] Ike advised Patton to apologise [15] to the victims, but said he still

---

[12] A "very nasty letter", according to Patton (Diary, 20 August 1943)
[13] Ike was "deeply shocked" to see more than 1,000 men with self-inflicted wounds in one hospital (p 713 Bodyguard of Lies)
[14] Ike cabled Marshall on 27 August that Patton was "apt at times to display exceedingly poor judgment and unjustified temper"
[15] Or make "other such personal amends...as may be within your power". (Letter, 17 August 1943)

might have to send the general home in disgrace. However, Ike assured Patton that the only record of the report or of his letter was in his secret files.

Not everyone condemned Patton's action. Ike's orderly wrote afterwards: "It always seemed to me that if the GI had battle fatigue, why couldn't General Patton have had it too? He'd certainly been in a lot of battles."[16] Later, the story broke in the US media. Without Ike's knowledge, correspondents were told that Patton was still commanding general of the Seventh Army (which was not true) and that he had not been reprimanded,[17] which was also untrue.

Meanwhile, the fighting in Sicily continued. On the evening of 16 August, the Americans entered Messina. Ike decided to cross the Messina Strait as soon as enough landing craft and guns could be assembled, and to attack Naples on 9 September. On 29 August 1943, at the end of a 40-day campaign on the island of Sicily, Ike flew from Algiers to Taormina to make Monty a Commander of the Legion of Merit, the highest order the United States could give a foreign soldier.

After a celebratory lunch in Catania, Monty and Ike took an open car up the windy coast road to Messina, a drive of nearly two hours. The day before, the road had been strafed by a dozen Messerschmitts, but Ike didn't even see an enemy plane on the journey. Cheering Sicilians greeted Monty and Ike with V signs. At Messina, Ike and Monty surveyed the Italian mainland across the two-mile-wide strait. On Monday morning, Ike was driven to Catania to a meeting in General Alexander's tent, in an olive grove swarming with flies. Afterwards, Ike flew back to Tunisia.

Once Sicily was firmly in Allied hands, Patton invited Kay and Beetle's secretary Ruth Briggs to his palace there. They turned down the infamous 'Patton 75', a cocktail of Champagne, brandy and "possibly other disastrous mix-

---

[16] Sgt Mickey and General Ike, p 54
[17] Ike had not formally recorded his action on Patton's 201 personnel file

tures", but accepted a gift of silk stockings. Patton then took them on a sight-seeing trip, ending at a church outside Palermo. There he "sank to his knees and prayed aloud for the success of his troops, for the health and happiness of his family and for a safe flight back" for Kay and Ruth. Patton was a high Church Episcopalian communicant who went to church most Sundays[18] though he often attended Catholic Masses because he thought God was "quite impartial as to the form in which he is approached".[19] Kay asked Patton about the slapping incident, and he said his "goddamned mouth" always got him into trouble, but he'd do the same again in similar circumstances.

When she got back and told Ike about the trip, he responded: "Georgie is one of the best generals I have, but he's just like a time bomb." He eventually sacked Patton for his remarks about the denazification programme in Bavaria. (Patton died in hospital 12 days after a minor car crash in December 1945.)

A peace feeler from Italy on 17 August indicated, not only that Italy would get out of the war, but that it was prepared to fight on the Allied side. Ike said that the Allies would support Italians who fought Germans, destroyed their property or obstructed their movements, but they must also free any Allied prisoners who might have been captured by the Germans.[20] Also, the Italian fleet[21] and merchant shipping must sail to Allied-controlled ports, Italian aircraft fly to Allied bases and any ships or aircraft likely to fall into German hands must be destroyed.

General Giuseppe Castellano contacted Ike from Madrid and said that Marshal Badoglio had authorised him to make urgent peace proposals because of the arrival of more German units in Italy. Badoglio had insisted that any Italian

---

[18] Diary 27 June 1943
[19] Letter, 26 September 1943
[20] CHAR 20/116/67-68
[21] The fourth-largest in the world (Vatican ambassador Myron Taylor memo to FDR, 26 July 1943)

surrender was subject to Allied troops landing on the Italian mainland, and protecting Rome and the Vatican from German reprisals. Ike told the Combined Chiefs he would send two staff officers to deal directly with Castellano in Portugal. He had "learned never to negotiate with an adversary except from a position of strength".[22] Brigadier Kenneth Strong and Beetle Smith flew to Gibraltar, from where a civilian plane took them in plain clothes to Lisbon for the secret meeting. Beetle went as Walter Smith and claimed that he was born at 20 Grosvenor Square (Ike's London HQ). Strong gave customs officers his correct address but dropped his military title. The two men talked to the Italian envoy, then returned to the farm on the evening of 20 August. They had given Castellano the unconditional surrender terms, plus a small transmitter and cipher.

But the Germans were still fighting. A week later in Algiers, in the first air raid in a couple of months, up to 40 Ju-88s dropped ten bombs and flares near Sailors' Delight. One plane dropped three bombs about a mile away, breaking windows at the farm. Nevertheless, in appreciation of his success in Sicily, Ike was appointed Brigadier-General (permanent) on 30 August and promoted to Major-General (permanent). FDR also announced the award of the oak leaf cluster to his DSM.

Three days later, a message was received via secret radio from Rome that the Allies' terms had been accepted. But Ike was concerned that he was the only person approved by the Russians to sign any armistice. Although he arrived in Sicily in time to sign the so-called "short-term" agreement, Ike decided that Beetle should sign for "operational reasons", and he would be merely a witness. On 3 September 1943, Castellano and Beetle Smith signed the surrender agreement in Cassibile, near Syracuse in Sicily. The document was to be superseded by a "long-term" agreement to be signed by Ike at a public ceremony later.

---

[22] at ease, p 30

Ike felt that the requirement for the Italians to surrender unconditionally was unreasonably harsh but, although he said it was a "crooked deal", he calculated that the terms of the surrender document might not become public for a decade. A premature leak of those terms would cost many Allies lives, as the Germans would begin taking over Italy and replacing Italian coastal units.

At the last minute, Badoglio asked for a postponement of the joint proclamation (or "was ratting",[23] according to the British) but Ike said he intended to broadcast at the hour originally planned, though he agreed to suspend the bombing of Rome. Eventually Badoglio broadcast his proclamation as originally planned, and Ike gave details of the armistice over Algiers Radio at 5.30pm on 8 September. "Fascism has been given its deathblow," wrote Ike in his diary. He said he would like to try Mussolini himself and would take great pleasure in seeing him hanged. But as Italy – the "birthplace of fascism"[24] – formally surrendered, German radio broadcast that: "A clique of Jews and elements alien to the Italian nation have brought about the treachery against the Italian nation. Germany and Europe are strong enough to punish the originators of that crime."[25] Berlin also announced that Otto Skorzeny had rescued Mussolini from the Gran Sasso, where the Italians were holding him, and a Free Fascist government, the so-called Salò Republic, was created in northern Italy.

Following the news of the Italian surrender, the battleship Roma, which had been undergoing repairs after an Allied air raid, was attacked by German planes. The Italians were under the impression that the Allies were bombing their ships and pleaded with them to stop, but Ike explained that it was the Germans who were doing the bombing. The Roma – part of a fleet of 19 Italian ships sailing to Malta to surrender – should have been attacking Allied ships taking

---

[23] Alan Brooke war diaries, 8 September 1943
[24] Daily Mirror, 9 September 1943
[25] Daily Mirror, 9 September 1943

part in the Salerno landings. But Dornier bombers armed with radio-controlled bombs sank the battleship with the loss of more than 1,250 Italian sailors, including Admiral Carlo Bergamini. Admiral Cunningham had ordered the Italian fleet and merchant navy not to scuttle their ships, but to sail them to North Africa, Gibraltar, Tripoli, Malta, Haifa, Alexandria or Sicily "and there await the outcome of events".[26] After 76 Italian ships had eventually anchored in St Paul's Bay in Malta, Cunningham signalled the Admiralty in London: "Be pleased to inform their Lordships that the Italian battle fleet now lies at anchor under the fortress guns of Malta." Eisenhower met Field Marshal Badoglio aboard the battleship HMS Nelson anchored off Malta 20 days after the announcement of the Italian capitulation, to sign a detailed version of the surrender agreement. Ike was keen for the Italians to see the damage they'd caused in Malta, the "most bombed spot in the world during the present war".[27]

Meanwhile, in North Africa the Allies celebrated the end of their campaign. On 4 September at Hammamet in Tunisia, Ike stood at attention on a reviewing stand for two hours while 12,000 Allied troops marched past in a victory parade. Later that day, General Clark met him to discuss the planned Salerno landings over which a thousand planes would form an air umbrella. The Isle of Capri, on which Ike hoped to install radar stations, was to be attacked as a diversion. But the Combined Chiefs of Staff also confirmed that four American and three British divisions would be withdrawn from the Mediterranean theatre starting on 1 November.

As the Italians were on the point of signing the armistice, Montgomery's British and Canadian troops crossed the Messina Strait at 4.30am on 3 September to attack the mainland of Italy on both sides of Reggio di Calabria in southern Italy. It was the fourth anniversary of Britain's and France's declaration of war. The same day, Anglo-American bombers carried out a "terror raid" on Paris, hitting targets

---

[26] Daily Mirror, 9 September 1943
[27] FDR diary 8 December 1943

on the left bank of the Seine and causing "very great" casualties, according to Paris Radio.[28]

On 5 September 1943, following a bridge party at Villa dar el Ouard, Kay drove Ike, Clark's Chief-of-Staff, Alfred M Gruenther, and Butch to the port, where Clark and Gruenther embarked for Sicily. Ike then transferred his HQ to Carthage and moved into an Italian-owned seaside villa. Almost every day, Kay drove him to visit Tooey Spaatz or Air Marshal Tedder, and the 50 miles to the British HQ in Bizerte, across the Bay of Tunis. By this stage, he was growing increasingly fed up with the constant fighting. After the war, he said, he was determined to go back to the US, find the deepest hole, crawl in and "pull it in after me".

The landings at Salerno Bay began on 9 September. The attack across the Strait of Messina met minimal resistance, as the Germans had apparently pulled back and the Italians were steadily surrendering. But Ike was worried when the Germans counterattacked with six divisions. On September 13, they drove a wedge between the two American divisions. The news was going "from bad to worse" and the landings were "doomed to failure", said General Brooke, adding that "neither Eisenhower nor Alexander will ever have sufficient vision to be big soldiers".[29] But the news from Salerno gradually started to improve. On 15 September, the Air Force bombed the counterattacking Germans, with B-17 crews flying two missions a day. An ammunition train blew up in Battipaglia, near Salerno Bay, wrecking the centre of the town. The Combined Chiefs invited Ike to repeat his request (which had been refused on 30 July) to use heavy bombers. Ike was "particularly careful to give clean-cut decisive answers".

Once again, the Italian campaign was not immune from "friendly fire" incidents. During the battle for Salerno, a

---

[28] Evening Chronicle, 3 September 1943. But according to the BBC's French service, "*Radio Paris ment, Radio Paris est allemand*" (Radio Paris lies, Radio Paris is German")
[29] Alan Brooke war diaries, 13 September 1943

shell from HMS Warspite hit HMS Petard, killing two British sailors and wounding six. Then a four-inch shell from Warspite hit the destroyer HMS Offa, killing one sailor and injuring several more. On 16 September, Warspite herself was hit by two rocket-propelled glider bombs, with two near misses. The four German glider bombs, each armed with 1,500 pounds of explosive, were controlled by a plane which stayed out of range, so jamming was ineffective. Nine sailors were killed and 14 injured.

Clark said the Allied naval and air bombardment had strengthened the soldiers' morale, but the Germans claimed that the Texas division (which Ike had earlier reviewed near Mostaganem) was in "headlong flight". Ike visited Salerno aboard HMS Charybdis on 17 September. He realised that he would probably be sacked as commander-in-chief unless the Italian landings were successful. One way of improving the situation was to allow Italians to fight on the Allied side. Ike recommended to the Combined Chiefs that they should accept the legal government of Italy under King Victor Emmanuel and Badoglio, and allow the Italians to be cobelligerents. Churchill approved Ike's recommendation but said the Italian forces must "work their passage". On 25 September, FDR said that Italy would be treated as a cobelligerent if the new government declared war on Germany. In the meantime, Ike should not sign a long-term agreement with the Italians pending further instructions, though the Italians should be allowed to wage war against Germany within the limits of military necessity and their fighting capacity.

King Victor Emmanuel said he preferred not to declare war on the Germans until Rome had been taken by the Allies (which didn't happen until June 1944, despite British newspaper headlines nine months earlier: 'Rome collapse at any minute'[30]). However, on 13 October, the new Italian government finally did declare war on Germany. In a message to Ike, Badoglio said: "By this act, all ties with the

---

[30] Sunday Express, 5 September 1943

dreadful past are broken."[31] But the Italians began badly in their battles against the Germans. An Italian brigade failed in its first attack and begged to be withdrawn from the line, but Clark insisted that it stay with the Americans. The attack was eventually successful. The other issue was food for the Italian people. The Italians estimated that 100,000 tons a month of food and other supplies would be needed for the four southern provinces of Italy alone.[32] The US had already sent almost 2,300,000 tons of food to Allied fronts in the previous eight months.

Mussolini had not been forgotten. On 20 September 1943, a cable arrived for Ike from Cape Town, South Africa: "I offer donate ten thousand pounds toward war funds if you arrange for Mussolini's personal appearance on the stages of our Cape Town theaters. Three weeks' engagement. Stodel African Theaters Ltd."

On the south side of the Gulf of Naples, Rear Admiral Anthony Morse took over as governor of the relatively untouched Isle of Capri. He lived in Villa Ciano, the hilltop home of Italy's former foreign minister, Count Galeazzo Ciano, and his wife, Mussolini's daughter, Edda. The villa, where the Ciano family used to spend their summers, was full of books containing pictures of Ciano with Mussolini and Hitler. Ciano was eventually executed on the orders of Mussolini after he was found guilty of treason in January 1944.

Meanwhile, cholera and typhus were reported in Naples, which Ike expected to be in Allied hands within ten days. In fact, the city fell to the Allies on 1 October 1943, after days of bitter fighting between Italians and Germans. The Germans had effectively destroyed the city's utilities. They had blown up the steelworks and chemical factory, cut the aqueduct and wrecked the telephone exchange and electric system,

---

[31] New York Journal American, 13 October 1943

[32] Even a year later, conditions in the Frosinone region were said to be "bad, very bad" (Report R/2466, 10 October 1944, from Colonel Charles Poletti)

but enough electricity was generated by three Italian submarines to light the dockyard. However, a delayed-action bomb which exploded in the post office killed dozens of people nearby.[33]

---

[33] Evening Standard, 11 October 1943

BACK IN AFRICA

Back in North Africa, Ike said he had a surprise for Kay. He had asked his tailor to make her two new uniforms. He told her she was "very special" to him, and she didn't realise how much he would like to do for her. But later he had a change of heart and told her to forget what he'd said, so she responded that she didn't want the uniforms. He reacted by calling her a "goddamned stubborn Irish mule" and *ordered* her to get measured. "Goddammit," he added, "can't you tell I'm crazy about you?"

It was the first time they had tried to make love, according to Kay. "It was like an explosion," she said in her auto-biography. "We were suddenly in each other's arms. His kisses absolutely unravelled me."

"We have to be very careful," he said. "I don't want you to be hurt. I don't want people to gossip about you. God, I wish things were different."

According to Kay, the romance continued. The two would often sit on a high-backed sofa in the living room of Ike's villa in Algiers, listening to records, drinking, smoking cigarettes and stealing a few kisses, "always conscious that someone might walk in at any moment". Ike gave Kay small tokens of his affection, for example, a four-leaf clover pasted on a card on which he'd written: "Good luck to Kay, a friend", Africa and his initials.

One night, Ike put several records on the turntable and, before the last, told Kay "I think you may like this one." It was 'I'll See You Again'. (Noel Coward later told Kay it was "probably the most popular song" he'd ever written.) According to Kay, Ike told her: "I'm not used to talking about love. It makes me uncomfortable...But I want you to know that I love you."

Ike said that the night he received the signal that the Strathallan had been torpedoed, "I felt as if the ground had been taken away from under my feet...I followed the progress of that convoy as I followed no other convoy....I spent that night worrying about you, cursing myself for not having had you fly to Algiers. I went through hell that night...I was never going to tell you how I felt. And sweet Jesus Christ, I don't know how I ever had the guts to."

But Ike knew he still had a war to win, not just in North Africa and Italy, but also in Europe. A new code name, Overlord, replaced the old one, Roundup. Preparations were also under way for a diversionary attack in southern France at the same time. Lord Louis Mountbatten (who was en route to Burma) was due to spend Sunday evening 26 September discussing Overlord with Ike at Amilcar, but arrived at the wrong aerodrome, so Kay spent three and a half hours driving Ike from one place to another trying to track him down.

On 10 October, Ike heard that Lieut John Winant Jr, son of the US ambassador to London, had been shot down during a bomber raid on Munster and was missing.[1] (Winant was actually captured and sent to Colditz, but was released at the end of the war. His father, who was having an affair with Churchill's younger married daughter Sarah, shot himself in November 1947.)

Moscow ambassador Averell Harriman and one of his daughters, Kathy, arrived in North Africa on Thursday 14 October, and stayed at Ike's villa. At the time Harriman was having an affair with Churchill's daughter-in-law, Pamela, the wife of Randolph Churchill and three years younger than Kathy.[2] (Later Kathy Harriman was responsible for a report on the Soviet massacre at Katyn which blamed the Germans for the killings.[3]) Secretary of the US Treasury Henry Morgenthau arrived the following morning, so Ike hosted

---

[1] Evening Standard, 11 October 1943
[2] She became his third wife in 1971
[3] http://www.nytimes.com/2011/02/20/us/20mortimer.html

both men for lunch. Secretary of State Cordell Hull arrived in the afternoon, so Ike had Harriman as house guest and entertained Hull to dinner.

Morgenthau wanted to discuss the rate of exchange in occupied Italy. US Senators were worried about the Allies printing their own money (the so-called Yellow Seal dollars issued in 1942 and 1943), but Morgenthau warned them that the Germans would use any public criticism for propaganda purposes. Many soldier-printers were assigned to run the presses, as so much money had to be printed.

Admiral Cunningham left on Sunday 17 October to become First Sea Lord in London. Sailors, soldiers and airmen from Britain and the United States formed a guard of honour in front of the Hotel St George on Saturday morning. The US Army Band played Auld Lang Syne and Rule Britannia, and Ike wrote a personal letter to be given to the admiral after his plane left. Meanwhile the war in Italy dragged on. The Allies had suffered 15,000 dead, wounded or missing so far, which Clark regarded as relatively light in view of the severe fighting.[4] Marshall criticised the "inadequate application" of the Allied Air Force to prevent the German build-up, but Ike thought the Allies would not be strong enough to risk an all-out battle in the Po Valley until spring, when they could use their superior air power. Marshall also wondered why this news hadn't been printed in the Yank newspaper, which didn't appear in the Mediterranean theatre, and why Ike appeared to have given exclusive privileges to the *Stars and Stripes* service newspaper. Ike explained that there was a critical shortage of paper, and he'd decided not to waste it by printing two similar papers for American servicemen.

Politics continued to intrude. A copy of the Washington Post of 6 October was sent to Ike with a headline saying 'Eisenhower Urged For President'. "Any man who wants to be President is either an egomaniac or crazy," he said. "Why

---

[4] Pope Pius XII asked on 19 October 1943 that the Allies might "circumvent Rome and thus oblige the Germans to retire without subjecting the city to havoc due to combat"

can't a simple soldier be left alone to carry out his orders? And I furiously object to the word 'candidate'." It turned out that former members of the Tanks Corps had suggested Ike as a presidential candidate. He told them they had "no right to speak for him on such matters".[5] But at the same time as he seemed to reject a political future, he realised the limitations of his present military career. He almost expected the press to start calling him the "paper general" because he had not yet taken part in a battle.

Harriman had meanwhile left Algiers and flown to Moscow for a conference which took place from October 18 to November 11. On 30 October, the governments of the United States, the UK and the Soviet Union signed the so-called Moscow Declaration, which included a joint three-nation statement and declarations regarding Italy, Austria and Axis atrocities. The three governments (four including France from 16 November 1943) agreed to continue hostilities against the Axis powers until they surrendered unconditionally. They also called for the establishment of a United Nations organisation to maintain international peace and security.

In the declaration on Italy, the signatories said that the influence of Fascism should be destroyed and that the Italian government should be based on democratic principles. The section on Austria declared the *Anschluss* null and void and said that, while Austria should be "liberated from German domination", Austrians had to be reminded that they had participated in the war "on the side of Hitlerite Germany". Account would "inevitably be taken" of Austria's own contribution to its liberation. The final declaration on atrocities, largely drafted by Winston Churchill, noted "evidence of atrocities, massacres and cold-blooded mass executions which are being perpetrated by the Hitlerite forces in the many countries they have overrun".[6] It said Germans should be sent back to the countries where

---

[5] Diary 10 April 1944
[6] Declaration on German atrocities, 1 November 1943

their "abominable deeds were done" and "judged on the spot by the peoples whom they have outraged". [7] "Major criminals" whose offences had no particular geographical location would be punished by the Allied governments (the basis for the Nuremberg Trials).

On Wednesday 20 October, Butch flew to Naples to look for new living quarters for Ike. He acquired a villa with three residences in one enclosure, the property of Prince Umberto, and the adjoining Villa Emma, named after its former occupant, Nelson's mistress, Lady Hamilton. He also stumbled on a hunting lodge in the hills behind the main palace at Caserta (where the German surrender in Italy was signed on 3 May 1945). The lodge[8] was furnished and supplied with hot water in preparation for Ike's arrival, and apartments were reserved in the palace for Ike and Beetle.

Ike then flew to Italy and toured the battle front with Clark before returning to Tunis to attend the marriage of Air Chief Marshal Tedder to divorcée Mrs Marie 'Toppy' Black, a former member of General Everett Hughes's staff.[9] He was back and forth across the Mediterranean during this period. On 17 November he met the British Prime Minister and others in Malta. Churchill was on his way to Cairo by ship, but as the Germans had "already published the fact that we were all meeting in Cairo",[10] the Prime Minister suggested that the meeting take place in Malta. (Churchill was used to avoiding German scrutiny and often used to disguise himself when travelling. In 1942, for example, he donned a false grey beard when flying to Gibraltar.[11] On other occasions, he suggested disguising himself as "an Egyptian demi-mondaine or an Armenian suffering from a toothache".[12]) Meanwhile, the Fifth Army had reached the line in Italy that

---

[7] This was a basis for Operation Keelhaul between August 1946 and May 1947

[8] Later taken over by General 'Jumbo' Wilson

[9] Black considered Tedder "a darling and so sweet and kind"

[10] Alan Brooke war diaries, 18 November 1943

[11] Alan Brooke war diaries, 30 July 1942

[12] Alan Brooke war diaries, 24 August 1942

the Germans intended to hold for the winter – the Gustav Line – but fighting was virtually stalemated because of torrential rain, which contributed to Ike catching another cold after he and Beetle went on a partridge shoot.

On Saturday 20 November, FDR arrived in Oran on a new battleship, the USS Iowa to be greeted by his sons, Elliott and Franklin, and by Ike. The secret service objected to Ike being driven with FDR to La Senia airport and flying with him to Tunis because they said Ike's prominence could affect the President's security. The head of the Secret Service, Irishman Mike Reilly, also refused to let Kay drive FDR because she was a woman. Kay told Reilly she was Irish too, but he replied "I wouldn't know, with that Limey accent".[13] The President eventually overruled Reilly.

At dinner in Carthage that night with Roosevelt's sons, FDR quizzed Kay about her work in the Blitz and about the use of women in wartime, particularly as factory workers, air raid wardens and on the buses. While the Women's Army Auxiliary Corps (WAAC)[14] had been created in the United States in May 1942, FDR assured Kay that there would never be female conscription in the US, as the "country would not stand for it". The President concluded, with his "almost androgynous intuition, that the general and his chauffeuse were sleeping together".[15] After FDR eventually went to bed, Kay attended a hot, noisy and smoky party at the villa, hosted by the President's two sons (one of whom fancied her).

The next day, Kay drove the President and Ike round the Tunisian battlefields in a Cadillac. Telek tried to attack Roosevelt (who smelled of his own Scotty dog, Fala) but was restrained and resigned himself to spending the rest of the journey quietly sitting on Roosevelt's lap. Approaching Medjez el Bab, Roosevelt suddenly said to Kay: "Child, that's

---

[13] Kay spoke with a very 'West Brit' English accent
[14] It became the Women's Army Corps on 1 July 1943
[15] Franklin Delano Roosevelt: Champion of Freedom by Conrad Black, p 895

a pretty grove of [eucalyptus] trees there ahead. Let's have our picnic there. Won't you come back here, child, and have lunch with a dull old man?" Kay moved into the back seat of the car while Ike handed out the sandwiches and drinks. Armed guards stood in a circle with their backs to the group, while the presidential party picnicked and chatted. Kay told FDR she'd like to join the WACs after the war but would need to become a US citizen first. "Stranger things have happened," said the President.

CAIRO CONFERENCE

Two main conferences took place in the autumn of 1943, in Cairo (22-26 November) and Tehran (27 November to 1 December). FDR flew to Cairo from El Aouina after spending the night with Ike, who was also ordered to attend the Cairo conference. Ike and Kay flew to Egypt on November 24 on a plane sent by Marshall. The two chatted and kissed on the night flight, though they moved apart to sleep in order to avoid even more scandal. After arriving at Payne Field ten miles outside Cairo, Kay and two other women were billeted with Ike. While he went to the conference in the Mena House hotel, the three women enjoyed Turkish coffee and highballs in the cocktail lounge of Shepheard's Hotel before going shopping (all they bought was bananas). At the conference, the Combined Chiefs of Staff were impressed by Ike's grasp of the military situation in North Africa.

The day ended with Kay and Ike attending a cocktail party. Kay went back to her quarters alone afterwards but Ike's orderly knocked to say Ike had invited her to "join him in a nightcap". She went to Ike's drawing room and they began kissing again. "This is where you belong," he said, holding her in his arms. But Ike was worried that he might be sent back to Washington as Chief-of-Staff. "If it has to be Washington, I'll find a way. I'm never going to let you go," he said. "I'm leaving tomorrow[1] and you're coming with me."

A day later, they flew in Tedder's C-47 (with Elliot Roosevelt) to Luxor to see the temples, statues of long-dead pharaohs and "rows of sphinxes in the moonlight". Ike held her hand and, at the Luxor Hotel, pressed a piece of paper into her hand which read "You know what I am thinking. Good night. Sweet dreams." The next morning they all went in a "caravan of decrepit cars" to the Valley of the Kings

---

[1] To see the pyramids

where they spent the day, lunching at a local inn on a nearby hillside. Afterwards, Ike slept for 14 hours and Marshall was so pleased at his obvious relaxation that he insisted on Ike taking another short trip straight away.

So Ike invited Kay to lunch in Jerusalem. The flight took only two hours, though the car journey from the airport in Palestine took another 90 minutes. They ate at the King David Hotel[2] then visited Bethlehem and, thanks to Ike, the otherwise-closed Garden of Gethsemane. Afterwards they went shopping. Kay paid $20 for a smelly sheepskin coat, while Ike bought postcards. On the back of one souvenir envelope from the Garden of Gethsemane, he wrote in pencil: "Good night! There are lots of things I could wish to say – you know them. Good night." (The note was found in Kay's wallet after her death.)

Meanwhile, at the Tehran conference – the first time that the three Allied wartime leaders had met – Roosevelt and Churchill (who had celebrated his 69th birthday on 30 November) told Stalin that a second front "would be possible" by 1 August the following year. The Russians thought that was too late and insisted that Overlord be launched not later than May 1944. Stalin refused to accept the assurance of the western leaders that no decision had yet been made about a Supreme Commander for Overlord.[3] So, on 7 December 1943, General Marshall announced the "immediate appointment of General Eisenhower to command of Overlord". Ike said he liked the title of 'Supreme Commander'; "it had the ring of importance, something like 'Sultan'", he said.[4]

Ike and Kay returned to Algiers on Wednesday 1 December.[5] Six days later Ike flew to El Aouina to welcome FDR on his

---

[2] Bombed by Zionists in July 1946, killing 91 people

[3] On 6 December 1943, FDR cabled Stalin that the decision had been made "immediately" to appoint Ike "to command of cross-Channel operations"

[4] at ease, p 268

[5] Ike was sick with a cold, according to Patton's diary

arrival back from Tehran. FDR's first words to Ike were "Well Ike, you'd better start packing", as he confirmed that Ike would head Operation Overlord in 1944. The Combined Chiefs of Staff did not formally notify Ike until 10 December that he had been appointed to head Overlord. The appointment was partly because FDR wanted Marshall to stay in Washington and partly because Winston Churchill got on better with Ike than with the humourless Marshall. At dinner that evening, as two Italian prisoners served them a regular GI meal, FDR said Ike should take up his new job as soon as possible after 1 January. Before assuming command, however, he should return to Washington for "two blessed weeks" for discussions with Marshall and the CCS "and see your wife and trust somebody else for 20 minutes".

Before FDR left, he and Ike flew in a C-54 (escorted by 20 Lightnings and Spitfires) to Luqa aerodrome in Malta on Wednesday 8 December so that FDR could present the governor, Lord Gort, with an illuminated scroll from America to 'courageous Malta'. "I wish I could stay," said FDR, "but I have many things to do."[6] They then flew to Sicily, where the President presented Clark with the DSC and Beetle with the Legion of Merit.

The President then intended to fly to Marrakesh for the night, but the hydraulic pressure failed on his aircraft[7] so he returned to El Aouina and stayed overnight. He left early on Thursday for a direct flight to Dakar in West Africa.

Roosevelt had planned to present Kay with the Medal of Merit, and asked Ike to write a citation, but a letter from FDR's White House secretary[8] three weeks later said that Ike had not sent any citation for his "young chauffeuress". So Ike wrote:

---

[6] Times of Malta, 11 December 1943
[7] The flaps had already failed before the landing in Malta
[8] Major Gen Edwin 'Pa' Watson, 21 December 1943

Citation For Medal Of Merit

Kay Summersby, British citizen.

"Kay Summersby has been employed as a chauffeur by the American forces for two and a half years, and for one and one-half years of this time has been the principal driver for the Allied Commander-in-Chief. During all this time she has established such an enviable record for attention to duty, skill as a driver and complete loyalty to the Allied cause that she has been detailed invariably to act as driver for the principal officials of Great Britain and the United States when visiting the North African Theater. Because of the confidence reposed in her she has acted in this capacity for the President of the United States, His Majesty the King of England, the Prime Minister of England and many other senior officials of both Governments. In addition to her other duties, she voluntarily undertook those of corresponding secretary of the Allied Commander-in-Chief, both of which positions she is now filling. Her loyalty, attention to duty, and utter disregard of her own convenience under conditions which have frequently been difficult and trying, have been outstanding."[9]

While Ike felt that the award would be "a very good thing", FDR eventually decided that the Medal of Merit could not be given to a British civilian. Instead, he sent Kay a signed photo.

Towards the end of 1943, Ike asked Kay to act as his secretary, handling up to 50 letters a week from members of the public. He listed five clerical duties for Kay, and told her "Sign my name – just on a scratch pad – over & over & over." She learned to imitate Ike's signature on letters and

---

[9] Letter of 30 December 1943

pictures, and used to send presents of cigarettes, scarves, gloves, hats, sunglasses, fudge and even hominy grits to local hospitals, orphanages and front-line troops.

Ike told Kay's mother[10] that Kay "continues to drive my car, but has now taken on the added task of working on my 'personal-public' correspondence. That is, she takes charge of the letters that come to me from strangers and casual acquaintances and gets the replies all ready for my signature". Kay even typed a letter to Mamie. "You sound more like me than I do myself," Ike commented to Kay. But Mamie saw through the ruse and insisted on no more typewritten letters so, from then on, Ike sent his wife notes in what he confessed was his "execrable" handwriting.

But if his handwriting was poor, his spelling and grammar were fine. Another secretary, Sue Sarafian, said that, when Kay finally started dictating some of the fan mail to her, one letter was not grammatically correct. General Eisenhower "would never have affixed his signature under that letter", she said.[11] Despite Kay's shortcomings as a secretary, however, she got on well with the rest of the staff. Eisenhower's personal pilot, German-American Kurt Heilbronn, said that Kay was "very, very easy to work with". She was "not only a very fine-looking person, but she was also very efficient, impeccably neat, and very devoted to the general".[12]

Ike was now looking forward to going to England to plan the Second (or Western) Front invasion of Europe. From the beginning of 1944, General "Jumbo" Wilson was to take over as Supreme Allied Commander in the Mediterranean and General Alexander was to take charge of the battle in Italy.[13]

---

[10] Letter of 2 December 1943

[11] www.ibiblio.org/lia/president/EisenhowerLibrary/oral_histories/ Jehl_Sue-Sarafian.html

[12] www.ibiblio.org/lia/president/EisenhowerLibrary/oral_histories/ Heilbronn_Kurt.html

[13] One of Wilson's tasks was to amalgamate the Allied Military Government (headed by a Briton) and the Allied Control Council (led by an American). "It was no love match, and like such weddings, it was unhappy".

Clark would stay in command of the Fifth Army until Rome was captured and then take command of the Seventh Army. Patton was to go to England eventually to command the Third Army in Overlord, while Monty was temporarily to be Allied ground force commander.

GAS!

The Allies pledged that they would not be the first to use poison gas, but claimed that the Germans were prepared to use gas to win the war, despite the ban on the use of such a horrific weapon.[1] In a British parliamentary debate about the "likelihood of the use of poison gas by the enemy",[2] Home Secretary Herbert Morrison said: "The use of gas is abhorrent to His Majesty's Government, and this country will in no circumstances be the first to employ the gas weapon." But Churchill described such an attitude as "squeamishness". "I am strongly in favour of using poisoned gas against uncivilised tribes," he once commented. "The moral effect should be so good that the loss of life should be reduced to a minimum."[3]

On 6 June 1943, President Roosevelt had threatened "full and swift retaliation" if the Axis ever used gas. It was the third such warning, based on unidentified sources which claimed that the Axis countries were making "significant preparations" for gas warfare. But in fact FDR had already sent gas bombs to Europe.[4] In Italy on December 2, an air raid on Bari harbour by more than a hundred German Ju88 bombers sank 27 cargo and transport ships. Among then was a ship carrying American gas bombs. The attack lasted more than an hour, and put the port out of action for two months. Ships were moored close together and an ammunition ship blew up, setting light to four others.

Deadly mustard gas was released from the SS John Harvey, but the British and US governments covered up the story. Eisenhower knew about the gas, but later claimed the wind

---

[1] Ike had warned the Germans against using gas after the Italians quit the Axis alliance (CHAR 20/117/138)

[2] Hansard, 27 March 1941, vol 370 cc 683-5

[3] War Office minute 12 May 1919 (Churchill papers: 16/16)

[4] http://archives.chicagotribune.com/1943/06/09/page/7/article/f-d-r-says-u-s-will-use-poison-gas-if-axis-does

was offshore. He wrote: "One of the ships was loaded with mustard gas, which we were always forced to carry with us because of uncertainty of German intentions in the use of this weapon. Fortunately the wind was offshore and the escaping gas caused no casualties."[5] In fact, 617 people (including 83 soldiers) were gassed to death.[6] A secret board appointed by Eisenhower to investigate the incident in March 1944 confirmed that the mustard gas was of US origin.

Even after the Bari incident, the Allies still considered using gas against the Germans. In February 1944, the British Prime Minister told Ike at dinner in Downing Street: "Politics are very much like war. We may even have to use poison gas at times."[7] Later that month, taking his own advice, Churchill ordered 250,000 four-pound anthrax bombs from the US for use during the invasion of France, but his chiefs-of-staff refused to use them on the basis that the chance of gas being used by the Germans against Overlord troops was negligible.

The German V-1s changed all that. On 4 July, the British Chiefs of Staff said they would consider using poison gas "as a general retaliation against Germany" for the V-1 attacks. And in a personal minute to General 'Pug' Ismay on 13 July, Churchill proposed using gas, "principally mustard", to "drench the cities of the Ruhr and many other cities in Germany in such a way that most of the population would be requiring constant medical attention. We could stop all work at the flying bomb starting points". The Prime Minister insisted that the proposals for using gas should not be considered by the "psalm-singing uninformed defeatists".[8]

---

[5] Crusade in Europe, p 204
[6] The Ju-88 bombers killed more than 1,000 soldiers and civilians (p 414 Bodyguard of Lies)
[7] Alan Brooke war diaries, 2 February 1944
[8] Memo D 217/4 and p 726, Bodyguard of Lies

Meanwhile, back in Italy, the battle for the "very nasty nut"[9] of Monte Cassino began on 3 December, with attacks on pockets of Germans on the ridge above the monastery. The Germans had agreed not to use the Benedictine monastery – founded in the sixth century by Saint Benedict himself – for military purposes.[10] Despite undertakings to the Pope by the Allies and the Germans that the monastery would not be attacked, the Allies bombed it on 15 February 1944, killing almost 300 civilians. Once the monastery was in ruins, German paratroopers made the most of the rubble to establish defensive positions. In all, nearly 100,000 Allied and Axis solders died in almost six months of drawn-out battles around the monastery.[11]

Eight days after the battle for Cassino began, the British PM arrived in Algiers. His personal Lancaster had first landed at a "closed" fighter airfield 40 miles beyond El Aouina before flying back. The PM had disembarked and was sitting on his suitcase on the runway for an hour on a very cold morning – the beginnings of his attack of pneumonia. When Ike and Kay eventually met him, the PM said that he felt very tired and hoped for several days' rest.

Ike had a pre-lunch military conference, followed by lunch and an hour's talk with the PM, then dinner and further talks. By nightfall, his voice was hoarse and he was worn out. Churchill agreed that Ike could keep Beetle as his Chief-of-Staff, though he turned down Ike's request for Telek and Caacie to enter Britain without the standard six months' quarantine. While the PM was visiting, Ike took the opportunity to write another letter to Kul warning her that Kay was sending her fruit and bank deposits. The letter was posted in London (possibly by a returning member of the PM's staff) on 14 December.

---

[9] Alan Brooke war diary notes, 17 December 1943
[10] General Frido von Senger und Etterlin, in charge of the Gustav Line during the Cassino attack, was a lay Benedictine
[11] http://www.theguardian.com/world/2000/apr/04/johnezard

On 19 December, Ike moved to Italy and took over the Villa della Ortensie, overlooking Naples harbour. After returning from the Italian front, he visited the ancient hunting lodge for the first time. The lodge included hundreds of acres of woods and miles of riding trails on the mountain behind his headquarters in the Duke of Naples' luxurious palace at Caserta.[12] There was a welcoming fire in the Italian-type high stove in the living room, but the building was infested with lice and rats. No sooner had Ike arrived than Telek cornered a rat in the bathroom. Ike took out his .32 automatic, put on his glasses and fired, hitting the toilet seat. The second shot hit the rat's tail and the third shot knocked the rodent to the floor where it was killed with a piece of wood.

In the evening, Ike took Kay to General Clark's for an Italian dinner cooked by an Italian restaurant owner. Afterwards, Kay drove Ike the seven hours to Monty's HQ at Bari and then joined Ike on a navy destroyer for a trip to the Isle of Capri. They spent Christmas Eve on the unspoiled island and, on their return, dined on GI rations at the hunting lodge, with guests who again included Butch's girlfriend, Mollie Ford. Several windows in the house had been broken by a bomb blast, but despite the cold, the guests got into the Christmas spirit by stringing tinned popcorn round a small Christmas tree.

Ike's main Christmas present was FDR's formal announce-ment, monitored on the lodge radio, that he was to be the Supreme Commander for the cross-Channel invasion of Europe.[13] Ike gave everyone old Roman coins as their presents, then Ike and Kay left Naples in the Flying Fortress on Christmas morning to return to North Africa. They stopped at Tunis to visit Winston Churchill who was still suffering from pneumonia. The Army Film and Photo-graphic Unit shot an informal group photograph of Ike with

---

[12] The palace was built in the style of the 17th century French Palace of Versailles

[13] FDR had agreed with Churchill on 20 December 1943 to announce the appointment on New Year's Day 1944

the Prime Minister in his 'siren suit' and Chinese dressing gown, then Kay and Ike flew on to Algiers later the same day.

The following day, Ike heard that the Royal Navy had sunk the German battle cruiser Scharnhorst, the pride of the German navy, in the Barents Sea while the German ship was attacking an Allied convoy. It was more good news, and Ike predicted at his final press conference of 1943 that the European war would be won "in 1944". On 30 December 1943, Ike met French leader Charles de Gaulle in Algiers and assured him that French troops would enter Paris first. As usual, de Gaulle was reluctant to speak English. However, at lunch with de Gaulle on 12 January 1944 while recuperating in Marrakesh,[14] Churchill, who was now 70, spoke French, remarking in a loud aside: "Now that the general speaks English so well, he understands my French perfectly." Everyone laughed – including de Gaulle.

On the last day of 1943, Ike flew to the US for a 12-day trip. He told Kay she would be with him all the time. "You have to know the things that are in my heart," he told her. "You know what I want to say."

At the airport, Ike gave Kay a slip of paper and said: "Will you tend to this for me?"

"Certainly General, have a safe trip," she replied. On the paper, Ike had written: "Think of me. You know what I will be thinking." Back in the car, Kay cried.

Ike first flew to Marrakesh, together with Butch and Mickey. They toasted the new year in Champagne then left Marrakesh at 5am on New Year's Day and flew on to the Azores. After three hours refuelling, they took off for Bermuda, which they reached after 11 hours. A couple of hours later, they were on their way again and, in four hours, reached Washington on the morning of Sunday 2 January.

---

[14] Pasha Hadj Thami Elglaoui presented Churchill with an engraved dagger as a reminder of his stay (6 January 1944, CH 2/493)

Ike and Butch took Telek's two puppies, Junior and Rubey, complete with Scottish tartan leashes and collars, as late Christmas presents for their wives. The dogs immediately urinated, first on Mamie's oriental rug and then Mrs Butcher's. Neither woman wanted a dog, so Ike gave Junior to his brother Milton, while Rubey was a present for Butch's daughter.

Despite FDR's promises, Ike had a busy schedule while in the United States. The first meeting was with General Marshall. The Chief-of-Staff's representative collected Ike at the back door of the Wardman Hotel, where Mamie lived, and drove him, with his general's stars covered, to a private entrance to the Pentagon. No one but the staff in the Secretary of War's office saw him enter but, in a secret memo to FDR,[15] the Chief-of-Staff conceded "if he is seen about town, the matter is bound to leak". When Ike returned to the hotel, he found a tray waiting for him with 50 oysters and several steaks, two chickens, dozens of fresh eggs and some butter, which was strictly rationed at the time.

On Monday evening, 3 January, Ike gave a speech at a dinner for visiting senior military officers and members of the House and Senate Military Affairs Committee. Marshall told Ike that the Germans hoped that the US war effort would disintegrate because of the US railway strike and the threatened steel strike. Ike agreed that the most difficult question he had to answer was "What about the strikes?" Ike was to have flown out of Washington on Sunday evening, but bad weather delayed him for 24 hours. Over the following 11 days, he visited his son John in West Point, conferred with Marshall again, spent several days with Mamie in a cottage at the Ashford army hospital in White Sulphur Springs, West Virginia, and flew to Kansas to see his mother.

While Ike was in the US, Kay was to fly back to London in Ike's luxurious new B-17 Flying Fortress, complete with

---

[15] Marshall memo, 4 January 1944

wood panelling, blue leather seats, carpeting, bunks and even a flush toilet. But the flight was grounded in Marrakesh for two days, so Kay took the opportunity to sightsee, sunbathe and go shopping for handbags. On the flight back to England, the navigator mistakenly nearly landed in neutral Ireland, where they all could have been interned. They eventually landed at Bovingdon US base on 14 January with only three of the four engines working. Kay immediately phoned her mother – the first time they'd spoken in 13 months.

Having finished his stay in the USA, Ike took off in a C-54 from National Airport on the evening of 13 January. After a three-hour flight to Bermuda, he had a late snack in the officers' mess, interrupted by requests to sign short snorter bills. The flight made a brief refuelling stop in the Azores and Ike finally arrived at a fogbound Prestwick where his former railway carriage, Bayonet, was waiting to take him to London.

OPERATION OVERLORD

The capital was experiencing the "worst fog London has had for years"[1] when Ike arrived on 15 January. Kay picked him up in a Packard at Addison Road station and, driving at "not over a half mile an hour", managed to find her way back to 20 Grosvenor Square, then to Hayes Lodge, Ike's new town house on Chesterfield Street near Berkeley Square. Harry Butcher recognised that Kay was "better than any man at driving that big Packard in a total blackout and through London's pea-soupers with those pinpoint headlights". In the drawing room at Hayes Lodge, after everyone had left, Ike put his arms round Kay and said he'd missed her. "Stay and have a nightcap," he suggested. He gave her an autographed photo of Roosevelt, then "I suppose inevitably, we found ourselves in each other's arms," wrote Kay in her autobiography. "Our ties came off. Our jackets came off. Buttons were unbuttoned." Later, they dressed again and kissed each other goodnight. Kay saluted at the front door at 2am – in case anyone was watching.

Patton arrived to see Ike on 26 January,[2] and Ike went to meet the newly-promoted Field Marshal Alan Brooke three times on 17, 24 and 27 January[3] to discuss Overlord and inspect tank developments. Brooke still didn't have much time for Ike as a military leader – he believed that Ike was "really totally unfit for the post he holds from an operation point of view. He makes up, however, by the way he works for good cooperation between allies".

Ike did not officially become supreme commander until the Combined Chiefs-of-Staff confirmed his appointment on 14 February 1944. In the meantime, he continued to plan Overlord with the staff of COSSAC (Chief-of-Staff to the

---

[1] Diary 15 January 1944
[2] Patton diary
[3] Alan Brooke war diaries, 17, 24 and 27 January 1944

Supreme Allied Commander).[4] At least twice a week, Kay would drive Ike to meetings with the Prime Minister. "There was luncheon on Tuesday and dinner with the Chiefs of Staff and others on Friday," he said. "Occasionally the dinner would be transformed into a weekend at Chequers."

Ike did much of the planning for Operation Overlord at Toll Manor, a six-bedroom 16th century country house in Hadlow Down, East Sussex, which he rented from a Colonel Lambert.[5] According to local rumours "passed down through the generations", Eisenhower's presence was kept top secret "because he was also using the house as a love nest with Kay Summersby".[6] Sometimes Ike and Kay would stay "briefly"[7] at The Grove, a Queen Anne house in the village of Sonning in Berkshire, where US troops were also billeted before D-Day.[8]

On 20 January, Ike called on King George who asked him to sign a blank card for the King's aunt, who collected autographs. The next day, Ike had a conference with Monty, Admiral Bertram Ramsay and Air Marshal Trafford Leigh-Mallory. (Two of the three were to be dead within a year. Leigh-Mallory died with nine others, including his wife, on 14 November 1944 when his plane crashed in the French Alps. Admiral Ramsay died in a plane crash in France on 2 January 1945 as he took off for a meeting with Monty in Brussels.)

In Italy, the invasion of Anzio on Saturday 22 January marked a new phase of the war. The following day, Kay drove Ike to a Sunday meeting of the Allied commanders at Norfolk House, the Overlord HQ. Despite Churchill's earlier

---

[4] The forerunner of SHAEF which was officially active from 13 February 1944 to 16 July 1945

[5] The house on nine acres was put up for sale for £1.45 million in 2010

[6] Eisenhower's 'love nest' goes on the market, 12 August 2010, kentnews.co.uk

[7] http://sonning-pc.gov.uk/svHistory.php

[8] The house was for sale at £1.2 million in 2001, and the sales brochure simply said that Ike "used the house for entertaining in the 1940s". (Eisenhower 'love nest' for sale, Financial Times, 27 October 2001)

proposal that Brooke should command Overlord, the British eventually accepted Ike, an American, as Supreme Commander, as most of the troops were American, although there were to be British commanders for land, sea and air forces. The British ground forces were to be commanded by Monty and, at the outset, the Americans would be under General Omar Bradley.

The meeting agreed that the Allies must take more French beaches than originally intended, including the peninsula and port of Cherbourg. Ike confided to his diary: "Whatever my orders are, I'll carry them out – but I am convinced that the original plan does not carry enough strength in the initial wave."[9] He wanted to use two airborne divisions on the Cherbourg Peninsula, rather than just one against Caen. It was therefore agreed that the initial Overlord assault force would be increased from three to five divisions on a wider front. There were to be three divisions in the first assault and two more as immediate follow-ups, with 35 divisions in all – 15 British or Canadian and 20 American. To ensure the strength needed, most of the commanders recommended a reduction in Anvil, the planned invasion of southern France. But Ike said a gateway into France must be found for French troops or all of the French investment would be wasted. Ike "earnestly" hoped to preserve Anvil, even though this would mean "a terrible additional burden on resources".[10]

The plans for Operation Overlord eventually comprised more than 1,000 pages with "endless" revisions.[11] It was "at once a singular military expedition and a fearsome risk," said Ike. Because of all the changes, it became clear that the invasion of Europe would have to be postponed from the start of May until at least the end of the month. The invasion might even have to be further delayed unless there were enough landing craft. The meeting also agreed to move the Allied Expeditionary Force (AEF) headquarters to Widewing

---

[9] 24 January 1944
[10] Diary 24 January 1944
[11] 2004 interview with Wren Fanny Hughill

at Bushy Park, near Kingston-on-Thames, the former head-quarters of the US 8th Air Force.

Meanwhile, the European Advisory Council drew up the terms for the unconditional surrender of Germany. These included the occupation of Germany (paid for by the Germans themselves), repeal of laws against the Jews, surrender of all occupied territory (with a return to the 1938 boundaries) and the abolition of the German General Staff. German press and radio would be controlled by the victors.

On 25 January, Ike heard that German planes had attacked three hospital ships off Anzio. The St David was sunk, and the Leinster was set on fire before the blaze was brought under control and she returned to Naples.[12] However, the Germans weren't the only ones to break the rules. Nine months earlier, British aircraft had torpedoed and sunk the Italian hospital ship Sicilia off Naples. A Red Cross ship carrying parcels for prisoners-of-war was also sunk during an Allied bombing raid on Marseilles.[13] Attacks on ships carrying wounded troops had been condemned by Rommel, who referred to a US Flying Fortress bombing a hospital ship leaving Tobruk and the RAF attacking hospital ships at sea. (He also criticised the "gangster methods" of New Zealand troops in North Africa who he said had bayoneted German wounded during a night attack at Minquar Qaim and had thrown a wounded German officer into a burning truck.[14])

On 27 January, Patton, who was to command the Third Army in Operation Anvil, was invited to dinner with Ike, Kay and Butch. He remarked to his diary that Ike was "very nasty and show-offish – he always is when Kay is present".[15] During dinner, Patton promised that he would be more

---

[12] http://en.wikipedia.org/wiki/List_of_hospital_ships_sunk_in_World_War_II
[13] Daily Mail, 15 September 1944
[14] Rommel The Desert Fox
[15] Patton Diary, 26 January 1944

careful in future about where he had his tantrums, and would not choose a hospital.

Even as Ike and his generals were planning Overlord, the air and sea war against the Germans was continuing. On 29 January, 930 US heavy bombers with more than 600 escorts – the largest number of American bombers yet to take part in a single operation – took off to bomb Frankfurt. The largest sea convoy from the US was also en route to the UK, with 83 merchant ships. A pack of 60 or more U-boats lay in wait off the western coast of Ireland; further north six U-boats attacked an Allied convoy en route to Murmansk and sank seven ships. But the German naval campaign was stuttering. By March 1944, only five of 7,100 ships in the Atlantic, UK coastal and Indian Ocean convoys were lost to enemy action.

BACK AT TELEGRAPH COTTAGE

At the start of 1944, London was suffering regular bombing raids. Up to 100 people were killed every night and 500 seriously wounded. Beetle had urged Ike to move out of London in case he became the victim of a German bomb, but Ike was becoming used to the attacks. When he was staying at Hayes Lodge, he could shelter in the old wine cellar of a nearby house which even had a small switchboard. On the last day of January 1944, Ike agreed to return to Telegraph Cottage, though Hayes Lodge was retained for overnight stays, meetings in Downing Street, dinners and nights when fog made it impossible to drive to the cottage. During dinner at the cottage the first night, the air-raid siren sounded and anti-aircraft guns went into action nearby. The windows rattled, but dinner went on with only occasional remarks about the raid. When the guests heard a plane diving, Tooey Spaatz explained: "There's a night fighter going after one of 'em."

Kay lived only two minutes from the cottage so she and Ike regularly used to "sit quietly in front of the fire" or on "our favourite secluded bench hidden in the shrubbery, hand in hand, my head on his shoulder". During one of their intimate times together, Ike mentioned to Kay that, when he'd been in the United States, he'd thought about Kay much of the time – to the point where he kept calling Mamie "Kay". "That tore it...she was furious," he recalled. According to Kay's autobiography, Ike said that, going to sleep, he used to think about the first time he'd seen Kay running towards him in Grosvenor Square. "You looked very glamorous. Beautiful...There are many times I look at you and want to tell you how beautiful you are and how much you mean to me, but something always stops me," he said. "I just don't have the right to tell you what I want to tell you."[1]

---

[1] http://www.parismatch.com/Actu/International/Kay-Summersby-l-amour-impossible-d-Eisenhower-579615

Ike also recalled the death of his firstborn son and said that he and Mamie were never able to rekindle their earlier relationship. "There's no tragedy in life like the death of a child," he said. "Things never get back to the way they were. Kay I guess I'm telling you that I'm not the lover you should have."

"Someday, things will be different," said Kay. "I'm not Irish and stubborn for nothing."

They spent hours horse riding together in nearby Richmond Park (which was closed to the general public) or with Ike planning a vegetable garden or cooking beef stew or chilli fried chicken. In the spring of 1944, they played golf, or bridge in the evenings. They enjoyed a "grand evening" on 19 March, riding bicycles and then playing bridge, at which Kay noted that she won four shillings.[2] Indeed, Kay's diary shows that she and Ike were bridge partners most nights at Telegraph Cottage, generally winning small sums from the opposing team.

Winston Churchill had encouraged Ike to take up painting – "daubs, born of my love of color",[3] as Ike said. He later presented a 1949 copy of a watercolour sketch of Telegraph Cottage to Master Sgt Moaney. On the back of the canvas, Ike had pencilled: "Telegraph Cottage – small house south of London where I lived while planning both Torch (1942) and Overlord (1944)."[4] He started to paint in oils because he was "fascinated by colours" – but the Supreme Commander had no illusions about his own abilities as an artist.

At the end of January, Beetle came back from Algiers with Telek, who went into quarantine at kennels just outside London for six months (at an "exorbitant" $4 a week). Putting the Scotty into quarantine was equivalent to "locking

---

[2] Diary 19 March 1944
[3] at ease, p 341
[4] http://www.rrauction.com/Dwight-D-Eisenhower-Original-Painting.html

up a part of my heart", said Ike. Caacie had begun her six months' quarantine in London on 27 January.

Ike had to continue with his everyday duties, as well as planning Overlord. On 1 February, an official group photograph was taken of a meeting of the Supreme Command, Allied Expeditionary Force, in London. It was a Who's Who of those who were to lead Overlord. Those present for the photograph included: Lieutenant-General Omar Bradley, Commander-in-Chief, 1st US Army; Admiral Sir Bertram Ramsay, Allied naval Commander-in-Chief, Expeditionary Force; Air Chief Marshal Sir Arthur Tedder, Deputy Supreme Commander, Expeditionary Force; Ike; General Sir Bernard Montgomery, Commander-in-Chief 21st Army Group; Air Chief Marshal Sir Trafford Leigh-Mallory, Allied Air Commander, Expeditionary Force; and Lieutenant-General Walter Bedell-Smith, Ike's Chief-of-Staff. But "Eisenhower's consistent refusal to have an overall Army Commander-in-Chief will always be a matter for discussion and criticism," wrote the military correspondent of The Sunday Times four years later. "He insisted on commanding the land armies himself; he is not in any way a battle commander, and he had had no previous experience; in fact he did not understand how to command *in the field*."[5]

The following day, Kay had her photo taken adjusting the flag on the front of Ike's car. Ike was also a guest at the PM's dinner for King George on February 2. The King didn't leave until 1am and Ike was detained by the PM for a further half hour discussing the Allies' lack of progress at Anzio, where the Germans were using remote-controlled tanks. Later that day, Ike visited Telek at Hackbridge Kennels. Kay brought her old handbag for the dog to sleep on. Ike refused a photographer's request for a picture of him holding Telek. But by holding a piece of meat above Ike's picture, the photographer made Telek appear to be licking his master's face. Kay also agreed to look out for a dog for Patton.[6] He

---

[5] Italics in original, The Times of India, 12 December 1948
[6] Patton letter of 20 February 1944

eventually decided on a 15-month-old white bull terrier, which took to him "like a duck to water".[7] Patton named the dog Willie.

On St Valentine's Day, Admiral Cunningham proposed Ike for London's Athenaeum Club. For only the second time in 130 years, the nominations book left the club so Cunningham could inscribe Ike's name in it. But the new member of the Athenaeum was more concerned with other domestic matters. He wrote to his Washington secretary, Jeanne Dixon, to tell her he was back at the cottage.[8] "We have got a fine rug for the living room and some comfortable chairs," he wrote. "As you know, I am very fond of the cottage and much prefer living in a small place." Jeanne replied asking Ike to give her best wishes to Kay.

On Sunday 26 March, Kay and Ike spent the whole day in one another's company with lunch at 1.30, horse riding at 3, a visit to the Tedders at 6 and dinner with the Gaults at 7.30.[9] Their social life was so hectic that, later that week, Kay "spent the morning in bed".[10] It was a rare break. For two or three days at a time, Ike and Kay would travel all over England and Scotland visiting bases. On one occasion, Kay met her brother, a Royal Engineer, and Ike invited Seamus to be in a photograph with him.

Throughout this period, there was an ever-increasing build-up of American troops. The first US soldiers (4,500 men from the 34th Division) had arrived in Northern Ireland only in January 1942 but, within two and half years, there were more than 1.5 million US military personnel in the United Kingdom. Their presence was only reluctantly accepted by most British ("overpaid, over-sexed and over here"). On 4 February, Ike left Addison Street Station aboard his special train and went to Plymouth to watch a US division training. He told the 8th Infantry that he would

---

[7] Patton letter 6 March 1944
[8] Letter of 10 March 1944
[9] Diary 26 March 1944
[10] Diary 31 March 1944

meet them "east of the Rhine" and personally make sure they celebrated their victory with Champagne, "even if I have to buy it myself".

But the Allies' preparation for Operation Overlord remained top secret. Because the Prime Minister and his War Cabinet feared a leak about the invasion, correspondents were only accredited to SHAEF just before the operation began. Decoy attacks were also planned to confuse the Germans. [11] The Combined Intelligence Committee hoped that an increase in air and naval operations in Norway would convince the Germans that the attack would come there. The Royal Navy was to attack Narvik, and Allied reconnaissance planes were flown close to the Swedish border. General Patton was put in charge of Operation Fortitude, which aimed to convince the Germans that an attack on Calais (by a non-existent army) was imminent.

In preparation for final victory, Allied commanders discussed the allocation of areas of a defeated Germany. Ike wanted SHAEF to control Germany after the war and said that, if the country were divided into "definite occupational zones on a national basis, we'd have trouble". [12]

But the British wanted to control northwest Germany, Denmark and the Low Countries because that was where the most significant German ports and air bases were. The US was to occupy the southwest of Germany, but FDR pointed out that this part of Germany contained only "scenery and tourists", and said he would prefer if US forces occupied the industrial northwest. The Americans were actually more concerned about their lines of communication passing through France, and were relieved when the British agreed that US communications could pass through their sector. [13] The Americans promised to remain in occupation of

---

[11] A "cover plan to mislead and mystify the enemy" was agreed at the Tehran Conference on 1 December 1943
[12] *Ibid*
[13] Alan Brooke war diary notes, 12 July 1944

Germany for just two years after the war finished,[14] but in fact they only returned full sovereign status to Germany in 1991.[15]

The pressure on Ike was telling. He developed a cold which lasted for months and he became increasingly depressed about problems with supplies, troop behaviour, de Gaulle, Churchill's ideas about the invasion of Europe and Monty. At lunch with the Prime Minister at Chequers, Monty expressed the view that there should be two major campaigns, Overlord and Italy. He said he would rather have plenty of landing craft for Overlord than use them for Operation Anvil (the Allied landing in southern France in August 1944, later called Operation Dragoon), but Churchill disagreed.

Life went on. On Wednesday 23 February, a dozen British officers who'd served with Ike in the Mediterranean presented him with a silver salver at a men-only dinner at Claridge's. Kay waited up for him, organising late-night food with Butch, Mollie Ford and General Everett Hughes. When Ike got back to the cottage, he warned Hughes to be discreet at supper in front of Butch's girlfriend.

On 29 February (1944 was a leap year), the Prime Minister again kept Ike and Beetle at dinner until 1.30am. He expressed disappointment at the lack of progress in the Italian campaign, though he didn't blame anyone specific. "We hoped to land a wildcat that would tear out the bowels of the Boche," said Churchill. "Instead, we have stranded a vast whale with its tail flopping about in the water."[16] Although Italy was to have priority over all other Mediterranean operations, the attack on the "soft underbelly of Europe", Operation Anvil/Dragoon, was to be launched

---

[14] Alan Brooke war diaries, 5 February 1945
[15] Elvis Presley, for example, did his national service as an army driver in Friedberg, West Germany, from October 1958 until March 1960
[16] Alan Brooke war diaries, 29 February 1944

shortly after Overlord.[17] The situation was to be re-evaluated three weeks later.

Holding the fragile alliance of Americans, British, Russians and French together was a continuing problem for Ike. For example, the Chief of the RAF Air Staff, Marshal of the Royal Air Force Sir Charles Portal, maintained that only part of the RAF's Bomber Command should be under Ike's control. The Prime Minister agreed with Portal that either Bomber Command should be independent (but work in conjunction with Ike), or else only some of the bombers should be under American control. But Ike said that if the British insisted on this less-than-all-out effort for Overlord, he would "simply have to go home". He said the Americans had a much larger air force in Britain than the British, and had put all of it under his authority. He could not face the US Chiefs of Staff if the British retained their "important striking force". Ike agreed that RAF Coastal Command could remain under separate control, but he said that Bomber Command must be directed by the Supreme Commander – him. Portal eventually agreed that the RAF's Tedder (who was deputy Supreme Commander of Overlord) would direct the strategic air plan.

---

[17] "Why should we bash in the back door when we have the latchkey of the front door?" asked Churchill. (CHAR 20/169/61)

WIDEWING

SHAEF headquarters moved to Widewing (or "Wide Wings" as Kay noted in her diary[1]) on Sunday 5 March, despite the opposition of some staff officers who were used to enjoying leisurely lunches at the London clubs. Ike pointed out that there were hourly shuttle buses from Widewing to central London, but eventually decided to "get rid of useless officers"[2] like these.

Camp Griffiss at Bushy Park was named after US Colonel Tim Griffiss, who was killed in February 1942 when his plane was shot down by Polish RAF pilots. The camp looked like an ordinary Army post. It had Nissen huts, a low PX and mess buildings, tents for the British and American troops and two long, single-storey buildings, covered with camouflage nets. A one-armed civilian guard controlled the entrance at Coombe Lane leading into Kingston Road. On the Kingston and Teddington side, the park was surrounded by a stone wall up to ten feet high and the entrances were guarded by white-helmeted MPs from the 888th MP Company. When Eisenhower wanted to go somewhere, he'd whistle and MPs armed with .38-calibre Smith & Wesson Victory revolvers and on Model 74 Harleys would lead off, followed by Kay's car. "We were his personal company," said Sgt Gene Stephens.[3]

Ike had a 20-feet-square office with a large walnut desk, and a globe of the world next to it. On the desk were framed pictures of his wife, mother and son, Mamie, Ida and John, flanked by the British and US flags and his general's flag. There were two phones: red line 6 (the same designation as during Operation Torch) and a scrambler. On the walls were

---

[1] Diary 6 February 1944
[2] Diary 16 March 1944
[3] http://www.reviewjournal.com/news/veteran-mp-recalls-world-war-ii-experiences

autographed pictures of Roosevelt, Churchill, [4] General Marshall and Admiral Cunningham, and there were two easy chairs next to the open fire. In the American fashion, there was a coffee break at around 11 each morning. Similarly, in the British style, the mess would send up tea at four in the afternoon and Kay would take it into Ike's office. "Bring yours in too, Kay," he'd say. "It makes more of a break to have someone to talk to."

Kay was now acting as Ike's appointments secretary and had her own office and secretary. She answered all his phone calls and, if visitors stayed too long, she'd go into Ike's office with a blank piece of paper saying: "Excuse me General, this message just came in." On 29 March, Ike presented Kay with a matching Parker pen and pencil set inscribed: 'Kay, for service in Mediterranean AFHQ, DDE'. He gave similar pens to nine officers who'd served as Commanders-in-Chief under him in the Mediterranean, and to four others. An accompanying letter said the fountain pen was "a personal present" and that Kay's "services" had been "of inestimable and constant value". She framed the letter and kept it on her desk. As well as being his secretary, Kay continued to be Ike's chauffeur. On 23 March, Kay drove him to Newbury to watch exercises involving 1,500 parachutists of the 101st Airborne.[5] After the "wonderful display" of red, yellow, white and green parachutes, Kay and Ike – who was "on wonderful form" – drank Champagne until 11.30pm.

Ike was still avoiding most social invitations, and British foreign secretary Anthony Eden was annoyed when Ike turned down an invitation to dinner.[6] But Ike did host a reception for most of the American and British top brass at Claridge's in March 1944, and the following month agreed to present the cup to the southern winners of the Football League War Cup final. (A capacity crowd of 85,000 at

---

[4] Replaced in June 1944 with an "immeasurably better" photo (72, CHAR 20/141A)

[5] Diary 23 March 1944

[6] Diary 16 March 1944

Wembley on 15 April saw Charlton beat Chelsea by three goals to one. Charlton then drew one-all with Aston Villa in the national final. Because of the difficulty of a replay due to transport restrictions and the threat of bombing, the two teams uniquely shared the 1944 Alexander trophy, receiving a trophy each.)

But soccer aside, Overlord was still at the forefront of Ike's mind. The three main problems of the operation – landing craft, aircraft and political relationships with the French – were discussed at a meeting of the British commanders-in-chief. Overlord would require 200 tugs to tow the invasion barges and Mulberry artificial harbours across the Channel to Normandy. The 128-ton concrete invasion barges, 84 feet long by 22 feet wide, were being built in England. (The record for building a single barge was 74 hours.[7]) But Admiral Cunningham said he might not have enough tugs to tow the two Mulberry harbours and invasion barges across the Channel in such a short time.

From 6 April, leave for all troops was cancelled. All travel had been suspended between Britain and Ireland on 13 March so that the Axis embassies in neutral Dublin would not discover the invasion date. The Irish Prime Minister, Eamon de Valera, had earlier rejected a call by FDR to close the German and Japanese embassies "for security's sake".[8] The British considered this "a substantial disservice to the Allied cause" and the British Prime Minister announced restrictions on travel between Britain and Ireland to isolate "Southern Ireland" from the outside world "during the critical period which is now approaching".[9]

Ike continued to review the troops and weapons to be used in the invasion. About 30 SHAEF officers including Ike took his train to Salisbury to see new weapons being demonstrated. At Bovingdon airfield north of London, where Ike's

[7] New York World-Telegram, 10 April 1944
[8] Alan Brooke war diaries, 4 February 1944
[9] March 1944 speech to House of Commons Hansard, 14 March 1944 vol 398 cc36-8

personal B-17 was kept, he saw a new B-29 from America which could carry ten tons of bombs 5,000 miles. He was also told that leaving Flying Fortresses in their natural aluminium finish, rather than painting them olive drab, could increase the bombers' top speed by six miles an hour. By then, 800- to 1000-bomber raids on Axis targets were standard. For example, Berlin was frequently targeted, once by 2,000 planes in March 1944.

Bomber crews often suffered heavy losses from anti-aircraft fire and defending Luftwaffe fighters, such as the loss of almost 12 per cent of the planes which bombed Nuremberg on 30 March 1944. Overall during the war, 55,573 Bomber Command crewmen, out of 125,000 aircrew, were killed. The US Eighth Air Force, which had 350,000 aircrew in the UK, suffered 26,000 killed and 23,000 crewmen taken prisoner. But Allied bombers killed around half a million civilians by "area bombing" of cities in mainland Europe.

By 31 May 1944, the target date for Overlord, 38 divisions were expected to be operationally available. The Americans were to have 21 divisions, including one parachute regimental combat team, five armoured units, two Ranger battalions and four parachute regiments. The British would have 17 divisions, one line-of-communication division, ten tank brigades, one infantry brigade, eight Commando groups and a flail brigade to deal with tank obstacles.[10] There were 224 motor torpedo boats available, as well as several coastal vessels, with a total cargo-carrying capacity of 313,000 tons.[11] The landings were also to be supported by six battleships for up to 48 hours, 21 cruisers, many destroyers and two monitors. There were also to be rocket ships and Allied artillery mounted on landing craft.

US air forces available for Overlord were to be 12 squadrons of heavy day bombers, 50 squadrons of day fighters, 42 squadrons of photo-recce planes, 32 squadrons of light and

---

[10] http://www.history.army.mil/documents/WWII/g4-OL/g4-ol.htm
[11] http://www.ibiblio.org/hyperwar/ETO/Overlord/NEPTUNE-OpsPlan/OpPlan-2-44-I.html

medium bombers and 12 squadrons of night fighters. In the US Air Force, a squadron of heavy bombers ('heavies') normally consisted of nine planes, and there were three squadrons in a group, with headquarters having six more planes. However, the 8th Air Force had 48 planes per group, instead of 33. American fighter squadrons had 25 planes, with 75 in the group. In the Royal Air Force, a fighter squadron was 18 planes, of which 12 were operational. The RAF was to have 18 squadrons of day fighters, 18 bomber squadrons, 18 fighter and reconnaissance squadrons, 18 night fighter squadrons, 38 light bomber squadrons, 20 heavy night bomber squadrons, 46 squadrons of troop carriers and 30 transport squadrons. [12]

Altogether, there were likely to be almost 1,400 planes available for airborne forces and transport on June 1, plus 2,000 gliders. A total of 90,000 parachutes were earmarked for use in Overlord. [13] Ike was told that he could use the heavy bombers in RAF Bomber Command and the US Strategic Air Force for air cover of the landings in Overlord, [14] but the ordinary soldier would have to defeat the Axis forces on the ground in order to win the war.

Secrecy was still vital, but the details of Overlord – including strengths, targets, equipment and the target date – were disclosed when an American soldier of German extraction in the US Ordnance Division sent documents to a private home in a part of Chicago where many German emigrants lived. The soldier said his mind was elsewhere because his sister, who lived in Chicago, had been seriously ill. Four unauthorised people at US army headquarters and at least ten post office employees who saw the papers were all put under observation, but nothing further was discovered. Ike also refused to comment on the widespread story that an Air

---

[12] http://www.history.army.mil/documents/WWII/g4-OL/g4-ol.htm
[13] "That's All, Brother", the Douglas C-47 that dropped the first paratroopers on D-Day, was found in a scrapyard in Oshkosh, Wisconsin, in June 2015 (Daily Mirror, 6 June 2015, p 10)
[14] Diary 3 April 1944

Force major-general at a cocktail party had offered bets on the date of the invasion. The officer had been reduced to his permanent rank of Lieutenant-Colonel and sent home. A similar breach of security by a naval officer was "so serious it gave Ike the shakes".

As Supreme Commander of the invasion forces, Ike was becoming well known. On 22 March, he asked the Judge Advocate General, Brigadier-General Ed Betts, if he had a legal right to prevent publication of his letters following publication of some of his personal letters and talks to small groups of soldiers. But he was advised that he could not prevent publication, as he was a prominent figure. The Judge Advocate also advised Ike about the best way for "Mrs Kay Sommersby" (sic) to be naturalised as a US citizen. [15] Betts said Kay should:

1. lawfully enter the United States on a visitors' visa,

2. live there as a civilian for a suggested 30 days,

3. become an officer in the Women's Army Corps (WAC) as a "citizen of a co-belligerent nation",

4. take up active duty,

5. serve honourably for a proposed 30-day period and then either

    a) remain in the United States and be naturalised by a US court (this section was crossed out in the original memo) or

    b) return to Europe and obtain US citizenship through a consular officer in London.

---

[15] Confidential memo JMP/147 to Eisenhower, 1 April 1944

General Betts said that Kay could be appointed a WAC officer, but enlistment in the WACs, which was limited to US citizens, [16] was "<u>not recommended</u>".[17] Possible future consequences of enlistment could include US government steps to revoke the naturalisation "on the grounds of fraud or illegal obtainment by those acting on behalf of the lady concerned".

---

[16] Kay was "the only non-American woman to hold a commission in the US forces". (p 3, Cork Examiner, 13 June 1945)
[17] Underlined in the original

RAILWAYS OR OIL PLANTS?

Relationships between the major Allies continued to be poor. American officers found "the British high-handed manner most difficult to stand – remembering the injunction that they must 'get along' with the British. They have found themselves pushed to the background; unconsulted when important decisions were being made; assigned to relatively unimportant jobs while the more important ones went to the British officers." To Americans, the order to 'get along' with the British "means that both sides must yield something in order to gain something. To the British, however, this injunction seems to mean that Americans must be willing to do all things in the British way and as the British wish." [1] A 'Memorandum concerning Anglo-American relations In Italy (particularly in the Allied Control Commission)' added: "One senior American officer, holding a responsible position, remarked that he could promote a British Lieutenant-Colonel to Colonel more easily than he could promote an American Private to Corporal."

One area where the difference was most marked was in the decision about bomber targets. The heads of the US and British air forces just could not agree whether Allied bombers should target railways or oil plants. US General Tooey Spaatz suggested concentrating bomber efforts on synthetic-oil plants, rather than rail transport. He said the Luftwaffe would defend the plants, leading to the continued destruction of planes and oil. Fourteen synthetic-oil plants produced 80 per cent of all German synthetic petrol and oil, whereas 14 marshalling yards constituted only a fraction of the German railway system. But Air Chief Marshal Tedder favoured attacking the railways because he said the Germans would then be forced to move by road and become targets

---

[1] Howard Barr memo to Myron Taylor concerning Anglo-American relations in Italy, 10 April 1944

for strafing. He said bombing the oil plants could not be really effective in time for Overlord.

The British Cabinet meanwhile criticised the proposals for concentrating bombing on transport targets in France because civilian casualties could lead to French ill-will.[2] But Ike said people living in the areas to be bombed would be notified by pamphlet and other means, so they could move to safety. The arguments eventually "became so heated that at various points Tedder, Spaatz, and Eisenhower himself threatened to resign".[3] Eventually Tedder's plan for bombing transport targets, rather than oil refineries, was adopted, largely because the oil plan would not seriously affect German military operations for six months. Once the Allies were firmly established ashore, the strategic bombers could attack the oil industry. But the primary effort of British and American strategic bombers was still to hit the production of enemy aircraft and to destroy as many as possible – in the air or on the ground.

Because of slow progress in Italy, Operation Anvil, the diversionary attack of two divisions (with ten to follow) in southern France was virtually abandoned for the time being. Ike conferred with the British chiefs-of-staff about US proposals for launching a modified Anvil by July 10, and abandoning the quest for Rome. The British Prime Minister insisted that the capture of Rome would have a negative psychological effect on the Axis forces. But US support was needed for Overlord too. Ike said the first five or six weeks of Overlord would be critical for the Allied armies and he hoped that Admiral King would provide gunfire support for the invading Allied soldiers before his battleships returned to the Mediterranean for what remained of the amphibious attack on southern France.

---

[2] Alan Brooke war diaries, 5, 13 and 19 April and 2 May 1944
[3] Eisenhower, p 28

Meanwhile, the Italians were showing more and more "sullen discontent"[4] because of the level of civilian casualties at the hands of the Allies. US Vatican ambassador Myron Taylor told FDR that US aviators had strafed civilians, including a tram full of workmen in Naples, in early April 1943, and US planes had also bombed the city of Grosseto in Tuscany on 6 May and machine-gunned civilians.[5] The battle for Monte Cassino was similar to the First World War Battle of Verdun in miniature. The Germans hid in tunnels while US bombers practically levelled the town (having the previous month destroyed the ancient Benedictine Abbey, killing monks and refugees). Allied troops then retook a substantial part of the town in bitter hand-to-hand fighting.

There were also problems with bombers flying from Italian bases to targets further north. On 1 April 1944, 50 USAAF B-24 Liberators mistakenly bombed Schaffhausen in neutral Switzerland, killing 40 people and injuring many others. Within six months, the apologetic Americans had paid $4 million compensation for the damage, with a further $10 million paid in restitution by 1949. But it wasn't the first time the war had come to Switzerland. Sometimes Allied bomber crews in damaged planes would land in the neutral country, ultimately leading to the internment of 1,700 American aircrew. Switzerland was frequently bombed and strafed by the Allies during the war, killing civilians and damaging property. In one case, where US planes bombed Zurich, the lead pilot and his navigator were court-martialled in England after the war ended, but were found not guilty. The Allies generally blamed the attacks on navigational errors, poor weather or equipment failure. The errors eventually got into the press, which also published the story about how the US navy had shot down 23 Allied transport aircraft in the Sicilian operation. This caused a headache for the public relations people who were worried that the delay over the reporting of this, the Bari gas incident

---

4 Winston Churchill Parliamentary speech, 27 July 1943, Hansard vol 391 cc 1397-402
5 Cable, 14 May 1943

and the Patton slapping episode would suggest that the Allies were reluctant to release bad news.

In England, rockets and pilotless aircraft interfered with the loading and shipping of landing craft in the Thames and Southampton areas, but ships and landing craft stayed there nonetheless. The Combined Chiefs were also making plans for France after the invasion. They approved supplies for up to 170,000 Frenchmen for policing areas of France occupied by the Allies. In return, the British wanted Le Clerc's French division from North Africa used in the follow-up to the invasion of the south of France. On 6 April, de Gaulle was made commander of all the French armed forces, but Giraud wasn't consulted and threatened to resign. Ike still insisted that the Supreme Commander must be allowed to direct the French resistance, though the French were still given no information which might compromise the secrecy of Overlord. The Russians were also not given exact details of the French beaches to be attacked. They were to launch a large-scale offensive on the eastern front on D-Day, which they were told would be two or three days either side of 1 June, depending on weather and tide.

Separately, Ike urged the Combined Chiefs to reach agreement on a number of questions following the invasion, including civilian labour, treatment of banks and exchange rates, transfer or seizure of enemy property, distribution of civilian supplies and handling of displaced persons. Ike said "unconditional surrender" should be defined in a new American-Anglo-Russian statement so that radio broadcasts and pamphlets could explain to the Germans about Allied proposals to:

- demilitarise Germany;
- purge Nazis from the government;
- arrest and try war criminals;
- move people in an 'orderly fashion' and
- restore freedom of religion and trade unions.

Overlord was now less than two months away. After a briefing session at St Paul's School in London on 7 April, Ike visited Dunmow in Essex on 11 April and saw 39 American bombers take off to attack the rail yards at Charleroi. Kay then drove him to Debden, where he met Colonel Donald Blakeslee, the commanding officer of the 4th Fighter Group which had notched up 500 kills by the end of April. Blakeslee had flown the first P-51 Mustang over Berlin to support a US bomber raid. He had told his pilots to learn how to fly the new planes "on the way to the target". Ike had awarded Blakeslee the DSC on 6 March 1944 making him the most decorated US Army Air Force fighter pilot in World War II. While in Debden, Ike took his first ride in a fighter – ten-minutes as a passenger in a new 'droop snoot' P38 Lightning, with a place for a bombardier in the extended Plexiglass nose. "Everyone held their breath" during the ride, said Kay, and Tooey Spaatz "didn't smile" until Ike landed.[6]

Fighters and bombers were a constant preoccupation. After 64 US bombers and 16 US fighters were shot down in a raid by 2,000 aircraft on targets east of Stettin on 12 April, RAF Bomber Command said it expected to cut losses from night fighters with a new detector installed from May 1. Several squadrons of 400 mile-an-hour Typhoons were also equipped with rockets, as were some American planes.

Next, Ike inspected training facilities and billets at Bassingbourne, where he christened a B-17 'General Ike' by breaking a bottle of Mississippi water over its nose. He was impressed by the mess food, though a sergeant told Butch that the mess officer was just putting on a show for Ike and that really "the mess stinks and the food is frequently cold". Ike later agreed that he had "made things miserable on occasion for young captains or lieutenants, responsible for messes, who limited their inspection to questioning whether pots and pans were shined brightly enough. Some had no

---

[6] Diary 11 April 1944

idea whatsoever about a balanced meal and others cared not at all whether food not only tasted properly but looked appealing". To Ike, food was important – particularly beans. His orderly, Sgt McKeogh, recalled that Ike "was always fond of baked beans, made with salt pork and molasses and onions...We never could get them just the way he wanted them. There would always be too much or not enough of something; too many onions or not enough, or too much molasses. I guess we were always a great disappointment to the General when it came to beans."[7]

Meanwhile, the US President's poor health was continuing to cause concern (he suffered from polio). Undersecretary of State Ed Stettinius (a former munitions salesman) told Ike that FDR was "far from well and that he is becoming increasingly difficult to deal with because he changes his mind so often". Neither man realised at the time that FDR had only about a month left to live.

On 14 April, Kay and Ike forgot the war for a time and went fishing at Colonel Ivan Cobbold's at Cairnton in Scotland. "No luck at all – beautiful weather though," said Kay.[8] "I fished a bit and caught a baby salmon, 3 ins. E [Ike] got a kelt [a salmon which had just spawned] which was bad luck as he has got to throw it back in river. We all had a lovely time, wish we could have stayed longer."

Lend-Lease was also occupying Ike's attention. He was furious when he learned that an HQ mess officer had bought a $600 silver tea service for the Yankee Doodle Room and charged it to Lend-Lease in Ike's name. Following an investigation, Ike also discovered that his name had also been used to acquire antique furniture for Hayes Lodge, even though he would eventually be leaving the house. The antiques were eventually returned for 90 per cent of the purchase price, as furniture was difficult to obtain in England at the time. Butch also returned four sofa pillows

---

[7] Sgt Mickey and General Ike, p 12
[8] Diary 14 April 1944

for which he'd paid 40 dollars for the hard davenport and two chairs at Telegraph Cottage.

By this time, the Allies had identified 51 German divisions in France and the Low Countries, of which eight were Panzer, ten field and 33 'lower establishment', that is below the normal standards for field divisions. Altogether the Germans were estimated to have 336 divisions available, but 199 of those were still on the eastern front. The Luftwaffe was estimated to have more than 5,000 aircraft, of which 1,680 were on the Russian front. To defeat these troops, there was to be mass aerial bombing of the beachhead within 45 seconds of Overlord H-Hour, starting about 200 yards inland and continuing for 800 or 900 yards, including possible targeting of underwater mines. Ike said he couldn't see any reason why troops in the leading assault wave had to stay 1,500 yards short of aerial blanket bombing. But he changed his mind when he saw a plane on exercises drop its bombs more than 500 yards short.

Ike also ordered an all-out effort against the Pas de Calais 'ski sites' which had increased in number from 20 to 30. Seven large sites were presumed to be connected to the long-range V-2 rocket. The accuracy of the V-1 had also been improved so that three out of five – rather than two out of five – successful firings landed in greater London. Ike and Tedder returned to Telegraph Cottage for lunch after an inspection of airfields, including a "fog dispeller," a British invention involving a series of petrol-burning jets shooting a flame into the air alongside runways, clearing the fog up to 400 feet. The machine required 60,000 gallons of petrol an hour, but was used only in emergencies.

On 28 April 1944,[9] Ike watched Exercise Tiger, the amphibious landing of the US 4th Division at Slapton Sands, between Dartmouth and Plymouth. No naval destroyers accompanied the convoy due to a signal failure. The

---

[9] The US Navy Secretary Republican Frank Knox died of a heart attack and was succeeded by James Forrestal

organisers of this large exercise expected it to be attacked by the Luftwaffe or possibly enemy E-boats – and so it transpired. Two LSTs were sunk and one damaged by E-boat action off Lyme Bay.[10] Casualties at the time were said to be 300 to 400, but 946 actually died, one of the biggest death tolls in England during the war. The defenders were said to have been armed with live ammunition, instead of dummy bullets, and a British cruiser is reported to have used live ammunition during the exercise. Many of those who died were apparently the victims of friendly fire.[11] Several of those killed carried papers with the details of Operation Overlord, though their bodies were all said to have been recovered.

And if the preparations for D-Day weren't enough for Ike, Patton was in trouble again. He privately told an Allied club[12] that it was the destiny of Britain and America to rule the world after the war – though he later insisted that he had added "and, of course, the Russians". US Republicans considered this an intrusion into politics on Roosevelt's side. Ike was "very upset at Patton's actions"[13] and later had a "distressing interview" with him. As Patton recorded in his diary, General Marshall said that this "crime" had destroyed any chance of Patton's permanent promotion, "as the opposition said even if I was the best tactician and strategist in the army, my demonstrated lack of judgment made me unfit to command".[14]

"Georgie should have done three things," said Ike. "Thought about what he wanted to say, watched his tongue and checked the roster" because a reporter was present at the meeting, unknown to Patton.

In the immediate run-up to Overlord, civilians were banned from a ten-mile-wide military strip along the south coast –

---

[10] Diary 28 April 1944
[11] The Observer, 16 May 2004
[12] At the opening of a Welcome Club in Knutsford, Cheshire, on 25 April 1944
[13] Diary 30 April 1944, though Patton regarded it as a "stink over nothing"
[14] Diary 1 May 1944

despite Churchill's initial opposition[15] – and diplomats and couriers were not allowed to leave the British Isles.[16] The Belgian, Dutch and other governments in exile in London objected to the ban which they said treated them as 'second-class allies'. In response to the British move, they withheld intelligence about the battle order of the Germans, which had arrived in their diplomatic bags. Ike wrote to the PM at the end of May asking him to continue the ban on diplomatic communications after the invasion; if the Germans learned that the Allies had used up all their troops on D-Day, they could move their reserves from the Pas de Calais area to the Normandy beachhead. But Churchill said the restrictions should not extend more than a week beyond D-Day.[17] The mail of British soldiers scheduled to take part in the invasion was also heavily censored, and Americans were not allowed to telephone or cable the United States for 10 days in May. American troops were confined to quarters from midnight on 16 May to facilitate the MPs' search for absentees.

Meanwhile, the fighting in other parts of Europe was continuing. In Italy on 18 April 1944, Marshal Badoglio's cabinet offered to resign, but King Victor Emmanuel invited Badoglio to form a new government – which lasted just over seven weeks. On 20 April, the US 8th Air Force bombed Paris La Chapelle, killing 670 civilians.[18] Beetle drafted a proclamation to be issued to the French when Overlord started, but said he was "walking on eggs" to find words which would be effective, yet not criticised in the US. The initial communiqué for Overlord was to read: "Allied naval forces supported by strong air forces began landing Allied armies this morning on the northern coast of France." The Combined Chiefs said the communiqué should also specify

---

[15] Alan Brooke war diaries, 9 February and 10 March 1944
[16] Diplomatic bags were opened and their contents censored (p 540 Bodyguard of Lies)
[17] Diary 1 June 1944
[18] The Allies bombed more than 1,500 French cities and towns, killing almost 70,000 civilians

"under the command of General Eisenhower". Before Overlord began, Ike lunched with the PM who became emotional when they parted. "I am in this thing with you to the end," said Churchill with tears in his eyes. "If it fails, we will go down together."

The Germans continued to attack shipping in Plymouth harbour with glider bombs, the guiding aircraft staying out of reach of antiaircraft guns. Anti-aircraft batteries and ships in Portsmouth were ordered to fire on all unidentified planes flying below 2,000 feet at night. As two more German divisions arrived in France, Ike decided that D-Day would be Y-Day (June 1) plus 4, i.e. 5 June.[19] On Y-Day plus 4, 5, 6 and 7, the tides were right and the moon was full, as Ike preferred. After asking the Combined Chiefs to allow him to give full details of D-Day to the French, he inspected yet more troops near Lydd and Hastings on the south coast.

Ike decided that H-Hour might be staggered for different beaches, depending on the underwater obstacles, such as angled steel gates, metal pyramids and steel rails blasted into the sand by water jets. Mines and barbed wire were also strung between the obstacles to obstruct any landing. Beetle said at lunch that underwater obstacles were the greatest concern. Beetle predicted that the Allied chances of holding the Normandy beachhead after the German build-up were only 50-50, and said he was "damned well" going to get out of the Army after the war. Leigh-Mallory, whom Eisenhower considered "excessively pessimistic and glum",[20] wrote to Ike saying he feared losses of up to 70 per cent in the paratroop operation.[21] Ike looked older now than at any time since Kay had been with him – though he seemed to improve after a good night's sleep or a few hours' riding.

On 15 May, with just over three weeks to go, Ike had a final review of plans for Overlord at St Paul's School, London.

---

[19] "D-Day means Death Day", said one German propaganda leaflet. (1324-3-45)
[20] Eisenhower, p 26
[21] Diary 30 May 1944

Among those present were King George,[22] the PM, Patton, Smuts and Brooke. The Navy said it had put together the biggest armada ever of transports, landing craft and warships. All the ground troops had to do was to land and capture some villas for the VIPs, particularly the King. The air forces said they would support the landings with 11,000 planes on D-Day. Ike said fighter bombers needed to provide special protection for paratroopers and gliders, as they could run into heavy flak. In all, 915 aircraft – 96 of them towing gliders – would fly across the Cherbourg Peninsula at less than 1,000 feet in full moonlight and through heavy anti-aircraft fire. The planes weren't armoured and didn't have leakproof tanks to prevent spillages of fuel in case of a crash-landing, but Ike insisted that the aerial attack was essential. He said four million barrels of high-octane aviation fuel should be kept in England as a back-up for the 'big push'. Churchill said that bravery, ingenuity and persistence were worth more than equipment, but General Alan Brooke said his main impression at the St Paul's meeting was that "Eisenhower was a swinger and no real director of thought, plans, energy or direction! Just a coordinator – a good mixer, a champion of inter-allied cooperation".[23]

On 18 May, German radio broadcast that 50 Allied divisions would invade Europe "any day", now that supplies had been concentrated around the English south coast. Field Marshal Gerd von Rundstedt, visiting Marshal Pétain, agreed that that the Allied invasion would begin "any moment now". Only 14 of Germany's 100 or more pilotless aircraft and rocket sites in Europe remained operational. But since the German defeat in Russia, there were now 58 Axis divisions in France – about three quarters of a million soldiers, including about 200,000 anti-communist Russians. The Germans had effectively lost the war in the east, but had killed many Russians during the invasion of the Soviet Union. Soviet military and civilian losses were estimated at

---

[22] It was "rather painful to watch the efforts he made not to stammer", wrote Patton (Diary 15 May 1944)
[23] War Diaries 1939-1945, p 546

sixteen million, while German losses were said to be around four million. (The Germans and Austrians also suffered 3.5 million civilians killed.)

As the Germans were keeping an eye on planes leaving neutral airports, 12 days before D-Day a soldier imper- sonating General Montgomery[24] was flown in Monty's plane from England to Gibraltar and then on to Algiers. This helped confuse the Germans, since Monty was the ground commander of the invasion troops. (A year earlier, the Germans had been informed that a heavily-built man smoking a big cigar had boarded a transport plane about to take off from Lisbon. The plane was shot down because the Germans believed that Churchill was aboard. In fact, the plane was carrying the actor Leslie Howard, among others.)

Ike now began to finalise plans for D-Day. He asked the US War Department to ensure that American visitors to Europe (including Mamie) be limited to those absolutely needed. To enable Allied soldiers to recognise one another in the heat of battle, officers commanding combat troops were to wear a narrow green band around their shoulder loop, with enlisted men wearing a narrow green stripe below their chevrons. FDR didn't want to call Overlord an 'invasion' of the Continent, but a 'liberation' (though Churchill continued to insist that Overlord was an invasion). The President also planned to broadcast to Germany on the day of the invasion, though Churchill was strongly opposed to this proposal. [25]

On 20 May, after considering "several nasty GCM [general court martial] cases", Ike and Kay had dinner with Beetle. [26] Ike took his mind off D-Day on 21 May by going for a drive "alone"[27] and, on 22 May, by playing badminton for half an hour at the cottage and then bridge for nearly three hours. He said other leaders were diverted by sketching or painting, which he might also try if he had the materials. American

---

[24] Lieutenant Clifton James – unlike Monty, a smoker and drinker
[25] Alan Brooke war diaries, 24 May 1944
[26] Diary 20 May 1944
[27] Diary 21 May 1944

Red Cross worker Betty Baker later gave him a short sketching lesson but, after drawing the big pine tree in the garden, he scrawled "baloney" on the drawing. At the end of the week, Ike spent a "most enjoyable two hours" at Buckingham Palace having lunch with the British King and Queen.[28] Everyone helped themselves to food from a side table. The Queen, who was chattier than the King, recalled the incident at Windsor Castle one Sunday afternoon two years before when they were in an area which Ike and Clark were visiting. They crawled away on their hands and knees so they wouldn't be noticed.

In Italy, the British Eighth Army had captured Cassino and the Poles "raised a triumphant flag" over the ruins of the monastery.[29] The "alarmingly high" total casualties in Italy to 25 May were 109,054, plus 33,241 for the Allied beachhead force. (A June 1944 proposal to the British government that the abbey be completely restored at German expense as a "memorial to the heroes who fell in storming it" was dismissed as premature.[30])

Kay and Ike took the train to Dulverton in Somerset on Saturday 27 May, and spent the day riding across Exmoor.[31] "It was lovely. Lunch at a little pub. London Inn – big cream tea." She and Ike had dinner on the train on the way back. The following day, after a late lunch, Ike relaxed in the garden of Telegraph Cottage and listened to the cuckoos. Later he recorded a message to be broadcast shortly after H-Hour.

In the north of Britain, 38 ammunition ships waited off the coast to unload. Ike planned to capture enough ports in Normandy and Brittany in about 90 days to supply a continuous drive into Germany. By 25 days after D-Day, 4,000 tons a day were due to be unloaded through the

---

[28] Diary 26 May 1944
[29] Eighth Army News, 19 May 1944
[30] Hansard debate, 6 June 1944, vol 400, cc 1199-1200
[31] Kay's pencilled diary entry for this date has "DE" – presumably Dwight Eisenhower – changed to "DP".

Continental ports. Ike visited about 20 airfields, 20 divisions and four US Navy ships in the final run-up to Overlord, including troops in Northern Ireland. He was impressed how American training had improved following the lessons learned in North Africa and the Pacific. He envisaged Allied armour making a major attack on the beachheads, with deeper penetration by airborne troops. Coastal defence and field batteries were to be bombed before dawn, and there would also be a naval bombardment. Assault troops would land at low tide to clear the obstacles which were then showing.

The weather in the English Channel for three or four days at the end of May was the worst for 20 years, and Allied air activity had to be limited. But there were 3,700 air sorties from England on 30 May as the weather turned balmy, with practically no wind. From June 1, the Commanders-in-Chief met Ike daily to consider weather reports. A final decision would have to be made by the morning of June 3. D-Day was initially set for June 5. Y plus 5 and Y plus 6 (June 6 and 7) were also suitable if the invasion had to be postponed because of bad weather. However, many units would be ready to move or already at sea if the invasion had to be postponed for 24 hours or more. The next suitable date for Operation Overlord would be June 19, but that night was moonless and, once ashore, the Allies would not experience good fighting weather. Ike said the ideal was clear weather with a five- or six-mile-an-hour onshore wind, so the smoke of the battle would blind the Germans, not the invaders.

SOUTHWICK HOUSE

In the run-up to D-Day, Ike moved on 2 June [1] from Telegraph Cottage to advance HQ near Southwick House, seven miles north of Portsmouth. There he discussed the invasion with Air Chief Marshal Tedder, Admiral Ramsay and General Montgomery at a 10am meeting. The HQ was in a wood about a 20 minute drive from Southwick House, and was equipped with "very comfortable" [2] trailers. Ike's trailer, which had been shipped from Africa, had "a bathroom with a shower, hot and cold water and everything you could want, including a very comfortable bed". [3] For Ike, the trailer meant he could be "free and independent".

Members of staff at Southwick House ignored the apparent close relationship between Ike and Kay. It was "not a topic of conversation," said naval operations officer Fanny Hughill. "I can think of other people who were having relationships at the time," she said, "and I didn't think it was of much interest." [4]

Later that evening, Butch arranged for everyone to attend a movie night in Ike's caravan at 8pm. However, Ike was due to have dinner with General Montgomery about that time and arrived in his caravan just as the operator was packing up to leave. The projectionist said he'd be late for a show for the GIs if he ran Ike's film. Ike lost his temper at Butch for arranging a film so late that the soldiers would have to stay up to watch their film.

The next day, at Ike's request, the RAF agreed to bomb high-powered radio stations on the French coast which could be used to jam Allied radar. By then, there were 2,876,000

---

[1] Ike set up HQ at Southwick House on 29 May 1944, and the US Chiefs of Staff were to arrive in London on 7 June (p 624 Bodyguard of Lies)
[2] Diary 2 June 1944
[3] Sgt Mickey and General Ike, p 105
[4] 2004 interview

Allied troops in southern England, more than 4,000 American, British and Canadian ships and more than 1,200 aeroplanes. There were meetings going on all the time at Southwick House, early in the mornings, through lunch and dinner and into the night with individuals like the Prime Minister, South African Field Marshal Smuts, Minister of Labour Ernest Bevin, de Gaulle and all the Allied generals.[5] Meetings to consider the weather were held twice a day, during daylight hours and around 1.30 in the morning. When the daytime meeting was over, Kay would often drive Ike back to main headquarters at Widewing.

The PM said he would like to witness the invasion,[6] but Ike said he'd just be a nuisance. Churchill and King George then asked to watch the D-Day landings from aboard HMS Belfast, but Admiral Ramsay refused to take responsibility for their safety. (The PM eventually crossed the Channel and visited France aboard the destroyer HMS Kelvin on 12 June, though he said the French "did not seem in any way pleased to see us arrive as a victorious country to liberate France. They had been quite content as they were, and we were bringing war and desolation to the country".[7] King George VI sailed to France aboard HMS Arethusa two days later, lunching with Montgomery and holding an open-air investiture less than six miles from the front.[8])

Secrecy was still paramount, so an error just before D-Day led to an outbreak of jitters. Early on Saturday 3 June, a girl in the Associated Press office sent out a tape saying that Eisenhower's forces were landing in France. Moscow and CBS repeated the report, the Germans circulated it, and AP took 23 minutes to quash the story. Later that night, the Prime Minister and South African Field Marshal Jan Smuts, who were on a special train parked at Southampton, decided to visit Ike. The PM and his group of ten arrived at 7.15pm,

[5] Sgt Mickey and General Ike, p 114
[6] Second World War, Winston Churchill, volume V p 546
[7] Alan Brooke war diaries, 12 June 1944
[8] Daily Mail, 17 June 1944

filled their petrol tanks from Ike's supplies and drank his Scotch, then left, with Churchill announcing that de Gaulle would visit Ike the following afternoon. Another conference took place at 4.15am, but there was still no break in the un-seasonably bad weather[9] which made Ike "very depressed".[10]

In Italy, the Allies entered Rome on Sunday 4 June and King Victor Emmanuel II handed over power to his son, Crown Prince Umberto. Unfortunately, some of the welcoming Italians were killed by flying shell fragments.[11] "One up [or 'down', as the British would say] and two to go," said FDR.[12] Italy was now only a sideshow but Ike sent Clark a congratulatory message nevertheless. The morning papers in American and Britain carried headlines about the Fifth Army's victory: "Rome Ours, 5th Captures Center of Capital"[13] and "Rome Falls, Allied Troops in City's Centre".[14] Ike read the news while resting in his caravan suffering from headaches and stomach pains, surrounded by overflowing ashtrays and new Westerns[15]. "Then I knew he was keyed up," said orderly Mickey McKeogh. "It was one of the ways I had of finding out how the war was going."[16]

Ike rang chief meteorologist Group Captain James Stagg to ask "What will the weather be like in a couple of days in the Channel and over the French coast?" Stagg hesitated then replied "To answer that question would make me a guesser, not a meteorologist." (Rommel's meteorologist, Major Heinz Lettau, who was captured by US troops on his way from Paris to Rennes, said he had advised his superiors that the invasion of Europe was impractical after June 4 because of stormy weather moving in from the Atlantic. Based on this

---

[9] Diary 3 June 1944
[10] Diary 3 June 1944
[11] Daily Mirror, 5 June 1944
[12] The Detroit Free Press, 6 June 1944
[13] Daily Mirror (US), 5 June 1944
[14] Daily Mirror (UK), 5 June 1944
[15] Reading Westerns was a habit he shared with Adolf Hitler, who enjoyed the stories of Karl May
[16] Sgt Mickey and General Ike, p 14

forecast, many German officers in Normandy took leave or were on manoeuvres. Rommel had gone to Berlin to celebrate his wife's birthday, and exercises had been cancelled. The Germans were taken by surprise on June 6, not only because of the weather,[17] but because the Allies had attacked at low tide, with all the underwater obstacles exposed. They had been expected to attack at high tide to try and float over the obstacles.)

While Ike was resting, de Gaulle was driven from the Free French HQ in Carlton Gardens, London, to the PM's train for lunch. Afterwards, at Southwick House Ike took him on a tour of the war room, and de Gaulle explained how *he* would run the invasion. They had already discussed the PM's proposal for a provisional Allied administration in France, a proposal with which de Gaulle disagreed. De Gaulle said Ike had no right to instruct the French people on civil administration matters and he refused to broadcast after Ike on D-Day unless Ike changed the wording of his message. Kay noted in her typed diary transcript that de Gaulle was "very difficult, sees only his own point of view".[18] Churchill was furious, accusing de Gaulle of treason, and was only slightly mollified when SHAEF's British political officer phoned him at 4am on 6 June to say that de Gaulle had agreed to broadcast an address to the French that evening at 6pm – though not immediately following Eisenhower.[19] De Gaulle eventually announced: "The supreme battle has begun...Of course it is the battle of the French and the battle of France."[20] But it is noteworthy that only 19 Free French soldiers were killed on D-Day, compared with more than 4,500 Allied soldiers who died.

---

[17] According to Generalleutnant Friedrich Dihm, the German met report for 6 June said: "Invasion possible, but not probable"

[18] In the original handwritten diary on 4 June 1944, Kay described de Gaulle as "impossible"

[19] On D-Day, as well as Ike, King Haakon of Norway, the Dutch and Belgian prime ministers and, at 6pm, de Gaulle, broadcast by radio from England (p 672 Bodyguard of Lies)

[20] *La bataille suprême est engagée...Bien entendu, c'est la bataille de France et c'est la bataille de la France*

Ike met senior officers for a "very short" conference at 9.30pm on 4 June. The weather situation was "most extraordinary and a mid-winter situation, rather than normal to a June period".[21] The forecast for the next day was for rough seas, high winds and heavy clouds, so Ike postponed D-Day from June 5 for at least 24 hours. Many of the 4,000 ships, which were already at sea, were notified soon after the meeting. Ike regarded the postponement as a letdown. "If you had to sit and wait, you would go nuts," said Kay.[22] At 4.15am on 5 June, Stagg predicted that the storm forecast for Sunday night and Monday morning would end and there would be a "quieter interlude" for 6 and 7 June, a change that was "almost miraculous". Considering the "vagaries of the weather", the problems with troops at sea for more than 24 hours and the "good chances of being forced into an even more undesirable situation", Ike confirmed that the invasion should go ahead on 6 June, with H-Hour about 6.40am.

"He really looked so serious as he got in the car," said Kay, "and he said: 'D-Day's on. Nothing can stop us now'."[23] Kay then drove Ike to Portsmouth where Ike inspected troops going aboard the invasion ships at 11.30am. "Good old Ike," they shouted.[24]

At an afternoon press conference to announce the invasion, Ike noticed a flash of sunshine through the tent door and told the four correspondents: "By George, there is some sun." (He didn't pay a fine for saying "By George"...) To while away the time before the invasion, Ike and Butch played Fox and Hounds and then draughts.

At 6.30pm on Monday 5 June, Ike went to airfields at Greenham Common near Newbury to see off airborne

---

[21] As Ike came out of the conference, "he told me the date of D. Day", wrote Kay in her diary
[22] 1972 Thames Television interview
[23] 1972 Thames Television interview and The World at War 1973 (episode 17)
[24] Original diary 5 June 1944

troops, including the 101st Airborne Division. They were to be the first parachute troops to land behind enemy lines in Normandy, dropping north of Carentan, to prevent the movement of enemy reserves into the Cotentin (or Cherbourg) Peninsula. The four stars on Ike's red plate were covered – "no parade, no fanfare"[25] – but, when he was recognised, the black-faced troops cheered him. (He wondered how "people somehow manage to call out, 'Hey, Ike!' when I think I'm hidden incognito in an unmarked automobile".) "The shouts that went up were tremendous," recorded Kay in her diary. "They were going to jump in Nazi-occupied Europe in a very short time, and you kept thinking 'I wonder how many are going to come back?'"[26] The paratroopers appreciated her presence too. "I came in for my share of whistling and shouting, too, in the good old GI sort of way."[27]

Ike moved among the paratroopers, stepping over packs, weapons and equipment and chatting to the soldiers. He was offered a cup of coffee before going up to the roof to see the troops off, but his hands were shaking so badly that a Red Cross worker had to take the cup back from him before he spilled the coffee on his uniform.[28] Hundreds of C-47s took off and circled in the sunset until they formed up, while Ike waved goodbye from the roof. "Visibility was perfect," recorded Kay, and "the stars were gleaming".

The following day, Ike told Marshall: "The enthusiasm, toughness and obvious fitness of every single man were high and the light of battle was in their eyes." But to Kay he said: "You know, Kay, it is very hard to look a soldier in the face knowing you might be sending him to his death for all you know."[29] In a letter to Mamie, he wrote: "Only time will tell how great our success will be. But all that can be done by

---

[25] The Milwaukee Sentinel, 26 September 1948, p 19
[26] The World at War 1973 (episode 17)
[27] The Milwaukee Sentinel, 26 September 1948, p 19
[28] http://edition.cnn.com/2014/06/05/opinion/lauder-eisenhower-d-day-anguish/
[29] 1972 Thames Television interview

human effort, intense devotion to duty, and courageous execution, all by thousands and thousands of individuals, will be done by this force. The soldiers, sailors, and airmen are indescribable in their élan, courage, determination and fortitude. They inspire me."[30]

At almost midnight, Ike returned to his Portsmouth HQ and stopped at naval headquarters for a last-minute check on news, before returning to the trailer and sitting in silence until 3am, when he finally went to bed.

---

[30] 9 June 1944

IT'S ON!

Ike's order of the day for D-Day, in "finely wrought words",[1]
said: "Soldiers, Sailors and Airmen of the Allied Expeditionary Force! You are about to embark upon the Great
Crusade, toward which we have striven these many months.
The eyes of the world are upon you...Your task will not be an
easy one. Your enemy is well trained, well equipped and
battle hardened. He will fight savagely. But this is the year
1944! Much has happened since the Nazi triumphs of 1940-
41...The tide has turned! The free men of the world are
marching together to Victory! Good luck! And let us beseech
the blessing of Almighty God upon this great and noble
undertaking."

Ike and Kay waited nervously and expectantly for news, Kay
occasionally massaging Ike's shoulders, as wave after wave
of bombers flew over. "It was the beginning of the end of the
war," said Kay.[2] English ports opposite the Pas de Calais
were still full of real and dummy landing craft to suggest a
cross-Channel thrust in that area. The Allies also bombed
Dunkirk and Calais to confuse the Germans further. Most
German night fighters stayed over the Pas de Calais area,
expecting a follow-up invasion. More than two months later,
the Germans were still expecting an Allied invasion of
Belgium, the Netherlands or Scandinavia.[3]

Around 13,000 paratroopers were dropped early on D-Day,
followed by almost 4,000 glider troops in two parachute and
six glider groups. But many of the drops were inaccurate
because the airborne attack was launched in darkness,
instead of waiting for first light. Newspapers at the time
claimed that the airborne troops "were landed with great

---

[1] at ease, p 99
[2] 1972 Thames Television interview
[3] Daily Mail, 21 August 1944

accuracy and very little loss".[4] Indeed, the British Prime Minister told the House of Commons that the landings "took place with extremely little loss and with great accuracy".[5] But total D-Day casualties for the US airborne divisions were calculated in August 1944 as 2,500, plus 700 for the British.[6] Some of the paratroopers landed in swamps or in French villages occupied by the Germans, where they were shot or taken prisoner. One was snagged by the spire of a local church. It could have been "the most ghastly disaster of the whole war".[7] But Leigh-Mallory phoned to say that the glider operation had not been the disaster he feared. Kay's diary said that only 21 of the 850 American B-47s went missing and only four gliders were unaccounted for.[8] In fact around 30 of the 1,250 Allied support aircraft were lost within the first couple of hours.

Altogether, almost 4,500 Allied soldiers died storming what the Germans called Festung Europa.[9] Some of them were casualties of "friendly fire". For example, the guns of the British light cruiser HMS Orion caused "heavy casualties" among British troops. Soldiers who withdrew to tend to the injured were attacked by an American Thunderbolt fighter. Naval gunfire also killed 64 Allied soldiers in the village of Colleville, and a shell from HMS Glasgow hit a British command post, killing the commander and wounding his deputy. The nervous crews of Allied ships fired at planes carrying reinforcements, downing one Dakota and killing all on board.

During the landings, aircraft of RAF Bomber Command dropped almost 6,000 tons of bombs on ten coastal batteries between Cherbourg and Le Havre. But there were several

4 Daily Mirror, 7 June 1943
5 Hansard, 6 June 1944, vol 400, cc 1323-4
6 'Casualties' include dead, wounded, missing and POWs, but the total Allied death toll for D-Day is estimated at 4,414
(http://www.ddaymuseum.co.uk/)
7 Alan Brooke war diaries, 5 June 1944
8 Original diary, 6 June 1944
9 Fortress Europe

incidents of Allied planes bombing their own troops. On 5-6 June, RAF Avro Lancasters aiming for the German artillery battery at Merville-Plage attacked British positions by mistake, killing 186 members of the Reconnaissance Corps and destroying the town. They also bombed the 6th Airborne Division in error, killing 78 soldiers and injuring 65. RAF fighters also bombed and strafed the 3rd Parachute Brigade HQ near Pegasus Bridge after mistaking them for a German column, killing at least 15 men and wounding many others.

In general, however, the Normandy landings went better than expected, although things were "not so good" on Omaha beach[10] where mortar and artillery fire[11] from the fortuitously present, battle-hardened German 352nd Infantry Division ensured that V Corps seemed to be "stuck",[12] with upwards of 2,500 US soldiers killed.[13] Dead Americans lay on the beach and in the shallows, with many more wounded nearby. Ike ordered Allied bombers to attack the beach – which was still full of US soldiers – at 1.30pm, but fortunately "this could not be done".[14] By about 3.30pm, naval guns, bombers and the landing of some guns had allowed Allied troops to advance two or three miles inland. French citizens were advised by radio and by leaflets to evacuate a 35-kilometer-deep strip from the coast and to make for the countryside, at least two kilometres from the nearest town.[15] Meanwhile, German-controlled Calais Radio announced: "This is D-Day. We shall now bring music for the [Allied] invasion forces."[16]

---

[10] 1972 Thames Television interview with Kay Summersby

[11] From the 352nd infantry division, made up of survivors from the eastern front

[12] Alan Brooke war diaries, 7 June 1944

[13] Original diary 6 June 1944

[14] pp 153, 172, 182 and 183, Fighting Them on the Beaches

[15] The Detroit Free Press, 6 June 1944

[16] *ibid.* The Germans broadcast propaganda radio ("Jerry's Front") by shortwave 15- 47.6 meters and on medium wave 221-491.8 meters which included American and British programmes, dance music and a "nightbirds' show" with "lovely (it's a pity you can't see her!) husky-voiced Helen"

The Royal Navy cleared some German mines, but two destroyers and one Landing Ship, Tank (LST) hit mines during the night, and a battleship and a dozen destroyers were lost to enemy action. Some landing craft hit Teller mines mounted on posts. Ten US landing craft were also swamped by rough seas on the approach to Omaha Beach, though ammunition barges and minelayers were continuing to move steadily towards the beachheads. Ike sent a situation report to General Marshall at 8am on 6 June saying that, although preliminary reports were "satisfactory", he had still not officially been informed that "leading ground troops are actually ashore", so a communiqué could not yet be issued. The Allied communiqué was eventually broadcast by the BBC at 9.30 am, but the Germans had already issued theirs at 7am, reporting operations around Le Havre, "in the area of the mouth of the Seine".[17] Ike knew that "successful penetration of a defended beach" was "the most difficult operation in warfare". The Prime Minister told the House of Commons: "This vast operation is undoubtedly the most complicated and difficult that has ever occurred. It involves tides, wind, waves, visibility, both from the air and the sea standpoint, and the combined employment of land, air and sea forces in the highest degree of intimacy and in contact with conditions which could not and cannot be fully foreseen."[18]

Early on the morning after D-Day, Ike – a "fairly good" sailor – visited the French beachhead aboard the fast minelayer HMS Apollo. He headed first for Utah Beach, then found Admiral Alan Kirk's flagship, USS Augusta, off Omaha Beach. All the beaches were "littered with damaged landing craft",[19] though Ike thought that most of these could eventually be repaired. During the afternoon, the weather cleared, the sky was blue and the sea grew calmer. Ike said it looked as if the weather would hold for the next several crucial days. HMS Apollo then hit a sand bank though it

---

17 Detroit Free Press, 6 June 1944
18 Hansard, 6 June 1944, vol 400, cc 1207-11
19 Original diary 7 June 1944

managed to free itself by using full power. However, the incident bent the ship's propellers and drive shafts, putting it out of action for two months. (Monty's destroyer ran aground the same day, and also suffered broken propellers.) Ike transferred to the destroyer HMS Undaunted and sailed back to Portsmouth, arriving at 10pm.

Apart from that brief trip to the Normandy coast, Ike and Kay waited in the trailer for days for news. Kay asked the mess to send over sandwiches for supper, and she made coffee while Ike chain-smoked. In a letter to Mamie on 9 June, Ike referred to the "intense periods of strain and effort". That same day, he approved the sentences for two black soldiers convicted of rape and murder.

Kay drove Ike to conferences in London and Bushy Park every other day. But Ike was annoyed because, by 10 June, there still appeared to be no information from Montgomery, who had agreed to radio his reports of the battle every night. However, because of the volume of traffic on D-Day, SHAEF staff were 12 hours behind in transcribing radio signals. On top of that, an Army decoding machine had broken down. In fact, Monty's signal had arrived the previous night – but in British cipher, which further delayed its delivery. When its contents were eventually phoned to Ike around 10am, he was happier.

One of Ike's fears was that the French Resistance would rise against the Germans too early so, on Monday 12 June, he and General Koenig both broadcast a plea to the Resistance urging them to obey orders exactly.[20] Later that day, Ike met General Marshall who had arrived by train after flying from Washington. Marshall crossed the Channel to France on a destroyer[21] and said the Germans seemed to be "at the top of the toboggan slide" and now faced "a grim prospect".[22] Back in England, Ike waited up until midnight for a message from

---

[20] p 691 Bodyguard of Lies
[21] He cabled FDR on 14 June that Ike and his staff were "cool and confident" and carrying out the operation with "superlative efficiency"
[22] Memo S-53824, 14 June 1944

the PM which eventually arrived about 2am. Churchill said a German message had been intercepted asking whether Allied troops carried their gas masks with them or in baggage cars. Ike told General de Guingand to make sure all the troops were carrying their equipment in case of German gas attacks (which never materialised). However, the Allies had "lots [of gas] on hand for counterattack if [the Germans started] the bad business", said Butch.

Later that day, Ike actually went ashore in France for the first time and met Monty, Bradley, King and other commanders. When he returned about 8.45pm, he said his visit had seemed more like a tour of peacetime manoeuvres, except that, by then, there had been nearly 11,000 casualties – 9,386 Allied soldiers killed and 1,557 missing. De Gaulle also returned to France two days later, accompanied by Monty. Within six days of D-Day, 326,000 troops and 54,000 vehicles were ashore on the beaches.

After dinner back in England, Ike managed to relax for the first time since D-Day. He played two rubbers of bridge – with an incomplete pack of cards – eventually losing three-pence. (In the makeshift deck, the joker represented the six of clubs.)

Caen was to have been taken by Monty on D-Day, yet the town was not taken until 9 July after the Allies were pushed back by a German counterattack. And in an operation reminiscent of the Dieppe débâcle, the Germans ambushed and destroyed 51 of 53 Canadian Sherman tanks on 11 June. But overall, while the Allied build-up was 24 hours behind schedule, so was that of the Germans. Up to the afternoon of 17 June, 589,653 personnel, 89,828 vehicles and nearly 200,000 tons of stores had been unloaded on the five beaches. The British brought 51,000 vehicles ashore, compared to the Americans' 38,000, though the Americans were soon unloading supplies more rapidly than the British. Despite an almost unprecedented four days of Channel storms after 19 June, disembarkation of supplies was greatly helped by the use of the two artificial Mulberry harbours and the four landing strips which had been built on the beachheads. By 1 July, there were 929,000 Allied troops and 177,000 vehicles ashore. The millionth Allied soldier landed in France on American Independence Day, July 4.

But Ike was still taking no chances. Later, he came across a pencilled draft message in his wallet saying: "Our landings in the Cherbourg-Havre area have failed to gain a satisfactory foothold and I have withdrawn the troops [changed from "the troops have been withdrawn"]. ["This particular operation" crossed out.] My decision to attack at this time and place [added to end of line] was based upon the best information available [Full stop added and "and" removed]. The troops, the air and the Navy did all that ["I asked"] bravery and devotion to duty could do. If any blame or fault attaches to the attempt it is mine alone. July 5 [Presumably should be "June 5"]." He said he had written a similar note for every amphibious operation, but had later torn up each one.

Meanwhile, Ike's son John, who had coincidentally grad-uated from West Point on D-Day, travelled to England to see his father and meet Ike's "family". John sailed from the US aboard the Queen Mary and arrived a week after D-Day after travelling from Scotland on the Bayonet train with 'Tex'. He was to return to the US by air after about two weeks to join the Infantry Training School at Fort Benning, Georgia. When Ike first saw "Johnny" in his army officer's uniform, he said he almost "burst with pride".[23] After a quick tour of HQ, Ike, Kay and John went to Telegraph Cottage. John said he'd handed in his gear early at West Point and had spent his last night sleeping on the bare springs of his bed. "Oh for God's sake!" snorted Ike. "Across the Channel, there are thousands of young men sleeping in foxholes if they're lucky, and my son complains about a restless night on a cot without a mattress."

---

[23] Letter to Mamie, 9 June 1944

On 15 June, John and his father flew to visit Monty on the beachhead.

John recalled in his memoirs[24] how, aboard a Flying Fortress on the way to the front, he asked his father: "If we should meet an officer who ranks above me but below you, how do we handle this? Should I salute first and when they return my salute, do you return theirs?" Ike responded: "John, there isn't an officer in this theatre who doesn't rank above you and below me!" On their return, Kay, Ike, John and others slept in the Telegraph Cottage bomb shelter because of the danger of V-1 attacks.

The next day, Ike had lunch in the Yankee Doodle Room with Lord Mountbatten's Chief-of-Staff who told a story attributed to Ike. In Algiers, an American and a British officer had become involved in a flaming row, and Ike himself sent for the men and talked to them "in the interests of unity". After giving both of them a dressing down, he dismissed the British officer but kept the American behind. "I don't mind your airing your differences with this British officer. I don't particularly mind that you engaged in fisticuffs with him. I must say that I think you were right in your position. Ordinarily I don't condone cursing and name-calling, and I forgive you for calling him a son-of-a-bitch. But I cannot forgive you for calling him a *British* son-of-a-bitch. Consequently, I am sending you home on a slow boat, unescorted."[25]

On the night of 17 June, the first air raid alert at the cottage sounded just after dinner, while Ike and John were watching a film of the Overlord landings,[26] and the alerts continued until daybreak. One V-1 exploded in a field nearby, breaking a window at the cottage and lifting a bunch of flowers out of

---

[24] Strictly Personal by John SD Eisenhower (Doubleday & Co, January 1974)
[25] http://archives.chicagotribune.com/1952/08/24/page/207/article/from-colonel-to-four-star-general
[26] Hitler had flown to France that day from the Wolfsschanze to oversee operations

a vase without breaking the vase.[27] Butch went to the shelter and, a few minutes later, Ike, Kay, John, Mickey, Williams and Hunt joined him. Ike eventually decided to lie on his cot while John sat on the bench. Soon Ike was fast asleep and snoring and, as the ack-ack firing had tapered off, John went back to bed in the cottage.

On June 26, Ike contacted the Ministry of Defence, seeking a suitable date for presenting his son to the Prime Minister.[28] At the end of June, John flew back to the United States. Ike asked whether Kay would like to go with John to Washington and maybe to New York for a few days. Ike would meanwhile spend five days in France meeting Monty, Brooks and others and inspecting Allied defences at Cherbourg from the air.

"I want you to go. John will take care of you," said Ike. "I'm putting all my eggs in one basket. Come back safe."

On Friday 30 June, Kay and John flew to the US with Lieutenant-Colonel 'Tex' Lee in Ike's Flying Fortress with three others. Kay arrived in Bangor, Maine, on 1 July, having obtained a US visa from the American embassy in London. She declared that her "only legal address" was "Office of the Commanding General, US Forces, European Theater, APO 757, New York".[29]

Mamie Eisenhower greeted Kay "pleasantly" at the airport before leaving with her son. Kay had been in Washington for just three hours when a siren sounded and she immediately threw herself to the ground. With some embarrassment, she explained that this could save your life in London when the bombs were falling. The following afternoon, John invited Kay to a cocktail party with his mother and others, but Kay was the only woman in uniform. For the first time, Kay became aware of the "virulent" gossip in the United States about her and Ike. John then suggested they all take the

---

[27] Sgt Mickey and General Ike, p 120
[28] CHAR 20/141A/75
[29] Alien Registration form, 29 June 1944

train up to New York to see the new musical Oklahoma!, for which Rodgers and Hammerstein had just won a special Pulitzer Prize. The record-breaking Broadway production had only opened three months earlier. Mamie replied: "Oh I'm sure Miss Summersby doesn't want to go to New York in all this heat." "Yes, she does," retorted John.

In New York, Kay went sightseeing but she was shocked by the ostentation and waste in the US, compared to England. Before she left, Kay went to see Dick Arnold's mother, Mrs GR Arnold, in southern Florida. Thanks to a White House priority pass provided by General Marshall's aide, Kay flew down to Miami by USAF cargo plane. She spent a day and a night in Hollywood, Florida, before being picked up in Ike's B-17 and flown back to Washington (where the plane developed engine trouble just as it landed at National Airport). She returned to England after a fortnight in the US.[30]

---

[30] NY District Director WF Watkins said 15 days while Kay's departure permit 1559805 said she left on 17 July

REVENGE WEAPONS

The first V-1s (or 'doodlebugs', as they were called) were launched from sites in the Pas de Calais area six days after D-Day. The V stood for *Vergeltungswaffe*, German for 'retaliation weapon'.[1] The German Overseas News Agency said the flying bombs were in revenge for the Allied raids on German cities. "Tens of thousands of civilian dead cry for revenge from their graves," said German-controlled Oslo radio.[2]

Ike called them "the devil's own contraption".[3] Winston Churchill was only restrained with difficulty from proving his "vindictive nature" by bombing more small German towns in reprisal for the V-weapons.[4] Kay's diary recorded the first raid on London by "pilotless aircraft" on 15 June. The rockets, armed with an 1,800-pound warhead, crossed the Channel into England between Dungeness and Beachy Head at speeds of up to 370 miles an hour (round about the top speed of a Spitfire aircraft).

The first doodlebug landed in Grove Road, Mile End, in London and killed six people.[5] Before it crashed, the V-1 was seen streaking across the sky with anti-aircraft shells bursting around it. Then it dived to earth followed by a huge explosion. The pulse-jet engine sounded like a two-cylinder motorbike or an old Model T Ford.[6] People were said to have two seconds to shelter when the hiss and putt-putt stopped;

---

[1] One German propaganda leaflet said: "The American Jew Baruch gave orders to 'Butcher' Harris to indiscriminately kill German women and children, our women and children. V number 1 is giving the answer." AI – 078-6-44)
[2] Daily Mail, 17 June 1944
[3] Sgt Mickey and General Ike, p 119
[4] Alan Brooke war diaries, 5 July 1944
[5] The first V-1 on 12 June killed six and seriously injured 13 when it hit a railway bridge in East London's Bethnal Green (p 719 Bodyguard of Lies)
[6] Patton thought the V-1 sounded "just like a regular plane with a bad cold". (Letter to wife, 20 June 1944)

in fact it was more than 12 seconds. More and more V-1s were fired at England, particularly targeting London. Within two weeks, the rockets had killed more than 1,600 people and injured another 4,500 in southern England. Up to 95 per cent of the flying bombs which got through fell within 12 miles of Streatham, only five miles from Telegraph Cottage. The Daily Mail reported "Pilotless attack may not last. Too costly to German material".[7] But Home Secretary Herbert Morrison was "in a flat spin about the flying bombs and their effect on the population" and suggested that Londoners could not stand the strain after five years of war.[8] As a result of the attacks, most of the inhabitants of the capital were eventually walking around like zombies due to lack of sleep, and jumping whenever a door banged or a motor backfired or cut out. One newspaper in neutral Sweden reported: "London has got the jitters. Day and night hundreds of thousands are rushing the barriers at Waterloo Station, Paddington and other stations trying to escape from this chaos."[9]

The Ministry of Home Security said the V-1s caused "relatively small" damage but, in a speech to the House of Commons three weeks after the attacks began,[10] Winston Churchill said: "It would be a mistake to under-rate the serious character of this particular form of attack. It has never been under-rated in the secret circles of the Government..." The British Cabinet regularly discussed the threat.[11] On 16 June, about 300 doodlebugs were fired from the Pas de Calais area but the weather was so bad that reconnaissance aircraft could not even spot the sites in operation. When Allied planes did attack the sites, they often also bombed the surrounding villages, which further

---

[7] Daily Mail, 17 June 1944
[8] Alan Brooke war diaries, 27 June 1944
[9] 29 July 1944, Nya Dagligt Allehanda
[10] Debate 6 July 1944, Hansard vol 401 cc 1322-39
[11] Alan Brooke war diaries, 4 January, 8 and 22 November 1944, 23 February and 27 March 1945

distressed local civilians.[12] On Sunday 18 June, a V-1 hit the Guards' Chapel, near Buckingham Palace, during morning service, killing 121 [13] and injuring 140, including Ivan Cobbold, with whom Ike and Kay had recently been fishing. (Beetle Smith had turned down an invitation to attend the service, as he was too busy.) The following month, London's Dulwich College picture gallery, which contained 100 Old Masters, was "severely damaged" by a flying bomb.[14]

The Prime Minister and the chiefs of staff had regular meetings to consider defence measures against the V-1s. "The fighter aircraft are not proving fast enough, the guns are not hitting them, the balloons may have their cables cut, the launching sites are not worth attacking with bombers etc etc."[15] Allied fighters tried to bring down the V-1s without anti-aircraft fire in good weather, but ack-ack was used in conditions of poor visibility. On 18 June, all anti-aircraft fire in the London area was stopped because, when the rockets were hit by ack-ack (anti-aircraft) fire, they simply plummeted to earth and exploded. They had to be shot down in relatively unpopulated areas. There was a 15-mile band of anti-aircraft batteries between London and the coast. Fighters needed practically the whole distance from the Channel to London to catch the rocket, and almost half of the Allies' air effort was devoted to "trying to stop these beastly bombs".[16] The fighters eventually knocked down 48 per cent of those that crossed the coast, though that still left a considerable number to wreak havoc in London.

On 19 June, radar recorded 78 flying bombs over southeast England, 25 of which reached the London area, while 15 were shot down. One V-1 landed near the house of Ike's British aide, Lieutenant-Colonel Jimmy Gault, breaking

---

[12] Allied bombing was "very inaccurate" admitted Alan Brooke in his diaries on 11 January 1944.
[13] Alan Brooke's diaries on 19 June 1944 said the attack had killed "about 60 people"
[14] Daily Mail, 3 August 1944
[15] Alan Brooke war diaries, 4 July 1944
[16] Alan Brooke war diaries, 5 July 1944

windows and doors. That night, there were 25 explosions near Telegraph Cottage between 7pm and 1am, and one shook the shelter at 4.20am. During the day at SHAEF Main, Ike ordered everyone to go quickly to the brick shelter or slit trenches as soon as the air raid alarm sounded. Senior staff should set an example to junior staff, he said. Most people in HQ were working with secret papers which had to be put in a locked safe before they ran to the air-raid shelter. Ike took to the shelters eight times in one day and probably would have been there more often had the loudspeaker system not been closed for a couple of hours for repairs. On the evening of 30 June, a flying bomb landed within 200 yards of HQ injuring five people but with no fatalities. One window pane was sucked out of each office in the wing. Ike later admitted that he "despised" the noise of the air raid warning. "The siren is an assault on the senses," he wrote. "Most of us, whenever we saw one of the V-1s, would devoutly hope the things would continue on its way and not blow us to pieces...If we were caught distant from a shelter, we, like everyone, would lie down along a curb or in a ditch if one was handy."[17]

On 4 July, a flying bomb landed near Telegraph Cottage while Kay was away, and half an hour after Ike had left for France. Days later, another flying bomb exploded close to the cottage, bringing down a ceiling and breaking windows. By 6 July, a month after D-Day, 2,754 flying bombs had been launched – almost 100 a day. Churchill told the House of Commons that only one life was lost for each doodlebug that reached England, with 2,752 dead and 8,000 hospitalised to date.[18] From 18-25 July, radar plotted 4,541 flying bombs, of which 3,407 crossed the British coast killing 4,175 and seriously injuring 12,284. Blasts damaged 70 factories, ten schools, three hospitals and 18 military installations. One bomb exploded in mid-air about 300 yards from Telegraph Cottage. By the start of August, most

---

[17] at ease, p 286
[18] Debate 6 July 1944, Hansard vol 401 cc 1322-39

of the V-1s were being destroyed by ack-ack, barrage balloons or fighter planes[19] but 90 "buzz bombs" were still getting through to London every day.[20] In the face of the doodlebug threat, the government launched a campaign for children to leave the capital.[21] Around 282,000 mothers and children under five were helped to leave London, and 500,000 more left of their own initiative before September 1944.[22] Ike's headquarters staff were moved from Widewing to a camp close to the former Advance Command Post near Portsmouth. Ike agreed with the PM that the rockets should take priority over everything except the urgent needs of battle.

As the Germans faced defeat in France, the morale of the German army was largely based on "rocket philosophy – on the dreadful things V-1 is supposed to be doing to London and on the much more terrible devastation promised for V-2".[23] An 18-year-old German prisoner told Allied interrogators that the V-2 rockets were Germany's last hope of avoiding defeat and were to be aimed at English ports to destroy supplies bound for the Continent. In September 1944, the British government's Flying Bomb Countermeasures Committee revealed that the Germans were also using specially-adapted Heinkel 111s to launch flying bombs. During 80 days' bombardment, 8,000 flying bombs were launched, of which 2,300 landed in London, causing 92 per cent of the fatalities, but static antiaircraft guns, automatically aimed by radar, started to be used against planes and doodlebugs in southern England, and brought down their first two flying bombs. Eventually the British claimed that they were shooting down 70 per cent of the flying bombs.[24] Altogether, the V-1s were said to have killed

---

[19] More than 4,000 V-1s were eventually destroyed
[20] Diary 1 August 1944
[21] Daily Herald, 21 July 1944 and House of Commons debate 6 July 1944, Hansard vol 401 cc 1322-39
[22] Daily Mail, 8 September 1944
[23] Daily Mail, 23 August 1944
[24] Evening Standard, 7 September 1944

5,817 people and seriously injured 17,086, with 870,000 houses damaged.[25]

(The man accused of inventing the V-1[26] was arrested by the Allies in September 1944. At the end of the war, he was tried and acquitted of helping to design the V-1, but was convicted of collaborating with the Germans and sentenced to life imprisonment.)

On 8 September 1944, the Germans began using the bigger and faster V-2 rocket – first against Paris, then against London.[27] The British government had been aware of the threat from the "large cigar shaped objects" for more than a year.[28] The ballistic missile, which had a one-ton warhead,[29] was propelled by a mixture of ethyl alcohol and liquid oxygen. It was said to weigh 15 tons, to have a range of 160 miles[30] at an altitude of 60 miles, and was even proof against radar. The rockets, flying at around 3,000 miles an hour, struck without warning, making craters up to 30 feet deep and 25 feet wide, and destroying everything within quarter of a mile. The head of the Flying Bomb Countermeasures Committee initially said that, while "quite a lot" was known about the V-2, "a great deal more" would be known in a "very few days".[31]

But for most people, "the abruptness of the V-2's arrival was its most terrifying feature. There was no time to do anything. It travelled faster than sound and it was on a person before they could even think about it. Londoners reported that,

[25] Daily Mail, 8 September 1944. Bodyguard of Lies says that 10,500 V-1s were eventually launched against England killing 6,200, seriously injuring 18,000 and destroying or damaging 1.5 million homes (p 727)
[26] French scientist Georges Claude
[27] "Death from the unknown. Secret explosions rocking London. Nothing can be seen – Nothing can be heard. But it's there. V2" (German propaganda leaflet)
[28] Alan Brooke war diaries notes, 29 June 1943
[29] Alan Brooke claimed the rocket had a "5 ton warhead", diaries 27 June 1944
[30] Alan Brooke war diaries, 21 July 1944
[31] Evening Standard, 7 September 1944

without question, the V-2s were worse than the V-1 attacks. The thunderous bang of the explosion, followed by the roar of the rocket's descent, made it seem bigger and more frightening".[32] Countermeasures centred on jamming the controlling radio stations. Seven rocket-launching sites, five in the Pas de Calais and two in the Cherbourg Peninsula, were hit by an "all-out bomber offensive", but the Allies agreed that air defences alone could not defeat the V-2.[33] The Combined Chiefs ordered Ike to send Allied soldiers into the Pas de Calais area to capture the flying bomb and rocket sites which were now threatening Britain's production facilities. Around a quarter of London's production had already been lost as a result of the V-1 attacks.[34]

Winston Churchill assured Parliament in the winter of 1944 that German stories about the V-2 were "highly coloured" and damage from "widely-scattered" attacks was "not heavy".[35] He told the House of Commons on 10 November that the V-2 contained "approximately the same quantity of high explosive as the flying bomb. However, it is designed to penetrate rather deeper before exploding". This resulted in a "less extensive blast effect". But because the rocket flew faster than sound high in the stratosphere, "no reliable or sufficient public warning can, in present circumstances, be given".[36] By 20 November 1944, about 210 V-2 rockets had reached England, with 95 hitting London. The most devastating attack on London came on November 25, when a V-2 demolished Woolworth's in New Cross Gate, south east London, killing 168 people. Eleven bodies were never even found. But the London deaths paled into insignificance next to those killed in Belgium. On Saturday 16 December 1944, a V-2 rocket hit the roof of the Rex cinema in Antwerp, killing

---

[32] http://www.v2rocket.com/
[33] Evening Standard, 10 November 1944
[34] Alan Brooke war diaries, 5 July 1944
[35] Evening Standard, 10 November 1944
[36] Hansard 10 November 1944 vol 404 cc 1653-4

567 and injuring 291. Antwerp became known as "The City of Sudden Death".[37]

Some of the rockets were launched from Holland, and Allied planes targeted those sites. But in March 1945, due to a navigation error, 56 US bombers hit an area of The Hague, destroying more than 3,000 homes and killing 486 Dutch civilians. One of the last rockets fired at England, on 27 March 1945, hit a block of flats in east London, killing 134 people and injuring 49. More than 3,000 V-2s were eventually fired at London (and later Liège and Antwerp), killing around 9,000 people.[38]

---

[37] March 1945, Time magazine
[38] The Germans promised more. "How about V number 2 to V number X" (Propaganda leaflet AI-079-6-44)

BACK TO THE WAR

Ike wrote to Montgomery on 18 June advising him not to allow visitors to take up his time. In response he received a handwritten letter from Monty asking Ike to help deter visitors. It was the second time Monty had tried to keep Churchill away. He had earlier asked General 'Pug' Ismay to dissuade the Prime Minister from visiting him on 4 June because Churchill was "not only a great bore, but may well attract undue attention here". The Prime Minister was furious.

Ike was keen to cross the Channel again, but the weather was the worst for 50 years and all ships were confined to port. A huge storm on 19 June had destroyed the Mulberry harbour at Omaha Beach. On 21 June, Ike and John returned from the Advance Command Post before lunch, the bad weather again having prevented Ike's trip across the Channel. The next day Ike again returned from the Advance CP, having for the third time been unable to make the trip across in the destroyer. Eventually Ike and John sailed to France on Saturday 24 June aboard the destroyer USS Thompson. They left Portsmouth at 7.30am and returned later the same day visiting the American sector which looked "as if hell had moved across the land".[1]

Monty's attack eventually started the following morning, but he had delayed so long that he was faced by at least two more Panzer divisions. The delay of ten or 12 days also allowed the Germans to prepare their defences. On the other hand, General Bradley kept moving, so the Germans never had much chance to consolidate. Ike was concerned about the slowness of Monty's attack and didn't even celebrate the fall of Cherbourg on June 26/7,[2] particularly as the harbour had been destroyed by the Germans. (A week earlier, British

---

[1] Sgt Mickey and General Ike, p 121
[2] Eisenhower and his son met Churchill on 26 June (75, CHAR 20/141A)

newspapers had reported 30,000 Germans trapped on the Cherbourg Peninsula.[3]) Ike was also alarmed that US pilots had again strafed Allied troops by mistake.

In the first three weeks after the invasion, the Allies had occupied more than 1,000 square miles of France, taken 20,000 prisoners and captured two rocket-launching platforms. During that period, Ike and Kay flew back and forth from France to England. On 26 June, for example, they drove all over Devon and Cornwall with Ike inspecting units which were still preparing to go to France. Ike deplored talk of post-war plans, which he said tended to take the public's mind off the day-to-day battle. But in the United States, FDR had invited 42 nations to participate in the "world money talks" at Bretton Woods, New Hampshire, from 1 July. The US delegation was headed by 54-year-old Henry Morgenthau.[4]

Ike and General Bradley celebrated US Independence Day by visiting an anti-aircraft battery in France where 1,100 US guns were to target the German positions at noon. Bradley fired a Big Tom gun to mark 4 July. Ike meanwhile noted that the "swamps, hedges,[5] weather etc" of Normandy presented a "great problem to the troops". He was also informed that American tanks were inferior to the German Tigers and Panthers, and that Allied mortars were not as good as the German six-barrelled *Nebelwerfer*. Ike returned from France the following day, having flown a 45-minute patrol in a two-seater P51 Mustang fighter over the German lines (with an escort of a half-dozen other fighter aircraft). When he landed after the "secret" flight, "the Signal Corps boys had their cameras out, and the Boss had to pose beside the plane and in the plane and getting into the plane and getting out of the plane".[6]

---

[3] Daily Sketch, 19 June 1944

[4] Daily Mail, 27 May 1944

[5] The so-called *bocage*

[6] Sgt Mickey and General Ike, p 122

Back at the cottage, Ike suggested that Kay catch up with the 'blue book' diary before they went home. She read in the diary that 'Tex' Lee had been organising for her to join the US Women's Army Corps.[7] A memo to Ike from the personnel division of the War Department[8] said that Lee had indicated Ike's "desire to have Mrs Summersby appointed a First Lieutenant in the Women's Army Corps". Assistant Chief-of-Staff Major-General MG White wrote: "Our first reaction to any request of this nature from you is to approve it without hesitation, but in this particular case the proposed action will put us in such a difficult position that I feel obliged to lay the facts before you before any final decision is reached." White explained that only US citizens could enlist in the WACs, but "by a peculiar twist of language in the law" and "relying on a rather hair-splitting legal technicality", a non-citizen could be appointed a WAC officer. White added: "As a matter of principle, however, I do feel that we are somewhat bound by the law to restrict the Women's Army Corps to [US] citizens only."

White wrote that, since the WACs were first organised, "We have adhered rigidly to the principle of requiring graduation from the OCS [Officer Candidate School] as a preliminary to officer appointments." The general said this avoided allegations of "favoritism or partiality (which is, unfortunately, more likely to be made when we are dealing with the opposite sex...)". The War Department had already "refused many requests, both from high commanders inside the Army and from influential persons outside the Army, to appoint civil women directly as officers". If Kay were appointed an officer, "there are many hundred WACs there in England to whom this appointment would immediately become known". They would realise that "a British woman, not a member of the Corps, could become a First Lieutenant over night.

---

[7] Initially set up as the Women's Army Auxiliary Corps in May 1942, it became the WAC on 1 July 1943
[8] Confidential memo WDGAP 210.1 WAC, 8 July 1944

"I need not elaborate on the inevitable reaction and on the explaining that we would have to do to Congressmen and others here in the States and to commanders in the Army whose recommendations for the direct appointment of enlisted women have been disapproved." But notwithstanding the potential embarrassment, White wrote, if Eisenhower insisted on ignoring the "whole picture" and Marshall approved the "seemingly small request", "I will, without further hesitation, recommend that the appointment be made".

"I told you once that I was never going to let you go," Ike told Kay. "If you're a WAC, I can keep you on my staff later on." But he had already responded to General Stoner: "Have read your memorandum to me of July 8th on subject of WAC Commission and now understand difficulties and possible embarrassments which I formerly did not realize. Please drop the matter." [9] The memo was countersigned by 'Tex' Lee. But despite his letter, Ike did eventually commission Kay as a WAC officer.[10] As the US papers said later: "The powers of a commanding general in the field are so absolute, it could be no more than a matter of a telephone call from Gen Eisenhower...In any case, whatever technicalities existed, they were resolved in favour of Mrs Summersby, and she donned the WAC uniform." By the end of the war, Kay was wearing an "olive battle dress blouse and fawn coloured US WAC skirt", and "three ribbons denoting the American bronze star for service, the BEM and the ETO".[11] Kay was the only Irishwoman – indeed, the only foreigner – to be commissioned into the WACs in the European theatre.

---

[9] SHAEF confidential priority memo, 16 July 1944
[10] According to SHAEF WAC Paula Burrows, the order making Kay a WAC "came from President Roosevelt" (Herald-Tribune, 16 January 2003)
[11] The Evening Star, Washington, 6 November 1945, and p 3, Cork Examiner, 13 June 1945

FRIENDLY FIRE

Ike's hatred of the Germans remained unalloyed. At lunch on July 10, he told Lord Halifax, British Ambassador to Washington, that he would execute leaders of the Nazi party, from mayors up, and all members of the Gestapo. Alternatively, the Axis leaders should be "shot while trying to escape", or extermination could be "left to nature" if the Russians were given a free hand. Ike also said the 3,500 members of the German General Staff should be "utterly eliminated". He said the general staff had used the world wars as campaigns to dominate Europe and the world. He would exterminate them, or maybe they could all be concentrated in a place, like the remote south Atlantic island of St Helena.[1]

Ike believed that zones of influence in Germany should be temporarily assigned to the small nations overrun by Hitler. He would give Russia the biggest portion and other areas to the Czechs, Yugoslavs, Poles, Danes, Norwegians, Greeks and French. Ike's loathing for the Germans pervaded everything he did. In Portsmouth, he told Henry Morgenthau that the Germans should "stew in their own juice". In a letter to Mamie, Ike said "God, I hate the Germans..." (He wasn't the only one. German General Siegfried Westphal told the Nuremberg Tribunal on 18 June 1946: "We knew the slogan of El Alamein: 'Kill the Germans wherever you find them'. We had also captured an order, issued by a British armoured brigade, according to which prisoners must not be given anything to drink." The German officers burned the order so it would not be seen by their troops.[2])

On the morning of 9 July, Kay drove Ike to Chequers for a 90-minute meeting with the PM, then he went on to the Advance CP. He was in Telegraph Cottage when he heard

---

[1] Where the British exiled Napoleon to die
[2] Rommel, The Desert Fox

that FDR's son, Brigadier-General Teddy Roosevelt, assistant commander of the 4th Division, had died of a heart attack on 12 July in France.

During the night of 13 July, Butch received a secret message from Monty in Ike's private cipher saying that he planned to set the Normandy battle front "aflame". He sought air support for Operation Goodwood which was due to start on 15 July on the eastern flank and 17 July in the west, weather permitting. Churchill had meanwhile asked again to visit Montgomery. Ike agreed that the PM could go to Cherbourg and the rear area, but told him not to distract commanders or troops in the forward area, particularly Monty. But Montgomery again asked Ike not to allow any visitors during the attack. When the PM heard, he was "literally frothing at the corners of his mouth with rage"[3] and accused Monty of "dictating" to him. The PM said the Cabinet would discuss the issue of Monty trying to say where the PM could or couldn't go. But Churchill calmed down when Monty wrote him a note – at General Brooke's urging – saying the restriction didn't apply to the PM, and Monty would always welcome his visits.

Once again the weather closed in and prevented Ike flying to France, so he stayed in his caravan and dozed much of the day, getting up for dinner. Goodwood was eventually launched on 18 July, preceded by a huge aerial bombardment. Ike asked Bomber Command to saturate an area near Caen and the RAF dropped 7,000 tons of bombs to help the ground troops break through the German defences. On 19 July, Monty "cracked through", to use one of his own favourite phrases, but in effect then ordered his armour to halt. Although the Allied troops pushed back the Germans up to seven miles, 140 Allied tanks were destroyed and many British soldiers killed.[4] Ike was furious that the British VIII Corps breakout had failed. He was "not pleased with

---

3 Alan Brooke war diary notes, 19 July 1944
4 Ike later wrote that the seven-mile advance had been achieved at a cost of 1,000 tons of bombs per mile

Monty's progress"[5] and told him that he should push on "with every ounce of strength and zeal". Monty seemed to have only one tactical style – send tanks or infantry (or both) into action behind overwhelming artillery and air support. The Germans simply moved their guns and armour out of artillery range and hid their tanks and infantry until the attack. Monty had tried moving his armour ahead, but lost a lot of tanks and crews, so halted until infantry could come up to deal with the antitank weapons. Ike said the British and American public were becoming impatient after seeing the Allied successes against Axis forces in Russia and the Pacific. Monty had also not learned the art of giving credit to all services and commanders for his victories. At a press conference on 19 July, he said that at least 156,000 Germans had been killed or wounded since D-Day. Yet in the big push east and south of Caen, his forces had taken only 2,500 prisoners.

At lunch with Churchill back in England, Ike again predicted that the war would end in the winter of 1944, but suggested that maybe the best thing would be for Monty to be removed from the battlefield by being made a peer or given a governorship, such as Malta (Lord Gort was leaving to take over in Palestine). The Chief of the Imperial General Staff also dined with the PM and Ike on 26 July but continued to be unimpressed by Ike. Afterwards he said it was "clear that Ike knows nothing about strategy and is *quite* unsuited to the post of Supreme Commander as far as running the strategy of the war is concerned!"[6]

Monty agreed with this assessment of Ike. He later wrote in his war diary: "The Supreme Commander [Ike] had no firm ideas as to how to conduct the war and was 'blown about by the wind' all over the place...The staff at SHAEF were completely out of their depth all the time. The point to understand is if we had run the show properly, the war could

---

[5] Diary 20 July 1944
[6] Alan Brooke war diaries, 27 July 1944

have been finished by Christmas 1944. The blame for this must rest with the Americans."[7]

One area where Ike thought the American practice was superior was in the media identification of fighting units to bring the war closer to the people – a practice on which Patton had already insisted. Ike said the British War Office should take a leaf out of the book of the US War Department which publicly named regiments and the commanding officers of units that had already been identified on the battle front. (The British censor was particularly strict about naming units. In one newspaper two months after D-Day, for example, a correspondent referred to "members of a division that is earning a great name for itself in Normandy – though for some inscrutable reason its name cannot yet be mentioned".[8])

On 20 July, the day of the ill-fated bomb plot against Hitler,[9] Ike visited Monty and Bradley then spent the night at Telegraph Cottage. The next day, he worked most of the day at his main office. Telek got "out of prison"[10] the following day and Kay collected him from quarantine. He was thin from poor feeding, but he could still chase his tail and roll over for his belly to be scratched. Caacie was due out on July 26.

A few days later, Ike asked Kay: "Would you like to have a child?" Kay said she would love to have a baby – not *any* baby, but *Ike's* baby – but that was impossible. Ike said he knew, but maybe things would be different later. "You don't think I'd be too old for the boy?" he asked her, assuming the sex of the unborn child. Not at all, Kay insisted. Later, Kay

---

[7] https://books.google.ie/books?id=NvfyLM8IyvwC&pg=PA450&lpg#v= onepage&q&f=false

[8] Daily Mail, 3 August 1944

[9] A German propaganda leaflet said: "Shame on murderers! Shame on those that by low cunning stab in the back!" The reverse said: "Almighty God has miraculously preserved the life of this man, showing that He wishes Adolf Hitler to bring his mission to a successful end, to lead us to Victory, the Victory of Europe." (Kr-031-7-44)

[10] Diary 21 July 1944

and Ike enjoyed a Champagne dinner together, then sat in the garden before going to sleep holding hands across the aisle in the shelter. If it hadn't been for the war, the couple would have enjoyed an idyllic life at the cottage. They would collect marrows or beans from the garden. They used to hold hands under the breakfast table and occasionally hug when nobody was around. Ike told Kay that he didn't have to keep up pretences with her. "You're not after rank, you don't blab to the press and you don't gossip with staff members," he said. Most days Ike wrote Kay messages on scraps of paper which he tucked surreptitiously into her hand. "*You* don't have to write to *me*," Ike told her. "Every time you look at me, I see a love letter in your eyes."

When they were able to relax, Ike read the papers which were full of the attempted assassination of Hitler at the Wolf's Lair in East Prussia. After it became clear that the plot had been unsuccessful, German radio broadcast solemn music instead of the arranged programmes. (The first cancelled programme was allegedly an item on 'The Extermination of Rats'.[11]) Doenitz and Göering broadcast after Hitler to the German people, but no one spoke for the Army. Former Chief-of-Staff Ludwig von Beck, who left the Army after Munich and opposed Hitler on issues such as the attack on Russia, was accused of leading the plot and "lives no more". Afterwards, Hitler put Himmler in command of all forces in Germany, including the regular Army. Göering announced that, from then on, all German troops would substitute "Heil Hitler" for the traditional military salute.

But Ike had too many other troubles to spend much time reading. The bad weather brought London's heaviest attack by flying bombs. One landed near Ike's camp, resulting in flak holes in some tents. Ike told the press that, in France, casualties since D-Day now totalled 110,000, of which 68,000 were American.[12] Of the more than 21,000 Allied

---

[11] Daily Herald, 21 July 1944

[12] Marshall gave slightly different figures. He said that there were *nearly* 100,000 casualties

dead in June and July, almost 14,000 were Americans. The Germans had about the same of dead and wounded, but Ike expected them to fight on in the hope of getting better peace terms. On 24 July, Ike attended a lunch aboard HMS Victory, the flagship on which Nelson had won the battle of Trafalgar in 1805. After posing for pictures, Kay drove to Southwick House, where Ike spoke to Monty's Chief-of-Staff for an hour. He then went fishing with Beetle.

The following day, US forces were due to try and break out of Normandy. A total of 1,500 heavy bombers, 380 medium bombers and 550 fighter bombers of the American Eighth Air Force dropped 4,000 tons of high explosives and napalm in support of Operation Cobra but, although they faced only 11 weak German divisions with limited fighting power, the attack did not go "too well".[13] That was an understatement – Ike was told that 77 planes had bombed a mile short, killing 36 Allied soldiers and wounding 80. (In fact, 111 were killed and 490 wounded, and it was the second time in two days that the Americans had bombed short.[14] The previous day, US bombers flying at right angles to the Allied lines had been unable to see the targets properly and had killed 25 Allied soldiers and wounded 131.[15])

One of the most senior casualties was General Lesley (sic) McNair, killed in his foxhole near Saint-Lô when an Allied bomb blasted his body 60 feet from his slit trench and left it unrecognisable, except for the three stars on his collar. He was the highest-ranking US officer to die in the war to date.[16] When the news broke in the US on 26 July, the War Department said McNair had died from "enemy fire".[17] But McNair's aide told friends in Washington that the general

[13] Diary 25 July 1944
[14] Life magazine, 16 April 1951, General Omar N Bradley, p 101
[15] According to pp 773-4, Bodyguard of Lies, 25 men were killed and 131 wounded by 300 Allied bombers in the first attack; 111 were killed and 490 wounded by 77 Allied bombers in the second attack
[16] McNair had been appointed by Ike on 15 July 1944 to head Patton's "paper army" (p 738 Bodyguard of Lies)
[17] The Evening Independent (Florida), 27 July 1944

had been killed by American bombers. General Marshall cabled Ike to ask why the officer had not been pledged to secrecy; Ike replied that the real story should be given to the American public. Earlier, in a broadcast on Armistice Day 1942, McNair had told US troops: "We must scheme and plan night anD-Day to kill...The struggle is for survival, kill or be killed." Now he had been killed.

Ike discussed the incidents at lunch with the PM after meeting Tedder and Leigh-Mallory, and swore never to support ground troops with heavy bombers again – though he did. Despite the "friendly fire" deaths, the British PM was "supremely happy" that evening after talking to Monty. Ike visited Monty and Bradley again then talked to Churchill for more than half an hour,[18] returning to his HQ for dinner. Ike slept late on the Sunday, "the first time" he had done so since D-Day.[19] When he got up, he announced that he proposed moving to France more or less permanently within the next few days. In France, fleeing German troops were strafed by the US Air Force, and Ike said Field Marshal Erwin Rommel had apparently died after being wounded in France by British fighters. (In fact, his skull had been fractured on 17 July when his car was strafed by an Allied fighter-bomber between Livarot and Vimoutiers in Normandy, but he did not die until 14 October. His funeral took place four days later, with full military honours.)

Up to 1 August, the Allies had captured 78,000 Germans, of whom the British had taken 14,000 and the Americans 64,000. In Brittany and Normandy, Patton had taken command of the Third Army, and had advanced against weak resistance. The same day, Eisenhower called General Edward Betts, the European Judge Advocate, and said he was anxious to see a "complete report" on the number of death sentences passed against US troops, "especially as between white and colored troops".[20] Betts used to ask Ike

---

[18] Ike sent Churchill a box of 50 cigars on 1 August (77, CHAR 20/141 A)
[19] Diary 30 July 1944
[20] Diary 1 August 1944

once or twice a month to confirm death sentences on US troops who had raped or murdered civilians.[21]

On Saturday 5 August, the Prime Minister came for lunch at the SHAEF Forward camp and stayed for dinner. The PM had been going to fly to France, but his plane had been cancelled after an earlier plane crashed in bad weather at the French field where Churchill had been due to land, and all the occupants had been killed. The Prime Minister (and Admiral Cunningham) said Ike would miss a great opportunity unless Operation Anvil (now called Dragoon) were shifted from the scheduled amphibious attack in the Toulon area to Brittany or the Channel ports. Ike agreed – then phoned Field Marshal Brooke on 6 August to say he was strongly opposed to any change in the plan. He said that Allied landings in the Toulon area and an advance up the Rhone Valley would further stretch German resources. Ike – supported by Marshall, King and Arnold – now insisted that the invasion through southern France must not be diverted.

A little over two months after D-Day, on 8 August, USAF Flying Fortresses were to support Canadian and Polish troops in Operation Totalize, a breakout from Caen. Unfortunately, two groups of planes again bombed short, killing 65 soldiers in the HQ of the 3rd Canadian Infantry Division and 1st Polish Armoured Division and wounding 250. It was "part of the inevitable price of experience", according to Ike.[22] On the same day, Ike moved to a caravan in a two-acre Normandy apple orchard at Le Molay-Littry. The camp, known as Shellburst, was surrounded by a ten-foot hedge, in which a gap had been cut so that Ike could see the adjoining field where planes could land. The camp consisted of Ike's caravan, two for the WACs and a spare for use as an office by Kay or for overnight guests. Kay slept in a tent near Ike's office, a 20 by 30 foot tent with a board floor.

---

[21] Such as on 30 August, 23 September, 20 and 27 October, 12, 19 and 20 November and 4 and 14 December, according to Kay's diary
[22] Supreme Commander's Dispatch for Operations in Northwest Europe, SHAEF

There were several slit trenches nearby for use in case of air-raids. The correspondents lived in a camp a quarter of a mile away. Ike re-started his nightly bridge games – this time Omar Bradley and another secretary, Captain Mattie Pinette, against Ike and Kay, who won the first rubber. Late one night, he stopped by Kay's desk and told her he was finishing work for the day. She explained that she was still answering his fan mail after handling his official business during the day. "And to think I'd never received even one fan letter when you drove me and Wayne Clark that first day in London!" he exclaimed.

Kay spent her days driving Ike to the front, flying back to England with him and then driving him to London to meet Churchill or to SHAEF HQ. The war in France was now going well. Ike pressed Montgomery to destroy the enemy straight away, rather than just be content with territorial gains. After dinner on 8 August, he drove over to Montgomery's headquarters to talk to him about the big Canadian attack which had started the previous night. The British press reported that this was the first time in Canada's history that it had a fighting force large enough to call an army, although the soldiers included Poles. As well as Monty and the Canadians, General Patton was also moving quickly ahead. Patton's thrust through Brittany towards Le Mans had been so rapid that communications could not keep pace. He called for new maps as his troops had run off the edge of the existing ones. His tanks were well supplied with fuel from the cross-Channel pipe line, Pluto, between Sandown Bay and Nacqueville. It was finally connected on 12 August, with the 70 miles of welded pipe rolled on huge drums like wire. Patton's Third Army took Le Mans on 9 August, and the four-division Panzer counterattack intended to split the Americans at Avranches was defeated, the enemy losing 80 tanks to Allied air attacks. There was hand-to-hand fighting at Saint-Malo and Patton ordered the bombing of Brest and Saint-Nazaire, despite the fact that many French civilians would also die. The Germans were ordered to fall back in groups of 50 or 60 at half-hour intervals. Back in England,

Ike went to 10 Downing Street to talk again to the PM about Operation Dragoon. He argued that there was an urgent need for the port of Marseille. But Churchill wanted to divert Allied troops from southern France to Italy and the Balkans.[23] If Ike continued to disagree with him, he said he might have to go to the King and "lay down the mantle of my high office".

For an hour on Friday 11 August, Ike reviewed the 12,000 men of the 82nd Airborne Division at Stoughton, Leicester (spraining his knee in the process). After the review, Ike and General Lewis Brereton were invited to tea at the divisional headquarters in Oadby. General James Gavin was surprised when Kay joined them.[24] When Ike was told that the Germans had about 500 tanks against the Allied armies in the Mortain area, he replied: "Well we've got 3,500, so what are we scared of?" Ike's twisted knee meant he had to be confined to bed[25] where he heard of the death of Brigadier-General James E Wharton. It was Wharton's first day as commander of the 28th Division and he was shot dead by a German sniper while visiting the front.

On 13 August, Ike dined with General Bradley who Kay said played bridge just as calmly as if he had come off the golf course on a Sunday afternoon. The following day, the Canadians attacked the Falaise pocket with four divisions of infantry and two of tanks in a bid to take the town. RAF heavy bombers again hit Allied troops in error during the operation, leaving up to 165 dead and total casualties of almost 500. The bombers also destroyed two Allied tanks, 30 field guns and 265 vehicles. But while tens of thousands of German prisoners were taken during the fighting for the Falaise Gap, 40,000 Germans escaped – according to the Americans, because of the slowness of the advance of

---

23 The Prime Minister would try to bring opponents round to his view by sustained argument (General Sir Ian Jacob)
24 www.leicestermercury.co.uk/Eisenhower-s-speech-sparked-furious-protest/story-16446063-detail/story.html
25 Diary 12 August 1944

Monty's British and Canadian forces. This caused "friction between the Allies."[26] The "carnage and destruction" around Falaise was so terrible that it became known as "the killing ground". "It was literally possible to walk for hundreds of yards at a time stepping on nothing but dead and decaying flesh," Ike wrote later. Kay added that the "dead were everywhere to be seen...Horses and equipment were all mixed up. The stench was awful".[27] It was "a regular shambles of broken tanks, lorries, carts and dead horses".[28]

During lunch, Ike explained why Allied heavy bombers had dropped bombs short when supporting troops in a ground attack. He said US bombsights were fixed to hit targets from high altitude but 'heavies' had been bombing from lower altitudes, so the bombsight was not so accurate. Until now, bombers had dropped their bombs perpendicular to Allied lines, but in future Ike ordered that bombing be parallel to Allied troops, causing fewer casualties. That afternoon, Ike visited the military hospital near Carentan and got "mad"[29] when he realised that more than a thousand of the patients had self-inflicted wounds. Soldiers often shot themselves through the hand or the foot, and it was difficult to prove that it wasn't an accident. One soldier said he had accidentally shot off his thumb while climbing aboard a truck. Many complaints of battle fatigue were also faked to avoid fighting. Not surprisingly, the Germans encouraged Allied soldiers to simulate injuries to get out of the front line. Propaganda leaflets showed how to fake illness by temporarily paralysing arms or legs with a "round stone, eraser or short piece of rubber tubing in gauze tissue", swallowing ginger, mustard or picric acid or rubbing tonsils with a silver nitrate stick.[30]

---

[26] The World at War 1973 (episode 17)
[27] Diary 26 August 1944
[28] Alan Brooke war diaries, 29 August 1944
[29] Diary 14 August 1944
[30] AM4, 5 and 6

Ike now had to decide which way to send the Allied armies. The decisiveness of the victory west of the Seine convinced him that the Allies should continue into Germany up to the Rhine before regrouping. Patton predicted that the Allies would be "in Berlin ahead of every one" and Montgomery believed that his army group could go straight to the German capital, but Ike said this was impractical, as the Germans could attack the flanks of such a narrow thrust.[31] While Ike thought the Germans would soon give up territory which was not useful to them, such as Finland, he believed that "Hitler and his gang" had nothing to lose by continuing the war. He said Hitler expected to be hanged by the Allies – if he didn't hang himself, which Ike thought likely – so would fight to the bitter end. Later Ike controversially claimed that he had diverted the Allied troops from Berlin because the German capital would be in the Soviet zone after the war, and the Allies would have to withdraw to their own zones of occupation.

On 15 August 1944, the Prime Minister watched Operation Dragoon from destroyer HMS Kimberley[32] in the Mediterranean. Allied troops quickly occupied Marseille and other major French cities.[33] Ike recalled that the PM had tears rolling down his cheeks at their meeting the previous Friday, claiming that the Americans were "bullying" the British by failing to accept their (or Churchill's) grand strategies for an invasion of the Balkans. But Ike reminded him that the invasion of Europe had to be postponed from the spring of 1943 to June 1944 because America had accepted the British point of view about beating Hitler before defeating Japan.

---

[31] "With a proper plan, we could have been in Berlin, Prague, and Vienna before the Russians," wrote The Sunday Times military correspondent (The Times of India, 12 December 1948)

[32] The destroyer had been torpedoed by a U-boat off North Africa in January 1942, but survived the war

[33] The operation was "a strategic blunder of the first magnitude, and it was an American blunder". (The Times of India, 12 December 1948)

PARIS

The Allied attacks on French towns and villages were having their effect. Ike visited the town of St Lô, now "just a mass of rubble".[1] But for the troops in France, Paris was the target. Moscow Radio reported on 18 August that the Allies had entered Paris.[2] But in fact this did not happen for another week. On 22 August, de Gaulle told Ike it was important for the Allies to take Paris "on account of looting, rioting etc".[3] But Eisenhower told the French leader that he was against taking the French capital when the required troops and supplies could equally be used to defeat the Germans. The Americans regarded Paris as no more than "an inkspot on our maps to be bypassed".[4] On 23 August, General Marie-Pierre Koenig – who had been military governor of Paris for two days – issued a communiqué claiming the Allies had taken the city,[5] but SHAEF refused to confirm this.

American and British accredited correspondents, as well as several from neutral countries, were demanding to cross the Channel before the fall of Paris. However, permission was needed first from camp commandants as press camps in France could each accommodate only 35 to 50 correspondents. Any of the United Nations could have its correspondents accredited to SHAEF, including Russians, Chinese, Dutch, Czechs and Poles. More than a thousand correspondents already had SHAEF ID cards, and around 700 of those were in Europe, mostly at the front with various armies.

Paris eventually fell on Friday 25 August. Six correspondents – three British and three American – who were in the French capital broadcast uncensored material over a French

---

[1] Diary 18 August 1944
[2] Daily Express, 18 August 1944
[3] Diary 22 August 1944
[4] A Soldier's Story, General Omar N Bradley (Henry Holt & Co, 1951)
[5] Daily Mail, 24 August 1944

underground radio station when the Allies occupied the city. They were suspended, pending a decision from Beetle about stiffer punishment. General de Gaulle told a radio commentator: "I have only one word to say: *Vive Paris! Vive la France!*"[6] In a speech at Paris's *Hôtel de Ville* that day, de Gaulle said that Paris had liberated itself with the help of the French army which had landed in the south of France from Italy; he did not mention the Americans.

The newspapers reported that General Leclerc's 2nd Armoured Division led the entry into Paris in the morning, followed by the Americans in the afternoon, though the Americans actually entered the French capital first, the US Army's 28th Infantry Division parading 24-abreast down the Champs Élysées. At a press conference afterwards, a British reporter asked why the "American parade in Paris" had not included British and French troops. Ike replied that, when Paris was about to fall, he had ordered that Le Clerc's French armoured division under Bradley be first in the city, but that a small contingent of British, American and other Allies should go into Paris to symbolise Allied unity. As Le Clerc's troops could not get into Paris immediately, there were more American troops than intended, though Ike had arranged for de Gaulle to review the American troops marching triumphantly through the city.[7]

But taking Paris meant the Allied supply lines were becoming increasingly stretched, as the citizens of the French capital – as well as the troops – now had to be fed by the Allies. As a former regimental supply officer, Ike was becoming more concerned about shortage of supplies, considering the burgeoning number of supply staff. According to General 'Windy' Gale of the First Allied Airborne Army, ComZone was unloading only 17,000 tons of supplies a day, instead of the 30,000 tons needed.[8] The head of the

---

6 The Daily Sketch, 26 August 1944
7 Montgomery was also invited, but said he was too busy
8 Diary 19 September 1944

Communications Zone, General JCH[9] (not 'Tex') Lee[10] had meanwhile taken over the best hotels in Paris for his 29,000 supply personnel.[11] The Majestic Hotel on Avenue Kleberg housed ComZone headquarters, while the Raphael next door was used by SHAEF for visitors.[12] The French military was deprived of even its minimum requirements. General Koenig said the demand by American supply staff for rooms in the French capital exceeded the capacity of all the hotels formerly used by the Germans.[13] Beetle approved the public relations and public works departments moving into Paris, but Ike ordered that no soldier below the rank of Lieutenant-Colonel should be given a private room because of the shortage of accommodation.[14]

The Scribe Hotel in Paris was the centre for war correspondents and for 250 public relations staff – American, British, French and Canadian. The hotel was equipped with desks and typewriters, telegraph machines, offices and radio studios. There were also censorship and cable offices and, on any given day, between 150 and 200 correspondents were at the hotel. Before the three daily press conferences in the former ballroom, two briefing officers – one British and one American – would phone each army group for the latest news and the positions would be noted on the huge maps.

The Scribe Bar was a major attraction because food in the Paris cafes was very expensive, but the Army mess in the Scribe, with breakfast at ten francs and lunch or dinner at twenty francs, was even more popular. SHAEF messes were run on a pay-as-you-enter basis, and the mess officer then used these funds to buy food from the quartermaster. The

---

9 Known as "Jesus Christ Himself"

10 Later, Lee tried to release many German prisoners-of-war but Ike forbade this on 15 May 1945

11 This figure reached 160,000 by April 1945

12 The SHAEF initials were said to stand for "Société des Hoteliers Americains en France"

13 Patton wondered why Ike did not order ComZone to use 10 per cent of its "vast army" as infantrymen (The Patton Papers, p 588)

14 Diary 24 October 1944

mess actually made a small profit, but could not feed everyone whom the correspondents or staff wanted to bring as a guest. Paris was also to be used as a recreation centre for combat troops, and hotel rooms were to be kept for them, even though Ike told Kay that the uniform, discipline and conduct of American personnel in Paris was sloppy. The French authorities had already told him they had "definite evidence" of looting by American troops. One US Brigadier-General was said to have stolen a case full of silver.[15]

On August 26, Kay drove Ike from his orchard HQ to Bradley's HQ in Chartres, six hours away. In the car they discussed the "friendly fire" incident that day in which 117 British sailors had been killed and more than 150 injured in the English Channel off Le Havre. RAF Typhoons had attacked and sunk the minesweepers HMS Hussar and HMS Britomart, and damaged HMS Salamander so badly that it had to be scrapped.[16] The incident came three days after a US B-24 Liberator crashed into a Holy Trinity Church of England school in Freckelton, Lancashire, killing 38 children and 23 others, including the three-man crew. It was the worst air crash in Britain in the whole war.[17] Kay also asked Ike if she could go to Paris with some newsmen, but Ike said absolutely not, it was too dangerous. However, the following day, after dinner with Bradley, Ike decided that the three of them should drive to Paris, where Ike and Bradley were mobbed as they paid their respects at the tomb of the Unknown Soldier.

On 31 August, while his headquarters moved to Granville and his accommodation was moved to a villa near St Jean de Thomas, Ike flew to England to see the Prime Minister to discuss the removal of Monty from command of the Allied armies. At a press conference at the Ministry of Information, he told a couple of hundred correspondents that

---

[15] Diary 15 August 1944
[16] http://ww2today.com/27-august-1944-friendly-fire-disaster-for-royal-navy-off-le-havre
[17] Bing Crosby sang for the survivors in hospital

Montgomery – who was to be promoted to field marshal the following day – was "one of the great soldiers of the war". Ike said that he had put Monty in tactical control of the American land forces until they broke out of the Cherbourg Peninsula because the initial Normandy beachhead was so restricted. It was then planned that General Bradley should take over this part of the job, reporting directly to SHAEF. Kay's typed diary notes said: "Bradley couldn't possibly keep in touch with his forces both in the North and the Sout (sic). That is the only reson (sic) Monty was given command of American forces."[18] Ike told the correspondents that it would be "most unfortunate" if this plan were interpreted as a demotion of anyone. Ike said Monty was a "great and personal friend" for whom he had a great admiration (though this was far from the truth).

Up till the end of August, about 83,000 British, Canadian and Polish troops had been casualties, of whom nearly 16,000 were killed. Montgomery's forces were now expected to defeat the Germans in the north, Bradley's in the centre and the Mediterranean forces in the south. Ike said there would certainly be one major battle before breaking through the Siegfried Line to the Rhine, but he hoped that, by that stage, most of the best German troops would have been captured or scattered.

At Telegraph Cottage during lunch, Ike complained that port capacity was not what it should be, the French roads were clogged with Allied transport trucks, bridges were down and communications were poor. After lunch, Ike and Kay flew back to France to check out the situation. Shellburst headquarters had been established with those of SHAEF Forward at Villa Montgomery,[19] Granville, overlooking Mont St Michel. Ike took over the dual role of commander of the land forces on 1 September, while continuing as Supreme

---

[18] "Absolutely untrue," said The Sunday Times military correspondent (The Times of India, 12 December 1948)
[19] The name was just a coincidence

Commander. Monty resented Ike's appointment, [20] even though it had been agreed before D-Day, but his promotion to field marshal [21] was considered compensation. He continued to command the 21st Army Group, which consisted mainly of British and Canadian soldiers, but would no longer command US troops.

The next day, Ike flew to Versailles without Kay to meet Generals Bradley and Patton. He intended to "give Patton hell" for overstretching the Allied lines and "causing supply difficulties". [22] Patton continued to race ahead of the other Allied armies, particularly Montgomery's, but had to be reined in, physically and verbally. Ike ordered that any quotations by Patton should be censored, except for formal citations for good fighting by Third Army units, "to protect him from his own flamboyant and sometimes hasty words". Later, the US War Department ordered Patton to write his reports in more official language, as his profanities made his daily situation reports "too florid". Patton's first report thereafter was a model of military correctness, until the postscript: "I peed in the Rhine today." [23]

After Ike had dealt with Patton, he changed from his B-25 to an L-5 liaison plane at Chartres for the return journey but there was a high wind and visibility was poor. The plane was forced down on the beach near Ike's villa. As Ike helped push the plane off the soft sand, he wrenched his good knee. He limped more than a mile to the road and flagged down a jeep, which took him home.

"Ankles are nearly always neat and good-looking, but knees are nearly always not," he told Kay – an observation he was to make more than once. [24] The knee swelled up and finally the doctors put it in a cast. For several days, Ike was forced

---

[20] Alan Brooke war diaries, 9 November 1944
[21] One rank higher than Ike's
[22] Diary 2 September 1944
[23] He said "peed" in his official report. He wrote in his diary that he took "a piss in the Rhine" (24 March 1945)
[24] Milwaukee Sentinel, 16 June 1967, p 3

to stay in bed, so was out of touch with the Allied front line. Kay looked after him, and they would hold hands and kiss "but always very hastily", she said. With Ike confined to bed, the HQ was a picture of domestic bliss. Shaef, the big black cat – a gift from Lady Tedder – was fed milk from Ike's two cows. Caacie used to beg for food at the table while Telek sat on Ike's bed and growled if Ike or Kay did not scratch his back. On 4 September, after the bedridden Ike met the 6th Army Group commander, Kay and Ike had lunch with General Everett Hughes, who noticed that Ike "blinked" at Kay whenever Mamie was mentioned. Four days later, Ike had to go to Paris to make a speech. A microphone was rigged up but didn't appear to be turned on. "Is this ******* microphone working?" asked Ike. It was – and his profane language echoed from the loudspeakers.

With the British and the Americans now less than 20 miles from the German border, Bulgaria quit the Axis alliance and declared war on Germany. Ike ordered operational secrecy for the Allied push. On 11 September, the US Third Army moved five miles into the Reich north of Trier. It was the first time Allied troops had fought on "the sacred soil of Germany".[25] But the Allies were now many months ahead of schedule and had "far outpaced their supply trains".[26] And there was another problem – the Allies still could not agree about the division of post-war Germany. In Canada, the Quebec conference from 12 to 16 September did not accept Ike's recommendation that SHAEF should be put in charge of an occupied Germany. Instead, the defeated country was to be divided into four zones controlled by the Russians, Americans, British and French and its industry was to be destroyed, in accordance with the Morgenthau Plan. The pastoralisation plan was proposed by Churchill's friend Viscount Cherwell (the German-born Frederick Lindemann [27]) and by Harry Dexter White, subsequently

---

[25] The Daily Sketch, 12 September 1944
[26] Eisenhower, p 38
[27] http://www.oxfordchabad.org/templates/articlecco_cdo/aid/457389/jewish/Oxford-Jewish-Personalities.htm

exposed as a Soviet spy. [28]   Churchill, who attended the Quebec conference, looked forward "to converting Germany into a country primarily agricultural and pastoral in its character". [29]   The Quebec conference also removed Ike's direct command over RAF Bomber Command and the US Strategic Air Force. Ike didn't like the decision, but his close relationships with "Bomber" Harris and Tooey Spaatz meant that the change made no real difference. Ike could still call for strategic bombers to support land and naval operations, though their main job was now to bomb enemy industry, especially oil targets. Rumours that the Quebec Conference would make Ike Supreme Commander of troops in the Far East[30] turned out to be inaccurate.

From Friday 15 September, at the insistence of the Combined Chiefs, Ike assumed command of the southern group of armies. Bradley's forces were very stretched south of Aachen and Ike realised that there could be "another Kasserine" if the enemy concentrated in the right place. Ike supported Monty's plan to concentrate forces in the north as the main effort against the Germans. Monty hoped that meant the war would end in 1944. [31] "It is now the middle of September, and I will go so far as to say that statement is absolutely right," he said. "There is no doubt about it." [32] However, Monty seemed to realise the stiffness of the opposition he faced, as he changed his mind and bet Ike £5 in mid-October that the war would *not* end by Christmas 1944.

But the Allies were moving steadily ahead, defeating the Germans in ever-greater numbers. Ike discussed transport

---

28 Patton said White was "damned near a communist". (Diary)
29 Text of official statement, 15 September 1944, though he and Roosevelt were subsequently "forced to back down by the Foreign Office and the State Department" – Churchill p 323
30 Daily Mail, 15 September 1944
31 Monty's "pencil-like thrust" could have saved "heavy casualties, particularly the 70,000 Americans in the Ardennes", said the Times of India (12 December 1948)
32 Daily Mail, 20 September 1944

priority with Monty in Brussels, but wanted to be certain that Allied operations would continue towards Brussels, as he needed the port of Antwerp for supply. It had become apparent that the Allied forces could advance almost at will, but "Petrol, armour and supplies have to be brought up before the commander can hit the Germans a real blow and follow up without halting," said the British newspapers. [33] There was little damage in Granville and the surrounding area, but at Avranches, abandoned or destroyed German tanks, vehicles and guns were strewn along the road.

Captured German messages (like this one from Generalfeld-marschall Günther von Kluge) recognised: "Whether the enemy can be stopped at this point is still questionable. His air superiority is terrific and smothers almost all our movements. At the same time, every movement of his is prepared and protected by his air force. Our losses in men and equipment are extraordinary. The morale of our troops has suffered heavily under murderous enemy fire, especially since our infantry units now consist only of haphazard groups. Behind the front, terrorists, feeling the end approaching, grow steadily bolder."

---

[33] Evening Standard, 7 September 1944

OPERATION MARKET GARDEN

The Allies launched Operation Market Garden in the Netherlands on 17 September. The British 1st Airborne Division, supported by the Glider Pilot Regiment and the Polish 1st Independent Parachute Brigade, expected a walkover at Arnhem in Holland, but landed some distance from their objectives and quickly met stiff resistance, especially from the 9th and 10th SS Panzer Divisions.

Only a small Allied force was able to reach the Arnhem road bridge, while the main force was halted on the outskirts of the town and Britain's 30 Corps was unable to relieve the airborne troops on schedule. British press reports that "the landing has definitely gone according to plan"[1] and that "nothing can stop us"[2] turned out to be over-optimistic. After four days, the small British force at the bridge was overwhelmed by the defending Germans. After eight days of fighting, the remains of the airborne forces were withdrawn. The 1st Airborne Division had lost nearly three-quarters of its men and was not in combat again. By this time, the newspapers were referring to "The Agony of Arnhem" and "230 hours of hell". The Germans claimed they had killed 1,500 paratroopers and captured 6,150 prisoners, which was reasonably accurate.[3]

The collapse of the Arnhem bridgehead caused Monty to alter his plans for crossing the Rhine and taking the Ruhr. In the United States, the US papers claimed that the British failure to cross the Rhine at Arnhem had delayed victory by three months. Although the operation was militarily a failure, Ike said the "action and tenacity of the British constitute a brilliant page in their history". On 20 September, during the battle for Arnhem, SHAEF Main moved from

---

[1] Daily Herald, 18 September 1944
[2] Daily Mail, 20 September 1944
[3] Daily Mail, 28 September 1944

Bushy Park to Versailles and joined SHAEF Forward (Shellburst), which had moved from Granville. SHAEF was expected to require accommodation for 2,000 officers and 10,000 soldiers but, within a week, those figures had more than doubled. Ike's office was in an annexe of the Trianon Palace Hotel in Versailles, where he entertained Patton to lunch on 21 September and which became known as the 'Hotel Eisenhower'. [4] Ike lived about four miles away at Saint-Germain in General Gerd von Rundstedt's comfortable former mansion, which had an elaborate air-raid shelter. Kay stayed near Ike in an apartment above what used to be King Louis XV's stables.

While Ike was in Versailles, crooner Bing Crosby came to lunch, and Ike happened to mention that he hadn't tasted hominy grits since he was in the United States. "Bing said he'd take care of that and when he got back to the States he said in a radio broadcast that the Supreme Commander couldn't get hominy grits and asked his listeners to send him some," said Mickey McKeogh. "He must have very responsive listeners, because very soon we began to get hominy grits. We got them in boxes and in cases; the whole place was piled up with hominy grits. We must have got a ton of the stuff." [5] Kay sent most of the grits to the troops.

Ike was later persuaded to move to 'Tex' Lee's apartment in the Shellburst compound and then to a house on the approach to the Trianon following rumours that he was the target of a German assassination squad. Kay was moved to a neighbouring apartment. She drove Ike's 'double', Lieutentant-Colonel Baldwin Smith, to the mansion daily in a bid to fool the would-be assassins. The assassination squad was led by Colonel Otto Skorzeny, the man who had rescued Mussolini from the Gran Sasso. Eisenhower later circulated "wanted" posters throughout France with a picture of Skorzeny. Eventually, 23 of the Germans were captured, and

---

[4] Ike often faced criticism for "his 5,000-strong staff, his pet dogs, his mistress, his personal PR man established at Versailles..." Siegfried, p 48
[5] Sgt Mickey and General Ike, p 34

18 executed as spies for wearing American uniforms. [6] (Skorzeny himself was acquitted at Nuremberg after the war, thanks to evidence from Wing Commander 'Tommy' Yeo-Thomas, and went to live in Spain. He subsequently bought a house in Co Kildare, Ireland, and died in 1975.)

Kay drove Ike to Paris where he presented a SHAEF plaque to be erected on the *Arc de Triomphe*, and spoke briefly to a crowd of Parisians. Whenever Kay drove Ike in the 1941 Packard Clipper saloon on the Red Ball route[7] from Orly to Versailles, they would encounter burned-out German tanks, trucks and Volkswagens all along the road. But it wasn't only the Germans who were the victims of the Allied armies. One of the issues Ike had to decide was whether to bomb the French rail yards and roads, with possible heavy French civilian casualties. "General Eisenhower made the decision to go ahead, and we didn't kill very many [civilians]," recalled Kay. [8]

While at the Trianon hotel, Ike had many visitors, including 75-year-old Bernard Baruch – an old friend from the War Industries Board – and Prince Bernhard of the Netherlands, who later awarded Kay the Cross of Orange Nassau. Within a fortnight, Ike and Kay had moved again to Gueux. Ike's office was a wooden building with walls so thin that you could hear voices through them. They drove or flew regularly to Brussels, Luxembourg and other cities in France, sometimes visiting three countries in a day. The "material destruction" in Aachen was "tremendous", said Kay. "It was a relief to see at last German houses demolished," agreed the head of the British army. [9]

There had been major counterattacks against Patton, yet, without any real advance, he had captured about 9,000

---

[6] http://www.gettyimages.ie/detail/news-photo/view-of-an-german-soldier-executed-by-an-american-firing-news-photo/95795099

[7] One-way US supply route. The trucks had three shifts of drivers so could be kept constantly on the move

[8] 1972 Thames Television interview

[9] Alan Brooke war diaries, 3 March 1945

prisoners and knocked out 270 tanks in seven days. He complained to Ike about the assignment of two American airborne divisions to Monty, as their use might have helped the Third Army to advance even faster. But Ike said it would help if the airborne divisions managed to get a bridgehead across the Rhine. Ike returned to Reims in a liaison plane and, on 28 September, spent his first night at his new advance camp on the golf course a few miles west of Reims.

At this stage, the only major ports in northern France remaining in enemy hands were Lorient and Saint-Nazaire and, on the north coast, Dunkirk and Calais, which was not occupied by the Allies until 1 October 1944. In all, 20,000 Germans surrendered at Orleans, 77,000 at Brest. The Germans had lost a million men and an enormous amount of equipment in France, yet there were no signs of collapse in morale, despite the Allied air superiority. On a single day, 5,000 Allied planes dropped 3,000 tons of explosives and 600,000 incendiaries over Germany and over the Channel Islands. The British Crown dependencies were still held by the Germans and showed no sign of surrendering. A German request to the Allies for food for the starving population there was turned down.

On 3 October, Ike had lunch at Downing Street with Churchill, who wanted to see him "alone".[10] Ike said the best way of destroying the Germans was to capture the port of Antwerp and then strike at the Ruhr and the Saar. Alternatively, airborne operations might secure bridgeheads across the Rhine to help Bradley around Koblenz and Cologne. Ike told the British on 5 October that he then planned to advance on Berlin, either from Frankfurt or from the Ruhr. On 6 October, Kay drove Ike, Bradley and Beetle to Orly airport to meet General Marshall who was to visit Bradley's headquarters and then stay with Ike for six days while visiting the forward area.

---

[10] 80, CHAR 20/141 A

The next day, Ike posed for a painting by Cathleen Mann, the Marchioness of Queensberry, in a sunroom next to his office in Versailles. He had sat for a picture only once before, in Algiers. A British war artist, Royal Academician Henry Carr,[11] had been commissioned to paint the commanders at HQ there. Three days later, Ike was posing again, this time for a group photo with his commanders at headquarters.

[11] Carr had been an official War Office artist since 1943 in Algiers, Tunis and Cassino

FRATERNISATION

Among Ike's main concerns now that the Allies had entered Germany was fraternisation between Allied soldiers and German civilians.[1] In the United States on 11 October, there was "adverse reaction" to a picture of GIs in a jeep appearing to be very chatty with a group of German women. An editorial in Stars and Stripes on 20 October – "Don't Get Chummy with Jerry" – denounced "favoured treatment" for German civilians when Aachen was finally captured. It said that GIs travelled in open trucks to the front in the rain, and it compared this to the "tender treatment" of civilians in Aachen.

The next day, at a press conference in the Scribe Hotel, Ike said the Allies would go into Germany as conquerors and there would be no fraternisation. The Germans would be treated justly, in conformity with the civilised standards of the Allied governments, but the Allies would have nothing to do with them, except for necessary official relationships. But the fraternisation ban didn't work. Ike decided in June 1945 that American soldiers should be allowed to "fraternise" – or play – with German children. The ban collapsed on 14 July and was formally abolished three months later. One result of the end of the ban was a dramatic rise in the incidence of venereal disease among American soldiers — about 235 percent between May and December 1945. The French and the Belgians suggested that the brothels used by the troops be closed down altogether.[2]

On 14 October, Ike's birthday, he lunched at the headquarters of Hodges' First Army in Liège with King George VI

---

[1] "*No* soldier will be allowed to mix with any Germans" (Kay's diary, 1 September 1944), but "nothing could stop fraternization", according to Patton

[2] Diary 18 November 1944, Later in Germany, Eisenhower ordered the death penalty for German women infecting Allied soldiers with venereal disease (Siegfried, p 49)

who presented Ike with the Order of the Bath. Patton was also a guest at the lunch. When the King asked Patton how often he had used his famous ivory-handled revolvers, Patton said those were only the ones he carried socially; he used his "fighting pistols" on campaigns. The King asked how many men Patton had killed in war. "Seven, sir," came the response. "How many?" persisted Ike. "Three, sir," replied Patton. In fact, Ike said Patton claimed to have shot only one man, during a mêlée in Mexico in 1916. "I think this was about the limit of his lethal accomplishments," said Ike.[3] (But whether Patton had personally shot men or not, there was no doubt his bravery was tinged with luck. Four days later, a 700-pound German railway shell fell within eight feet of him – but it was a dud.[4]) To mark Ike's 54th birthday, Bradley laid on a "very fine dinner" that evening, with a cake featuring crêpes suzettes, Champagne and the SHAEF insignia in icing.[5]

One continuing problem for Ike was the rate of attrition among the Allied troops. The British Prime Minister cabled FDR to say that so many soldiers had been transferred from the Italian front for Operation Dragoon[6] that victory in Italy would be impossible unless fresh troops were committed there. But more Allied troops were also needed in France. For example, the US 1st Division lost 150 men killed and 1,200 wounded taking Aachen, where the German garrison surrendered on 21 October. FDR agreed with the Joint Chiefs of Staff that none of Ike's divisions should be diverted to Italy.

At headquarters in France, the shortage of artillery ammunition was also worrying Ike. The shortage was caused by limited port capacity, restricted distribution, inadequate shipments from the US and the limitation of production

---

[3] at ease, p 279
[4] The Stars and Stripes, 20 October 1944
[5] Diary 14 October 1944
[6] Churchill is said to have named the operation because he was "dragooned" into it

there. The port at Antwerp, which was still surrounded by Germans, was the key to the logistics problem. The Allies had to supply their superior forces with the resources for fighting, but this could not be done during the winter months without the continued use of the port at Antwerp. Antiaircraft weapons were brought in to protect Antwerp and Brussels, and the British Chiefs of Staff agreed that some of the defences used to protect London against V-1s should be moved to the Continent. Ike was ready to fight an all-out battle to cross the Rhine if supplies could be assured through the port. But not everyone agreed with Ike's concentration on taking Antwerp. "When Eisenhower issued these orders he was at Granville on the Cherbourg peninsula, about 500 miles behind the front, he was out of touch," said The Sunday Times military correspondent after the war.[7]

Ike also proposed to launch "flying bombs" against the Germans in the Ruhr. His staff agreed that the rockets would have a major effect on German morale.[8] But although the US Air Force developed a copy of a German flying bomb, SHAEF eventually said that it would require too much shipping, which could not be spared. As winter approached, the weather was also worsening. By 29 October, Ike's caravan near Reims was parked "in a sea of mud". He told Marshall that the Strategic Bomber Forces could not support the infantry because of the bad flying weather. Although the 'heavies' could bomb through cloud using radar, bitter experience showed this technique was not suitable for bombing near Allied ground troops.

Despite Ike's best efforts, there was still friction between the Allies. On 31 October at Versailles, General Joseph T McNarney, US army commander in the Mediterranean, told Ike that the American troops were fighting "much better"

---

[7] The Times of India, 12 December 1948
[8] Diary 20 October 1944, where Kay wrote about the "moral effect" of the rockets

than the British in Italy.[9] Consequently, General Clark in Italy was "very bitter" about General Alexander.[10] Another report said "Americans in Italy are easily angered at any consideration of the relative accomplishments of the Fifth [American] and Eighth [British] armies. The Fifth Army captured Naples, Rome and Florence, as well as many fairly large cities in Western Italy. The Eighth Army has done comparatively little. The casualties on the American side have been far greater and American private soldiers, even, comment on this." But Ike had other things to think about – he wanted the area around the Dutch town of Vlissingen bombed to limit infantry casualties in a forthcoming attack, but Churchill objected to civilians being killed.

In Monty's sector, the British press were again calling for a deputy ground commander for SHAEF, in the hope that Monty would be put in charge of the entire battle front. But 62 of the 94 Allied divisions were American and 11 were French, with the remainder under Monty's command, split between the British, Canadians and Poles. Ike's new directive for the ground battle, superseding his directive of 4 September, outlined three general phases:

1) the battle west of the Rhine, taking any opportunity to seize bridgeheads;

2) operations leading to the capture of bridges over the Rhine and deployment of Allied forces on the east bank and

3) the advance from the Rhine into Germany.

On 3 November, Monty reported that the Germans were no longer interfering with the approaches to Antwerp, and the Royal Navy could now ensure full use of the port. Ike was elated – and his mood was improved even further when he

---

[9] 10 October 1944, Memorandum concerning Anglo-American relations in Italy
[10] Diary 31 October 1944

was presented with a gold watch by grateful Americans and British for liberating Paris.[11] But his elation was shortlived. General Betts told him a couple of days later that "disciplinary conditions in the army" were worsening. The high incidence of rape, murder and pillage had led to numerous complaints from the French and Dutch authorities. Ike and Beetle discussed the particularly poor discipline of the 101st and 82nd US Airborne Divisions. Ike said that "strong measures" would have to be taken in the cases of "rape, pillage etc".[12] He even suggested public hangings, particularly in the case of rape. Officers were assigned to investigate the complaints and report back to Ike personally.[13]

Ike – whose bad leg was examined on 19 November by a doctor from London – was also worried about soldiers getting trench foot, of which there were "numerous cases" in the evacuation hospitals.[14] He knew that General Patton was providing troops in foxholes with dry socks every day. Meanwhile, wounded American soldiers returning to the US were complaining about their poor treatment. Marshall ordered Ike to inspect the hospitals, rehabilitation centres and replacement depots in France and England to find out the cause of the complaints. In the United States, the presidential election was held on Tuesday 7 November. President Franklin D Roosevelt, seeking his fourth term in office, beat Republican Thomas E Dewey,[15] despite FDR's worsening health.[16] Election results were played over the loudspeaker at the Scribe Hotel, but no one seemed particularly interested. (Within six months, FDR had died; he was replaced by Vice President Harry S Truman.) There

---

[11] Diary 3 November 1944

[12] There was "a lot of drunkenness, some rape and several score desertions" in the 82nd and 101st Airborne Divisions (Siegfried, p 75)

[13] Diary 5 and 6 November 1944

[14] Diary 16 November 1944. Siegfried (p 75) says the US 84th Division lost 500 men to trench foot

[15] By 53.39% of the popular vote to 45.89%

[16] He was a "dying man", according to a Connecticut businessman, Chicago Tribune, 19 April 1953

was another piece of good news on 12 November – the RAF had sunk the German battleship Tirpitz in Norway, killing more than 1,000 German sailors.

In France, the thick wintry fog and snow continued. Churchill and de Gaulle inspected French units 12 miles from the front, but the worsening wintry weather meant that 20 of the group's 30 cars could not complete the journey.[17] Ike said tanks and infantry could take the offensive only if there were a spell of good weather, instead of mud, ice and snow. But notwithstanding Ike's concerns about the weather, he still seemed "fairly vague as to what was really going on". Field Marshal Brooke suspected it was "another case of Eisenhower's complete inability to run the land battle as well as acting as Supreme Commander".[18]

In Paris, crowds at the *Arc de Triomphe* cheered as General de Gaulle presented Churchill with the freedom of the city. The next day, 14 November, Ike met the French presidential train at Reims, and took the PM back to the camp for lunch where they discussed changes of command.[19] One of the lunch guests was British Field Marshal Alan Brooke, who afterwards wrote: "When we lunched with Ike I was interested to see that Kay [Summersby] his chauffeur had now been promoted to hostess, and sat at the head of the table with Winston [Churchill] on her right. In Versailles she had been promoted to personal secretary and ran the lobby next to his office. Now she had moved one step up the ladder. In doing so Ike produced a lot of undesirable gossip which did him no good."[20] Brooke seemed unaware that Ike often asked Kay to preside as hostess at his more formal dinners. "We have no secrets from Kay," Ike once told Churchill, who was sitting on her right.

In the autumn of 1944, Eisenhower had a brownish nodule (which could have been skin cancer) removed from his

[17] Daily Herald, 14 November 1944
[18] War Diaries 1939-1945 p 624
[19] CHAR 20/174/111
[20] Alan Brooke "Notes on my Life", Vol XIV (14 November 1944)

trunk. Kay Summersby's book refers to an "infected cyst", but the 'cyst' proved to be harmless. While Ike was ill, he was visited by Merrill 'Red' Mueller, an NBC broadcaster in the pool assigned to SHAEF Forward.[21] Ike was furious that Mueller seemed attracted to Kay, even though she maintained that she was not interested. Ike then replaced the press pool with one correspondent who would travel in a car with the official photographers.

In the United States, the newly-created Women's Army Corps[22] did not seem to be fulfilling its potential. General Marshall said that "very poor use" had been made of publicity possibilities.[23] "The first group of WAC officers sent to Africa were on a boat which was torpedoed and they made the shore with a loss of most of their clothing," he said. "General Eisenhower's driver has been a WAC throughout the entire African campaign[24] and I presume she has gone with him to London." Kay wasn't yet a WAC, but Ike was still keen that she should be commissioned. Marshall told the head of the Women's Army Corps, Colonel Oveta Hobby, on 31 October 1944 that Ike had decided to commission Kay directly, and that his decision was "final". Kay was the only non-US woman in the European theatre to be commissioned in this way.

On 20 November 1944, Kay was sworn in as a WAC second lieutenant,[25] SHAEF'S Adjutant General TJ Davis pinning on her gold bars. Now she was no longer a "shadow freak civilian". She still breakfasted with Ike and drove to the office with him, but now sitting next to him in the back of the car. Three days after Kay became a WAC, Shellburst was

---

[21] Diary notes, 5 January 1945

[22] Formerly the Women's Army Auxiliary Corps

[23] Memo for Bureau of Public Relations, 26 January 1944, Washington DC

[24] That was inaccurate, as Kay only became a WAC in October of that year

[25] US Dept of Justice naturalisation form, 16 January 1951. As a lieutenant, Kay earned "£45 a month, plus overseas allowances". She joined the WACs "for the duration plus six months" (p 3, Cork Examiner, 13 June 1945)

moved to the schoolhouse in Reims, where the Germans were eventually to surrender.

At a news conference at the Scribe on 21 November, Ike praised the British for clearing the port of Antwerp despite heavy losses. The bombing of Germany was continuing, despite the poor weather, but the enemy's morale was still not broken. Ike blamed the secret police. "As early as August it became evident all along the front, the German was fighting in many instances because the Gestapo made him," said Ike. "The Gestapo's control is as firm as ever, as far as we can see, so the German is going to battle it out to the end." But where and when would the end be? One of the correspondents said that, two weeks earlier, Stalin had said that the Red Army would be in Berlin soon. "Good for him," said Ike. "He will do a good job there, I think."

All the Allies had their own plans for the future of Germany and the German people. The Morgenthau Plan envisaged the destruction of all German industry and its replacement by a pastoral economy. German industrialists were not only buying agricultural property in Germany but were sending their funds abroad, particularly to neutral countries like Switzerland through banks such as the *Schweizerische Kreditanstalt* of Zurich and the *Basler Handelsbank*. Some Swiss agencies would also buy property in Switzerland for a 5 per cent commission. But who would work on those properties? Neither FDR nor the British Prime Minister could give the Germans assurances about the post-war employment of German labour without consulting the Soviet leader. Stalin wanted several million Germans to be transported to the Soviet Union for years to repair war damage. Churchill reminded FDR that the Germans were terrified of occupation by the Russians and feared that they could be shipped to Siberia to be worked to death.

Meanwhile, in Reims, while Ike was busy winning the war, he still found time to play golf with Kay. Indeed, Brooke commented in his diary that Ike was "detatched [sic] and by himself with his lady chauffeur in [sic] the golf links at

Reims...Personally, I think he is incapable of running the war even if he tries". [26] But Brooke wasn't the only one concerned with Ike's fixation with golf to the apparent exclusion of his other duties. It was just like Ike's games of golf with Kay at Telegraph Cottage. [27] Brooke said that matters had got so bad that Beetle Smith "and a few others went up to tell him that he must get down to it and RUN the war, which he said he would". Brooke proposed that Omar Bradley be made commander of land forces in France, with Tedder working closely with him as air commander. The front should then be divided into two groups of armies, one north of the Ardennes under Monty and the other south of the Ardennes under Patton. This would have deterred the Germans from attacking the weak American troops between the two other army groups in the subsequent Battle of the Bulge.

But fighting was not the only problem. Cigarette supplies were also becoming scarce. The PX (Post Exchange) allotment was down to two packs a week in the rear areas, including the Scribe, and five at the front. (Ike smoked four packs a day. [28] The ration of cigars – which Ike didn't smoke – was five a week.) Because of the cigarette shortage, Ike told Kay to cut down his smoking to the rear-area ration. But as she couldn't smoke during office hours, she secretly shared part of her own ration with him.

Smoking was a habit Ike had developed over many years, since West Point. "Cigarette smoking, if discovered, brought serious penalties. So I started smoking cigarettes," he said. [29] As a 'roll your own' smoker, he was disciplined for "smoking

---

[26] Brooke said this caused "widespread offence" in the US while Ike was President (War Diaries, footnote p 628). The White House denied that Ike had played golf in Reims: (The Victoria Advocate, 6 November 1959)
[27] Even as president, there were signs that Americans were fed up with "his frequent absences from his desk to play golf in Washington or at his retreat in Augusta, Ga"
[28] at ease, p 354
[29] at ease, p 16

in room during call to quarters".[30] After the war, Ike was told to cut his smoking from four packs of cigarettes a day to one. After a few days, he decided that counting his cigarettes was worse than not smoking at all, so he stopped smoking permanently. "I just put smoking out of my mind," he said, "and developed a scornful attitude toward those weaklings who did not have the will power to break their enslavement to tobacco." He later told a news conference: "I'm a little like the fellow who said I don't know whether I'll start again, but I'll never stop again."[31]

But cigarettes weren't Ike's only vice. So was the use of bad language. Reading the US papers, Ike would wince when he saw himself quoted as saying "hell," yet it was part of his everyday speech – like "Now let me tell you something..." or "This world and then the fireworks". But whenever anything was printed about him that hinted even slightly at profanity, he received mail from soldiers' parents, particularly Americans. After the US newspapers reported that Ike used "a good deal of profanity, "one nice lady out in Texas wrote him a letter about it; she said he ought to pray, instead of cursing. The General was sort of annoyed by that, and hurt, too. He said: 'Damn it (but he didn't really say just 'Damn it') I don't curse, I just use some words as adjectives'".[32]

The continuing row between Ike and Montgomery about who should command the US and British forces raised its head once more. On 30 November, Monty said the main thrust into Germany must be so strong that success would be certain, but he repeated that there should be one commander north of the Ardennes (and suggested that *he* should be that commander). Ike's reply – to "Dear Monty" from "Ike" – said he didn't know what Monty meant. As far as Ike was concerned, the primary objective should be to

[30] 17 January 1915
[31] http://archive.tobacco.org/resources/history/Tobacco_History20-2.html
[32] Sgt Mickey and General Ike, p 50

defeat Germany. The rear was clear of the enemy[33] so the Allies could face forwards. More than 40,000 Germans had been captured, which greatly exceeded Allied losses.

The British field marshal responded in a letter dated 2 December saying he was disturbed by Ike's request that Monty "not continue to look upon the past performances of this great fighting force as a failure". Monty said he had simply declared that the SHAEF directive of 28 October had not been carried out. But he said there would be a lot of advantages to having General Bradley under his command. "Of course he is completely crazy to even think of such a thing," Kay wrote in the diary.[34] Ike apologised (through gritted teeth) for misreading Monty's original letter, and then added in the diary: "One of Monty's main troubles is that he is never very willing to listen to any view point except his own."[35] But Monty had the ear of then-Field Marshal Brooke who believed that "Eisenhower completely fails as Supreme Commander and just does nothing". Brooke said Monty had sent him a "long and despondent letter" about the Normandy campaign "drifting in a rudderless condition".[36] (In his 1958 memoirs, Monty accused Eisenhower of prolonging the war for a year by his poor leadership.)

Later in December, Monty wrote asking permission to spend Christmas with his son in England. He reminded Ike that he had bet him £5 on 11 October in Italy that the war would still be continuing by Christmas 1944. "For payment, I think, at Christmas," he noted. Ike protested that he still had nine days until Christmas 1944. By then, the weather was absolutely freezing. It was so cold that, when Butch took Mollie Ford to the *Folies Bergère* in Paris on 2 December, everyone wore their overcoats. SHAEF was informed that

---

[33] It wasn't. German troops on Alderney, for example, did not surrender until 16 May 1945
[34] 2 December 1944
[35] Diary 9 December 1944
[36] Alan Brooke war diaries, 20 November 1944

Allied prisoners in German custody would not have enough fuel, clothing or bedding for the freezing weather.

But Ike's spirits were lifted when the chairman of the House Military Affairs Committee arrived in France with a bottle of Kentucky bourbon. Butch asked the censor to add in the story that "General Eisenhower sent the whisky to a near-by field hospital." But Ike told Butch that the committee would know that was a lie because he and the Congressmen had drunk the bourbon before lunch! On 12 December, Ike and Tedder met Churchill and the British chiefs-of-staff in London. Ike outlined his plan to advance on two broad fronts, north of the Rhine and via Frankfurt, by May 1945. However, Brooke said that Allied troops should be concentrated for a single thrust against the Germans.[37]

But the form of the battles was not the only topic of conversation. The big story in mid-December was the disappearance of American band leader Glenn Miller. On 15 December 1944, Miller went missing during a flight from London to Paris in a small single-engine Norseman plane. Some suggested that the plane had been hit by a jettisoned bomb from an RAF Lancaster bomber returning from an aborted raid on a town near Cologne. Another suggestion was that Miller was killed by the Germans while on a mission for Ike to discuss peace terms with von Rundstedt.

The following day, Ike announced that he was being promoted to General of the Army with 5 stars – only the sixth in America's history.[38] (Washington and Pershing were appointed 'General of the Armies', an even higher rank.) Ike decided to wear a small circle of five stars, despite staff speculation that he would wear a straight line of five big stars. This collar insignia was worn with Ike's combat jacket, and only the new licence plates on his car showed that he was a General of the Army. Ike had risen from Lieutenant-

---

[37] Alan Brooke war diaries, 12 December 1944
[38] Churchill had teased General Marshall earlier in 1944 that the reason why America didn't have field marshals was that he didn't want to be known as "Field Marshal Marshall"

Colonel to five-star general in three years, three months and 16 days, after being a major for 16 years. But the promotion coincided with the start of the month-long Battle of the Bulge. Ike joked: "It was fortunate that no higher rank could be conferred."[39]

Ike also had to deal with more reports of misconduct by American troops. He was concerned at the growing "avalanche of reports from every type of source" about the misbehaviour of American troops. Every week there were more reports of rape, murder and looting in France and Holland, despite the fact that Ike later claimed that US troops were "on the whole, free of ruthless vindictiveness or the looting of mercenaries".[40] It was Ike's policy "not to give death sentences to any American soldier accused of raping a German woman".[41] However, on 14 August 1944, black GI Private Clarence Whitfield of the 494th Port Battalion had been executed for raping a Polish farm girl near Omaha Beach two months earlier. Whitfield was hanged on a gallows in the garden of the Chateau de Canisy near Saint Lô. The hangings continued into the new year. On 10 February 1945, on the Cherbourg peninsula, hundreds of black US troops were made to watch the hanging of black US Privates Yancy Waiters and Robert Skinner. They had been convicted of raping a 19-year-old French girl and murdering her boyfriend.

And it wasn't only rape, murder and looting. Desertion because of the fierce fighting was also a problem. On 23 December 1944, during the Ardennes offensive, Ike approved the death sentence imposed on 24-year-old Private Eddie Slovik for desertion. There were 21,049 convicted US deserters, of whom 49 were sentenced to death. At any other time, Ike might have recommended clemency, but now he

---

[39] at ease, p 263
[40] at ease, p 307
[41] Patton diary, 13 November 1945: "This seemed somewhat at variance with Anglo-Saxon customs."

said the execution would discourage other deserters. Slovik was executed by firing squad on 31 January 1945.[42]

---

[42] Slovik's remains were reburied in Detroit in 1987.

BATTLE OF THE BULGE

In what came to be known as the Battle of the Bulge (because of the German bulge in the Allied lines), the Germans – supported by tanks – planned to attack through the Ardennes forest in Belgium and recapture Antwerp. The Germans referred to the battle as *Unternehmen Wacht am Rhein* ("Operation Watch on the Rhine").

The "counter-offensive of considerable strength"[1] caught the Allies off guard. The 200,000 soldiers included fresh troops and Ike saw this as the Germans' "last throw of the dice".[2] The Germans – who even used women in their tank crews[3] – attacked on a 60-mile front, pushing back the Americans 35 miles in Belgium and Luxembourg. If they managed to seize the port at Antwerp, they hoped that the western Allies would negotiate a separate peace treaty, allowing Hitler to concentrate on the continuing battle against the Soviet army on the eastern front. The Germans planned to reach the Meuse in two days and Antwerp in three weeks, cutting off 38 Allied divisions. Ike met senior commanders at Verdun on 19 December to plan an Allied counterattack. Patton said: "We should open up and let 'em get all the way to Paris, then saw 'em off at the base."

During the battle, Ike was also a target again. A German officer captured at Liège on 19 December admitted being part of Operation Gryphon, an assassination squad of 60 Germans equipped with acid capsules to help them escape capture.[4] German agents in Paris provided information about Ike's movements, his security guard and his house in Versailles. All Allied troops were ordered to be off the streets by 8pm, because German paratroopers in American uni-

---

[1] Daily Express, 18 December 1944
[2] Daily Express, 18 December 1944
[3] Daily Express, 11 January 1945
[4] Daily Express, 11 January 1945

forms were being dropped behind US lines. Paris radio also broadcast a warning about Germans driving British or American vehicles and wearing captured Allied uniforms. It was the first time that the Germans had used this ruse which meant "an automatic death sentence for anyone taken prisoner".[5] "Using captured vehicles and weapons is an old trick and perfectly permissible," said the Daily Mail. "In some of the Western Desert mix-ups there were moments when the opposing armies seemed to have exchanged vehicles. But exchanging uniforms is another matter."[6] However, Wing Commander "Tommy" Yeo-Thomas – known to the Gestapo as the White Rabbit – confirmed at the Nuremberg Trials that his men had used the same ruse in France. Late in the war, German radio warned listeners to be on the lookout for four men, "presumably enemy agents", wearing German's officers' uniforms.[7]

US soldiers took various precautions to defend themselves from Germans wearing American uniforms. One MP at a road block asked Butch his native state. Butch answered "Iowa" but, to make certain, the MP asked what large river formed Iowa's eastern boundary. Fortunately Butch knew – unlike General Bradley who was stopped and questioned three times on the way to Spa. He knew that the capital of Illinois was Springfield (though the GI insisted it was Chicago) and he knew where the guard was in American football,[8] but he didn't know who Betty Grable's husband was.[9] One of Patton's officers, Brigadier-General Bruce Clarke, was held for several hours after mistakenly saying that the Chicago Cubs played in the American League.[10] Another victim of the general paranoia was General Montgomery who was held for several hours after failing to convince American troops that he was who he said he was.

---

[5] Daily Mail, 22 December 1944
[6] Alexander Clifford, 22 December 1944
[7] News Chronicle, 26 March 1945
[8] Between the tackles and the centre on the offensive line
[9] Trumpeter Harry James
[10] Rather than the National League

Several genuine Allied soldiers were shot dead in the general confusion.

Because of the assassination threat, Ike was confined to his office, which made him "mad".[11] Soldiers with machine guns guarded the house, and an armed guard accompanied him by jeep to and from the office. When he left the house for a walk in the snow, the security officer hustled him back.[12] By 22 December, the atmosphere at the 12th Army Group headquarters was reminiscent of the German breakthrough at the Kasserine Gap in Tunisia, even though officially the situation in the Ardennes remained "fluid".[13] Ike's order of the day[14] said: "The enemy is making his supreme effort to break out of the desperate plight into which you forced him by your brilliant victories of the summer and fall. He is fighting savagely to take back all that you have won and is using every treacherous trick to deceive and kill you. He is gambling everything, but already, in this battle, your unparalleled gallantry has done much to foil his plans. In the face of your proven bravery and fortitude, he will completely fail. But we cannot be content with his mere repulse. By rushing out from his fixed defenses the enemy has given us the chance to turn his great gamble into his worst defeat. So I call upon every man, of all the Allies, to rise now to new heights of courage, of resolution, and of effort. Let everyone hold before him a single thought: to destroy the enemy on the ground, in the air, everywhere – destroy him!"

For "tactical, geographical and supply reasons", Ike decided to give Monty temporary command of the First and Ninth American armies.[15] However, if the Germans became aware that Monty commanded the northern flank of the bulge and Bradley the southern, the Germans could adapt their tactics,

---

[11] Diary 20 December 1944

[12] Now he knew how it would feel to be President of the USA. "You'll never have to worry about me being President," he responded. (Milwaukee Sentinel, 26 September 1948)

[13] Daily Mail, 22 December 1944

[14] 22 December 1944

[15] New York Journal American, 5 January 1945

being familiar with the two generals' different types of fighting. The London papers suggested the move meant that Monty had come to the rescue of the Americans, and headlines in the US papers said "Monty leading 2 Yank armies",[16] but such reports only further damaged Allied relationships. The British Prime Minister put it another way: "Let no-one lend himself to the chatter of mischief-makers when issues of this most momentous consequence are being successfully decided by the sword."[17] The Allies' weakest spot was around Namur, where the enemy was expected to attack using tanks. Patton was to organise a major counterattack on 23 or 24 December. The general plan was to plug the holes in the north and to launch a co-ordinated attack from the south.

The Battle of the Bulge wasn't the only bad news. On Christmas Eve 1944, Ike and Kay heard about the deaths of 762 US soldiers from the 66th Division whose transport ship, the Léopoldville, had been torpedoed three miles off the coast of Cherbourg. "Very few were saved," wrote Kay.[18] The survivors were ordered not to mention the incident and their letters home were censored for the rest of the war. The files were only opened in the mid-1990s.

Christmas was a period of "storm and stress".[19] Christmas Day was not a holiday for Ike, despite a Christmas turkey being provided by the mess. The fighting was intense and, at Bastogne, the 101st Airborne was fighting an epic battle. German attacks were repelled, thanks to supplies and ammunition dropped from aircraft and gliders, and Patton's 4th Armoured Division got within two and a half miles from the beleaguered American troops. "This time the Kraut's stuck his head in a meat grinder – and this time I've got hold of the handle," said Patton.[20] Butch's girlfriend, Mollie Ford,

---

[16] New York Journal American, 5 January 1945
[17] Statement to House of Commons, 18 January 1945
[18] Diary 24 December 1944
[19] Marshall 'top secret' message to Eisenhower, 22 December 1944
[20] Life magazine, 23 April 1951, p 104

unwittingly drove into the battle at Bastogne while delivering Christmas packages to Red Cross personnel, but wasn't hurt.

The fierce US resistance around Bastogne continued to block German access to key roads. It was "one of the greatest American efforts of the war",[21] said British correspondents. On Boxing Day, Monty said he could not take the initiative until he had more troops. Ike travelled by train to Monty's headquarters on 28 December because fog and ice prevented driving. At the conference, he lent Monty a C-47 plane because Monty's had been "shot up" by the Germans. Monty – who wouldn't let his Chief-of-Staff be present during the conversation with Ike – continued to press to be appointed commander of all the ground forces and "was not very co-operative".[22] But Ike told him that one Army Group commander could not give orders to another; he hoped that he would not have to ask the Combined Chiefs to resolve the matter.

When Ike got back to St Germain, he moved house closer to the office but had to abandon Shellburst again (leaving 25 guards) on 6 January when the Germans broke through the Allied lines. Six days earlier, on New Year's Day, 900 German aircraft had launched a surprise attack on Allied airfields, but the attack was kept so secret that even German anti-aircraft batteries weren't told. Many of the Luftwaffe planes were shot down by the Germans themselves – in all, one third of the attacking aircraft were lost and 237 pilots killed, missing or taken prisoner, the biggest one-day loss for the Luftwaffe in the entire war.

But there was good news for Kay at the start of 1945. In Reims, Ike told her that, on the recommendation of Churchill, she had been awarded the British Empire Medal in the New Year's Honours List "for meritorious services" as "driver to the Supreme Commander, Allied Expeditionary

---

[21] Daily Express, 11 January 1945
[22] Diary 28 December 1944

Force (now serving in the United States Forces)".[23] A letter dated 21 November 1944 from Churchill's Downing Street secretary Kathleen Hill to Sir John Miller Martin, Churchill's principal private secretary, said: "The Prime Minister would like inquiries made about Miss [changed in manuscript to Mrs] Kay Summersby, General Eisenhower's driver, including particulars of her past history. He says that she is English and not American. I understand that Mr. Churchill is thinking of recommending her for a small decoration."[24] The handwritten response of Mr Martin (as he then was) five days later on the letter said: "Mrs Hill, I have taken up the question of an award for Mrs Summersby. JMM"

The medal was presented, with a signed photograph of the Prime Minister,[25] aboard the MV Britannic in New York more than three years later. Kay replied on Shaef notepaper on 13 June 1944: "Dear Prime Minister, I am most grateful for your kindness in sending me an autographed picture. Thank you so much. Yours sincerely, Kay Summersby (Miss) (General Eisenhower's driver)".[26] But there was bad news too. The following day, Ike and Kay heard that Admiral Bertram Ramsay had been one of five people killed when his Hudson crashed at Toussus-le-Noble, near Paris, as he took off for a conference with Montgomery in Brussels. Ike was "very upset" at the news.[27]

Once again, General Betts arrived to discuss courts martial for rape and murder, as he did again on 5 January. Men who had been court-martialled were offered a pardon if they would volunteer for the front. Those who had been sentenced to 15 years' or more hard labour accepted the offer. Very few of those with lighter sentences "chose to abandon the stockade for the risk of combat", said Ike.

---

[23] She was one of 1,070 civilians who received medals in the 1945 New Year's Honours list
[24] 21 November 1944 (12, CHAR 2/493)
[25] Churchill normally made it a rule not to sign photos (70 CHAR 2/493).
[26] 11 CHAR 2/493
[27] Diary 2 January 1945

On 3 January, the Prime Minister arrived with de Gaulle to study the progress of the Battle of the Bulge, which Ike "did not even then seem to quite understand".[28] Ike had ordered the 6th Army Group to withdraw from Alsace and Lorraine[29] to the Vosges to reinforce Patton's troops, but General de Gaulle feared that negative reaction in France to the withdrawal could lead to "an outcry throughout France"[30] and the collapse of his putative government. Ike then modified his order and left two US divisions in the city of Strasbourg to avoid having his supply lines endangered by "massacres". He urged de Gaulle to use French infantry divisions to do the work of US troops, but said privately that "one cannot rely too much on the French".[31]

The following day, Monty began a successful counterattack against the Germans.[32] To relax, Kay and Ike had dinner and played bridge together. [33] On 8 January, Ike attended Admiral Ramsay's memorial service in London then, just as the Germans started to pull back, he ordered all able-bodied men in the rear areas to be retrained and sent into combat.[34] The order included black troops. More than 100,000 black soldiers in Com Zone were to be allowed to volunteer in black combat units.[35] When sufficient infantry platoons were available, Ike hoped to make the black platoons into independent battalions.

Improved weather conditions after Christmas allowed renewed air attacks on German forces and supply lines, though one Allied bombing attack hit a French village which

---

[28] Alan Brooke diary, 3 January 1945
[29] General Giraud, in a message to Churchill more than two years earlier, had said: "I am certain today that, thanks to the efforts of all, Alsace and Lorraine will remain French" (Telegram, 8 November 1942)
[30] Alan Brooke war diaries, 3 January 1945
[31] Diary 12 January 1945
[32] Some German prisoners were shot. "I hope we can conceal this," said Patton (Diary 4 January 1945)
[33] Diary 6 January 1945
[34] Daily Express, 11 January 1945
[35] Diary, 4 January 1945

was supposed to have been evacuated.[36] On 9 January, the British Chiefs again suggested a single commander for ground operations so that the Allies' overwhelming strength could be used in one major thrust, preferably in the north. They told Marshall that Ike had too many pressing duties involving supply and political difficulties – clearly indicating that Monty should take on the role.

Ike was asked to report by 28 January on the progress of his operations, the effect of the German counteroffensive in the Saar and his plans for the rest of the winter and spring. Only now were the Allies starting to count the cost of the Battle of the Bulge. About 19,000 Americans had been killed – the heaviest total in one battle of the whole war – but the Germans lost 83,000 troops killed and wounded and 110,000 who became prisoners of war.[37] The Germans also lost up to 5,000 tanks, assault guns and motor vehicles.[38] Ike sent a review of the campaign to date and his future plans to Marshall on 10 January. He argued that the appointment of a separate commander for ground operations would lead to duplication in personnel and communications. Although the current command organisation might not be ideal, it was practical, as the Germans were now concentrating on battles elsewhere. In the east, the Russians began their advance on 12 January so the remnants of the Sixth Panzer Army were rushed to the eastern front.

On 15 January, Ike was annoyed to find that $100-worth of liquor had been stolen from his headquarters at Shellburst. It was part of a growing problem of theft of Allied supplies by US troops, who sold the goods on the black market.[39] "Thousands of gallons of gas, tons of food and quantities of clothing were being siphoned off each day into the French black market," said General Bradley.[40] Ike said: "That some

---

[36] Diary 9 January 1945

[37] Diary 15 January 1945

[38] Life magazine and diary, 15 January 1945

[39] Diary 15 January 1945

[40] Life magazine, 23 April 1951, p 94

men should give way to the extraordinary temptations of the fabulous prices offered for food and cigarettes was to be expected. But in this case it appeared that practically an entire unit had organized itself into an efficient gang of racketeers and was selling these articles in truck and carload lots."[41] [42]

The following day, Monty reported that his task in the Ardennes had ended, so he was returning the First Army to Bradley's command, as Ike had ordered. (In an earlier newspaper interview, Monty had suggested that he, not the Americans, had beaten the Germans in the Battle of the Bulge. This resulted in an uproar.) The US Ninth Army remained temporarily under Monty's operational command, but all administrative matters, such as supply and replacements, became Bradley's responsibility.

As the Battle of the Bulge ended, domestic matters came to the fore once more. On 22 January, Caacie had a litter of six pups, two of which died. Ike tied a red ribbon around the neck of one of the male pups, which he called "Lop Ear" because one ear was floppy. On Thursday 25 January, Ike had dinner with FDR adviser Harry Hopkins,[43] who went on to spend three nights with the Prime Minister in London. On his return, Hopkins told Ike that up to 15,000 troops could be spared for Europe from US bases elsewhere. Hopkins also expressed the opinion that, after the war, while the military would do its usual job of "getting the water turned on", stopping the sniping and restoring law and order, German commercial life should not be revived. Later Hopkins went to Rome to see Pope Pius XII, and then to Malta for discussions with the Prime Minister and de Gaulle. (Ike

---

[41] Brisbane Courier-Mail, 27 November 1948, p 2

[42] German propaganda claimed: "The black-market crooks find an endless supply of contemptible customers eager to pay preposterous prices for beefsteaks, whisky, nylon hose and gasoline." (Leaflet 331-11-44, November 1944)

[43] Divorced from Ethel Gross, by whom he had three sons, he was later accused of being a Soviet agent and of allowing his third wife to accept a gift of $500,000-worth of emeralds from a media tycoon

believed that Pope Pius XII was really on the Allied side, following a secret session at the US embassy with FDR's emissary to the Vatican in early October 1942. In fact, the Pope had sent a blessed rosary and a special Papal blessing for the wedding of Ike's orderly in Paris in December 1944.)

Back in England, General Montgomery talked about his "depression" with the American strategy and with Ike's "inability to retain a definite policy without waffling about". [44] The British agreed that Ike's appreciation of strategy was "awful". [45] The French also came in for some criticism. At SHAEF Main on Saturday 27 January, Ike had a heart-to-heart with General de Gaulle about the fighting prowess of the French Army in the Colmar pocket. De Gaulle's Chief-of-Staff, General Juin, asked whether Ike felt that the First French Army was not doing its job properly. De Gaulle said the French combat troops were tired, but Ike pointed out that the American soldiers moving from the Ardennes to reinforce French troops in Alsace had been fighting since July and were also tired! Butch said afterwards that Britain and America were treating the French like a spoiled child getting over the mumps. The more that was done for the patient, the more fractious he became.

While Ike was in England, Kay borrowed skis to go skiing in the Versailles hills, but quickly gave up because she feared breaking her leg on the frozen snow. Later, back in France, Ike went by train to meet General Marshall at Château Valmante, near Marseille, before the meetings of the Combined Chiefs of Staff (or the "Charlie-Charlies", as Ike called them) in Malta on 29-30 January and at the Yalta conference.

On Sunday, FDR arrived in Gibraltar on his way to the Malta meeting, but Ike told the President he couldn't leave his command in France to go to Malta. He arranged for Beetle

---

[44] Alan Brooke war diaries, 25 January 1945
[45] Alan Brooke war diaries, 31 January 1945

to represent him. Ike returned to his HQ after Marshall confirmed to him that he was against appointing a separate ground commander-in-chief, the main topic that was expected to be considered in Malta. In fact the big argument at the meeting on 30 January would be between Marshall, who wanted to finish the war against Germany first, and Admiral King, who preferred to concentrate on the Pacific. Beetle told the Combined Chiefs that the Rhine would be crossed in the north as soon as the situation in the south allowed.

Back in France, Ike said the fact that the Russians were not taking large numbers of prisoners on the eastern front indicated that the Germans were withdrawing towards the west, rather than standing and fighting. Stalin reckoned his armies would have to stop at the Oder and await the build-up of supplies before pushing on. The Soviet leader said there were German saboteurs and spies in areas recently overrun by the Russians, and he warned Ike to look out for spies when the western Allies occupied Germany. There was more snow on 2 February, followed by sleet and rain.

The Yalta Conference from 4-11 February at the Livadia Palace in Crimea was the second wartime conference involving the Big Three,[46] FDR, Winston Churchill and Josef Stalin.[47] The Allies agreed to prioritise the unconditional surrender of Germany. They confirmed that, after the war, Germany (and separately Berlin) would be divided into four occupied zones. France's zone would have to be carved out of the American and British zones[48] but, according to FDR, France was to be left out of the post-war security talks.[49] Germany would be demilitarised and denazified, and German reparations were to be partly in the form of forced labour. There would be a 'reparation council' based in the

---

[46] The Tehran Conference was in 1943, and the Potsdam Conference in July 1945
[47] General de Gaulle was not invited
[48] Churchill pressed at Yalta for France to be given an occupation zone – Churchill, p 327
[49] Daily Express, 25 October 1944

Soviet Union. Land would be transferred from Germany to western Poland. Soldiers fighting for Germany who had been citizens of the Soviet Union or of Yugoslavia or the Baltic states (and their families) were to be handed back to their countries of origin, whether they agreed or not.

On 9 February, the Canadians began Operation Veritable, intended to prepare the way for the large-scale Rhine crossing planned by Monty. An 11-hour artillery barrage blasted German defences, with 1,500 planes in support on a five-mile front – a typical Monty attack.

Since 6 June, the Germans had lost 860,000 prisoners-of-war to the Allies, while those killed or seriously wounded numbered well over 400,000. Enough German tanks and assault guns had been lost to refit 30 Panzer divisions. The battle for the Roer dams, which had begun three months before, ended the following day when the First US Army took control of the intact Schwammanuel Dam. The Germans had not completely blown up the dams but had jammed the floodgates to flood the Roer River for as long as possible. Despite the German losses, many Allied soldiers believed the fighting would continue until they were eventually killed. They had good cause to worry. If Germany wasn't conquered by June 1945, the improving production of German jets[50] and rocket planes would make the Allies' 1,000-bomber raids too expensive in terms of lives and planes.

Meanwhile, Ike hadn't forgotten about Kay becoming a US citizen. On 13 February 1945, Col 'Tex' Lee wrote to the US authorities about Kay's application. A reply from Acting Commissioner TB Shoemaker[51] said his office was "deeply desirous" of fulfilling Kay's ambition, but he pointed out that Kay had not been in the US before 1 July 1944 and was not a US resident when she was made a WAC officer almost six months later. At least three years' service in the US military

---

[50] The jet planes travel at "470 miles an hour", said Patton (Diary, 16 January 1945)
[51] Letter of 22 February 1945

was required as an alternative to the usual five years' continuous residence in the United States. Shoemaker suggested that Kay return to the US, leave the WACs, establish a residence in the States and then re-enlist as a WAC.

DRESDEN

Ike spent Valentine's Day[1] defending the previous night's attack on the ancient eastern German city of Dresden. Up to 100,000 civilians had been killed in the attacks by 8,000 Allied bombers. Ike had already indicated his support for Allied bombing policy. "I am feeling enthusiastic about the destructive air raids on German towns," he said. "If I could, I would pick out every day a German town in order to have it obliterated."[2] In 2005, Sir Michael Beetham, president of the Bomber Command Association, said the 'bomb Dresden' order had come down "from then Prime Minister Winston Churchill and US Allied Commander Dwight D Eisenhower".[3]

The historic Saxon city had so far not been bombed[4] and was full of refugees. But the Allies were determined to "cause confusion in the evacuation from the East",[5] even at this late stage of the war. The British press said that "more than 1,350" US bombers, escorted by "more than 900" fighters, took part in the raid after a night attack by "1,400 planes of RAF Bomber Command".[6] The bombers created a firestorm with a new 30-pound fire-bomb which was "dropped by parachute and shoots out a roasting jet of flame 15 feet long and two feet wide...An aerial 'blow-torch' of terrifying power, the bomb drifts down to the roofs and into the streets of German cities in clouds".[7] The flames of the burning city could be seen hundreds of miles away.

---

[1] He turned down FDR's invitation to attend a conference in Egypt "due to urgent need for his presence at his headquarters"
[2] United Press, 28 December 1943
[3] http://www.dailymail.co.uk/news/article-337667/British-anger-Dresden-portrayal.html
[4] Because Churchill's niece lived there, it was rumoured
[5] Memo from the chief of the air staff, Marshal of the RAF Sir Charles Portal, January 1945
[6] Evening Standard, 14 February 1945
[7] Daily Mail, 24 August 1944

One nine-year-old survivor recalled the horror of the aerial attacks more than half a century later.[8] Lothar Metzger lived with his mother and four sisters in Dresden. His soldier-father had gone missing the previous summer and his five-month-old baby twin sisters died in the bombing attacks. "Explosion after explosion. It was beyond belief, worse than the blackest nightmare," said Metzger. "We saw terrible things: cremated adults shrunk to the size of small children, pieces of arms and legs, dead people, whole families burnt to death, burning people ran to and fro, burnt coaches filled with civilian refugees, dead rescuers and soldiers, many were calling and looking for their children and families, and fire everywhere."

The Allies initially claimed that the city was a strategic target. "The Germans may be using Dresden – almost as large as Manchester – as their base against [Soviet marshal] Koniev's[9] left flank," said the Evening Standard. In fact, the movements were not of troops moving eastwards to fight, but of refugees fleeing westwards. The Russians were now within 50 miles of Berlin. As the scale of the civilian casualties became clear, the Allied leaders began to disclaim responsibility for the raid. According to a report from General Spaatz: "The heaviest attacks were made by the RAF on the night of 13/14 February 1945 and by Eighth Air Force the following day. Due to the proximity of these two attacks and the absence of intervening photographic coverage, it has been impossible to allocate damage to the attacking air forces." Yet the report was careful to point out that "the RAF dropped 1181.6 tons of incendiaries, whereas the Eighth Air Force dropped only 296.5 tons of incendiaries".[10]

Six weeks after the attacks, Churchill sent a top-secret letter to his chief military assistant, General 'Pug' Ismay, saying that the policy of bombing German cities "simply for the

---

[8] Lothar Metzger, Berlin, May 1999
[9] The Soviet marshal's name was Ivan Stepanovich Konev (in Russian ко́иев)
[10] US Strategic Air Forces in Europe HQ reply to W-49485

sake of increasing the terror" should be reconsidered, otherwise the Allies would "come into control of an utterly ruined land" and would not even have access to building materials. Churchill said the destruction of Dresden remained "a serious query against the conduct of Allied bombing" and there should be a "more precise concentration upon military objectives, such as oil and communications behind the immediate battle-zone, rather than on mere acts of terror and wanton destruction, however impressive".[11]

Separately, in France, Ike was still fighting the Germans on French soil – a strong German garrison held out at the mouth of the Gironde, preventing use of the port of Bordeaux. But even while the Allies were fighting to free France, the press criticised the Allies for their lack of deference to the French government, and for failing to bring in more railway rolling stock and food to the country. However, not everyone was short of food. The new quarters of Ike – known as the "château general"[12] – in Reims were in a château on the golf links built by the "big champagne merchants".[13] At the schoolhouse, Ike promoted Kay to First Lieutenant (though she was still signing herself "2nd Lt., W.A.C., Secretary" in April 1945[14]) and made her his official aide with a special insignia, a circle of five white stars on a blue shield topped by an eagle.

Allied military operations were continuing to go well. Early on the morning of Friday 23 February, six US infantry divisions crossed the Roer River in Operation Grenade, leading to the occupation of a large area of Germany west of the Rhine. At dinner, Ike talked until midnight about the military successes. The next day, he held his first press conference since November at the Scribe. In a one-hour address, he said the Battle of the Bulge had been a "dangerous episode", but he had not been afraid until he

---

[11] Top secret telegram (later withdrawn and amended), 30 March 1945
[12] War Diaries, p xvii
[13] Alan Brooke diary, 14 November 1944
[14] Letter to Herbert Dessert, Fall River, Massachusetts, 9 April 1945

read the American newspapers two weeks afterwards. The US troops had eventually "wrecked the Nazis' time schedule".[15] But Ike was to be rudely reminded of the war when he took a trip to the front in a snowstorm from a small airfield nine miles from Cologne. Just as the plane got airborne, a German artillery shell landed about 100 yards away.

Meanwhile, the Prime Minister hoped to appoint Field Marshal Alexander deputy supreme commander, a British position in the SHAEF organisation. The British hoped that Alexander would make good the perceived deficiencies of Ike who they considered had "a very very limited brain from a strategic point of view".[16]

---

[15] at ease, p 291

[16] Alan Brooke war diaries, 6 March 1945

DISARMED ENEMY FORCES

Hundreds of thousands of German soldiers were now being taken prisoner by the Allies. One of Ike's most controversial decisions in 1945 was to hold them in camps as Disarmed Enemy Forces (DEFs), rather than prisoners of war (POW). On 10 March, Ike sought Washington's authorisation not to release German POWs held on German soil, but to classify them as Disarmed Enemy Forces. DEFs would not be subject to the Geneva Convention,[1] their accommodation and food did not need to be up to a certain standard, they were not entitled to medical care or food parcels, and the Red Cross had no right to inspect their camps. Ike said they were to be given "no shelter or other comforts", including medical attention. He said the Swiss Red Cross had no jurisdiction to inspect the 19 camps, because DEFs were not covered by the Geneva Convention. The Third Geneva Convention (in 1949) specified that soldiers who "fall into the power" of the enemy following surrender are protected, as well as those taken prisoner while fighting. By September 1945, 692,895 German prisoners were held by the US Army as prisoners of war, while 363,587 were classified as Disarmed Enemy Forces. The DEFs were provided with inadequate rations – the whole of Europe was suffering from the shortage of food – but the prisoners were also held without shelter, toilets or medical treatment. The few US soldiers who tried to help them said they were threatened with court-martial.

The German prisoners were held in the camps for five months, from mid-April until September 1945. Thousands of all ages – particularly the very young, very old, sick, injured and women – died of disease, brutality and starvation in the

---

[1] When the US declared war, the State Department declared that the US would comply fully with the 1929 Geneva Convention. (Prisoners of War: Repatriation or Internment in Wartime, Charles H Murphy, 20 July 1971, CRS-13)

Rheinwiesenlager (or Rhine Meadow Camps). Colonel Ernest Fisher of the 101st Airborne Division, said that German soldiers in the American and French zones "were crowded into barbed wire cages, many of them literally shoulder to shoulder...Open to the weather, lacking even primitive sanitary facilities, underfed, the prisoners soon began dying of starvation and disease".[2]

While the Germans endured their harsh treatment, Tooey Spaatz brought his guitar and three WAC entertainers to Ike's house. Two of the WACs played the piano, while Spaatz strummed the guitar and everyone sang. During dinner on 7 March, Ike took a phone call from General Bradley with some surprisingly good news. "It's the best break we've had," he said. "To hell with the planners. Get across with whatever you need – but make certain you hold that bridgehead."[3] Ike told his dinner guests that Hodges had come across an intact bridge across the Rhine at Remagen and already had troops across. Ike authorised five more divisions to hold the bridgehead.

Several German officers who had been ordered to destroy the intact Ludendorff Bridge in Remagen were subsequently court-martialled, and Hitler relieved Generalfeldmarschall Gerd von Rundstedt of command in the west. The Germans then attempted to destroy the bridge by various means, including attacks by jet bombers, frogmen planting explosives on the supports and even V-2 missiles. The original bridge eventually collapsed on 17 March, but by that stage the Allies had built three more pontoon bridges half a mile downriver. By then, the bridge, with its centre span hanging from the stone piers, had not been used for five days. Engineers with welding torches were trying to strengthen the steel beams. Another 24 hours, said Bradley, and the bridge would have stood for generations. Now it was a monument to those soldiers who had taken the bridgehead, and to the 18 engineers who fell to their deaths when

---

[2] Foreword to Other Losses by James Baque. The statistics are disputed
[3] Life magazine, 30 April 1951, General Omar N Bradley, p 64

the span collapsed. Eight days after the collapse, Allied forces broke out of the bridgehead across the Rhine.

Now the issue was who would reach Berlin first: the western Allies or the Russians. Ike later claimed that, even if the western Allies had occupied Berlin, they would then have had to pull back out of the Soviet zone. Ike said that the capture of Berlin itself would not lead to a collapse of the Nazi regime – despite the fact that his own diary had talked about "a single dagger thrust to Berlin". He said the conquest of the Ruhr would have more serious repercussions, as it provided almost two thirds of Germany's crude steel capacity and more than half of its coal production.

On 14 March, Ike said in a memo that censorship was needed only for military security, and the term "blackout" should never be used. Normal censorship procedures should eliminate "glaring inaccuracies or statements damaging to Allied progress". It had also been the practice not to name units. (During the battle of Normandy, one British correspondent wrote: "Tomorrow perhaps we shall be able to write of one or two things that are secret at the moment."[4]) But from now on, armies should be referred to by the name of the commander and the army's numerical designation, such as "Hodges' First Army".

The next day, Kay drove Ike from the *École Supérieure* near the station in Reims to the headquarters of the 101st Airborne Division to present a Presidential citation. Ike took the salute as more than 200 Kansas paratroopers marched behind the Stars and Stripes and the official state flag of Kansas. It was rare for Ike to meet soldiers from Kansas; even more rare for them to come from the same town as him. "He found boys from Kansas, and sometimes boys who lived near Abilene, or had been in Abilene. But he never actually got to talk to any boy from Abilene," said Master Sgt

---

4 Daily Express, 18 August 1944

Mickey McKeogh.[5] After a lunch with pie and ice cream for dessert (banned for British troops in Belgium because of the danger of typhoid[6]), Ike drove to a nearby field where the whole division was drawn up for review.

Despite his hatred for the Germans, Ike had to contact them on 16 March 1945, when 131 German prisoners suffocated in boxcars – 104 at Mailly le Camp and 27 at Attichy. Ike sent his "profound regrets" to the German high command via the US legation in Berne. Ike said he had "taken steps" to prevent the recurrence of a similar incident. "If it is found that United States personnel were guilty of negligence, appropriate action will be taken," he said. Speaking to Kay, Ike expressed his irritation about having to apologise to the Germans for anything.

It wasn't only the Germans who were causing problems. General Patton wrote to the "scurrilous"[7] Stars and Stripes newspaper, saying that, if the paper continued to carry the cartoons of Bill Mauldin, he would bar the newspaper's reporters and photographers and would not allow the paper to circulate in his Third Army area. Patton objected to the slovenly, dirty and unshaven appearance of GIs portrayed by Mauldin in his characters Willie and Joe. (Patton's colleague, General Terry Allen, said he would not tolerate "Mauldins" in the 104th Infantry Division,[8] but Mauldin was later used to illustrate Life magazine's excerpts from General Bradley's book, A Soldier's Story.)

Ike's physical condition was worsening, with his bad leg being tended by a London doctor and a continuous cold so, on 19 March 1945, he took advantage of the offer of a "very rich American" to stay at a villa, *Sous le Vent* (Under the Wind), at Cannes on the French Riviera. The b*elle epoque* villa had six bedrooms and bathrooms on three floors. Its

---

[5] Sgt Mickey and General Ike, p 58
[6] Daily Mail, 19 January 1945
[7] Patton diary, 13 January 1945
[8] Terrible Terry Allen (Presidio Press, 2003) by Gerald Astor

secluded gardens overlooked the Mediterranean and had direct access to two sheltered sandy beaches.

Kay and a few other members of "the family" accompanied Ike on the "super secret" train trip and, once they arrived, Ike never left the villa. Omar Bradley brought two WAC girls but no other staff. For the first 48 hours, Ike slept. When he had recuperated, he would take lunch on the terrace, with two or three glasses of white wine. Apart from one trip to Monte Carlo, Kay stayed with Ike for the four days and they sunbathed together on the terrace overlooking the Med. General Everett Hughes, who was another visitor, spoke to 'Tex' about the relationship between Ike and Kay, but they agreed to do nothing about it.

Meanwhile, with the Remagen bridgehead enlarged, and Patton across the Rhine further up, Monty crossed the river supported by two divisions of the First Allied Airborne Army. Later he took Winston Churchill across the Rhine too.[9] The Allied armies had trapped five or six German divisions by seizing the Ludendorff Bridge. Its capture had "rendered tremendous dividends to the Allied cause" and Marshall said that "certainly a citation apparently would seem to be called for".[10] Patton was able to cross the Rhine because of the "crucifixion" of German forces east of the river and because the Americans were now building more bridges across the Rhine. (One engineer built a bridge over the river in a record ten hours and eleven minutes.)

Returning to the front, Ike watched the progression of the Ninth Army. "The most terrible job in warfare is to be a second lieutenant leading a platoon when you are on the battlefield," he murmured. (His orderly had been told that "the average life of an officer in combat was less than a minute"![11]) Ike notified the Combined Chiefs that the battles west of the Rhine had resulted in the destruction of many of the enemy forces. The two bridgeheads seized by Bradley's

---

9 News Chronicle, 26 March 1945
10 Memo from General Marshall to Ike, 16 March 1945
11 Sgt Mickey and General Ike, p 8

soldiers could now be exploited to support Monty's operation. At sea, however, things did not look so good. For five or six weeks, U-boats had been waging a very successful campaign against Allied supply ships, and there were indications that losses would become even more severe.

In Paris on 28 March, at a press conference, Ike reviewed the campaign to date. He then had about 4,600,000 troops under his command. The Allies had now reached the end of one phase of the campaign and were entering another. He had believed from the beginning that the Germans must be decisively defeated west of the Rhine. If they stood and fought, the Allies could "knock off a very large proportion" of their forces. The Rhine was "a definite geographical and military feature that any military plan must take into consideration", he said. Quarter of a million Germans had been captured since 1 March "and, without making any allowances at all for their killed and wounded, you see what a quarter of a million Germans left today on the east side of the Rhine would mean". However, Ike said that not all of the Germans were of the quality of SS troops, nor did they all, "like Ramcke[12] at Brest, fight to the bitter end". (Ramcke eventually surrendered on 19 September 1944 after destroying the port facilities. Saint-Malo had been captured on 17 August 1944, but its port facilities had been sabotaged by the defenders. A German garrison at nearby Cézembre Island only surrendered after days of heavy shelling by warships and air strikes involving the use of napalm.)

Ike praised the Navy's defence of sea communications and transport of supplies, maintenance and reinforcements, but said there was no such word in his dictionary as air support for ground or vice versa. "It's a ground-air war." Ike expected German resistance to be heaviest in the Ruhr. However, he said he would not like the correspondents to think he was writing off the Germans elsewhere. "No one knows yet what the German can do within his own country and it's certain that he's trying to do everything he possibly

---

[12] General der Fallschirmtruppe Hermann-Bernhard 'Gerhard' Ramcke

can. But it is equally certain that he has suffered defeats since June 6 [D-Day] that he could not afford." Ike said he honestly believed that "there will be no negotiated unconditional surrender. It will be an imposed unconditional surrender". (FDR had promised that "unconditional surrender" meant only that the "enemy war machines" would be broken up; it did not mean that the victors had any intention "of starving the peoples of Germany".[13])

"Civilians attacking American troops will be dealt with sternly and on the spot," said Ike. "I will not tolerate civilians, people out of uniform, bearing arms, firing on our troops. There is fraternisation and it would be silly to deny it, but the general conduct of our troops...in public has been almost exemplary. I would be the last one to deny that soldiers don't [sic] get in the back door and get Rhine wine and whatever else they are after, but I do say that the thing so far, while the battle is going on, has been well observed by our soldiers."

Ike added: "If the Germans were reasoning like normal human beings, they would realise the whole history of the United States and Great Britain is to be generous toward a defeated enemy. We observe all the laws of the Geneva Convention." (He said this less than three weeks after deciding that he would not abide by the Geneva Convention.[14])

On the issue of German weapons, Ike said that it was "perfectly true" that the Tiger and Panther tanks could knock out Allied tanks in a tank-to-tank duel, particularly at extreme ranges. German bazookas were also "more penetrating", but it was nonsense to say that three quarters of the Allies' equipment was inferior to the equipment used by the Germans. If the war "unfortunately lasts a number of weeks longer", Allied battlefield equipment would beat the Germans "head to head in a duel". Ike was again asked:

---

[13] Daily Mail, 11 August 1944
[14] The Germans meanwhile insisted that they were "strictly observing Geneva Convention" (Propaganda leaflet AI-069-7-44)

"Who do you think will be into Berlin first, the Russians or us?" He answered: "Well, I think mileage alone ought to make them do it. After all, they are 33 miles [away] and we are 250. They have a shorter race to run, although they are faced by the bulk of the German forces." (The Russians were 29 miles from Berlin in the spring of 1945, according to the US papers,[15] and Ike sent a telegram direct to Stalin trying to co-ordinate the offensives of the Russians and the western allies.[16] But the western allies' main advance was directed towards Leipzig, rather than Berlin,[17] and Stalin eventually declared the Russians had taken the German capital at 3pm on 2 May 1945.[18])

After the news conference, Ike went to a projection room on the Champs Elysées for a preview of the official film about fighting since D-Day. Afterwards, Ike complained that the film should have featured more about Bradley and the landings in southern France. That night at the Hotel Raphael, Ike spoke about his trip to the front where he had watched the preliminary bombardment by 1,250 guns. He had observed from a church tower as US and British landing craft ferried British, Canadian and American troops across the Rhine. But the Germans were already effectively defeated. Allied air superiority meant that German communications could be destroyed at will. By the end of March, V-Day (the announcement of victory) was predicted "within a week and almost certainly within the next month". [19] Germans were being taken prisoner at such a rate that they were not even guarded, just disarmed and sent to the rear. In one instance, a train full of convalescent German soldiers who were sent to the front to stem the Allied advance pulled into Hanau station, instead of Frankfurt, thanks to damaged signals. The soldiers were all taken prisoner by Allied

---

15 Daily News, 8 March 1945
16 Alan Brooke war diaries, 29 March 1945
17 Alan Brooke war diaries, 1 April 1945
18 Daily Express, 3 May 1945
19 News Chronicle, 31 March 1945

troops. [20] Housing and feeding such a large number of prisoners caused Ike one of his biggest headaches.

In April 1945, Ike was informed he was to be military governor of the US occupation zone in Germany. The next day, there was a rumour that he was to take over from Marshall as Chief-of-Staff in Washington. [21] Ike ignored the rumours and concentrated on finishing the war. He said Monty had done a fine job crossing the Rhine and could be relied on to hold what he took. Monty was feted in England, while the colourful and audacious Patton dominated the headlines in the USA because his Third Army's assignment had been perhaps the most difficult. Bradley, who had never "paused to regroup" when he saw an opportunity to advance, now said he intended to move his headquarters to Bad Ems, a popular watering place, but Allied bombers had already destroyed all the suitable buildings.

On 4 April, [22] Ike wrote to Kay's mother thanking her for sending him some 'Sphere' magazines. He said: "Kay continues to go her accustomed way – answering letters furiously to get all caught up, in the hope of taking another trip. The place doesn't seem to be so important, but the going is. Her health seems definitely better than it was during the winter." Wishing Kul "some relief from flying buzzers and rockets", he signed off "Sincerely, 'Ike'."

The following day, General Alexander said the Germans wanted to surrender in Italy. However, while "Smiling Albert" Kesselring's representatives were talking to Alexander's staff, German agents were telling the Russians that the western Allies were about to make a separate peace, following the approaches of General Karl Wolff, head of the SS in Italy. The Russians protested, but FDR wired Stalin asking: "What kind of ally do you think we are?" By 8 April, the Allies could go anywhere they wanted in western

---

[20] News Chronicle, 31 March 1945
[21] He eventually did so after the war, in November 1945
[22] Letter to Mrs Vera McCarthy-Morrogh (sic), 25 Holland Villas Road, London W14

Germany.[23] The Germans had blown up most of the bridges on the autobahns – two-lane motorways – but Allied bulldozers cleared passages through the rubble. (The sight of the autobahns later persuaded Eisenhower as US President to embark on a major road-building programme in the United States.)

Not everything was peaceful though. A sniper shot at Patton's Chief-of-Staff, General 'Hap' Gay, in a field near his caravan, but did not hit him. Patton ordered that the two houses closest to the shooting should be burned down. GIs (and reporters) wanted to keep going until they reached Berlin, but Bradley reckoned taking the city would result in 100,000 casualties, which he described as a "pretty stiff price for a prestige objective".[24] Ike said it was more important militarily to divide the Germans and prevent them from continuing to fight in Scandinavia or the so-called southern redoubt. (One captured German general told the Americans that the redoubt in the Bavarian Alps was "a myth",[25] and so it transpired.[26])

On 12 April, 63-year-old FDR died at Warm Springs, Georgia, from a stroke. He had been President of the United States since 1933, but had been unwell since at least the previous spring.[27] FDR's mistress, Lucy Page Mercer Rutherfurd, his wife's former social secretary, was also in Warm Springs when he died. FDR was succeeded by Vice-President Harry S Truman.

In a speech to a joint session of congress the day after FDR's funeral,[28] President Truman said the "armies of liberation" were bringing to an end "Hitler's ghastly threat to dominate

---

[23] But the Germans were still trying to persuade Allied soldiers to surrender. "Are you going to let yourself be killed in a fight the world says is already won?" (Leaflet 719-4-45)
[24] The War Between the Generals, p 399
[25] Daily Express, 28 April 1945
[26] A "figment of the imagination", according to Patton at a press conference on 27 April 1945
[27] Alan Brooke war diaries, 7 May 1944
[28] 16 April 1945

the world". But he confirmed that: "Our demand has been, and it remains – unconditional surrender! We will not traffic with the breakers of the peace on the terms of the peace." Truman said the United States did not wish to see "unnecessary or unjustified suffering. But the laws of God and of man have been violated and the guilty must not go unpunished...Lasting peace can never be secured if we permit our dangerous opponents to plot future wars with impunity at any mountain retreat – however distant".

Back in Europe, Ike went to see a hoard of German treasure in a salt mine, 2,000 feet underground in a town in Thuringia. The estimated haul was $100 million in gold bullion, $3 billion in Reichsmarks and $2 million in US currency.[29] Ike said the gold bars were too heavy to carry – he'd tried. When the SHAEF censor passed a media story about Patton's troops discovering the German gold and art treasures, Patton fired him. But Ike said Patton had no authority to sack a SHAEF censor.[30] This was at least the fourth time that Ike had rebuked Patton.

One thing they did agree on was the horrific state of the inmates of the "internment camps". Ike had seen a camp near Gotha and said the treatment of the inmates defied description. Their stories of starvation and cruelty were so overpowering that he said he felt sick. In one room, 20 to 30 naked men had starved to death. Patton had refused to enter, as he said he'd vomit if he went in. US troops continued to find German "concentration camps for political prisoners" and reported conditions of "indescribable horror", but no specific targeting of Jews.[31] After the mayor of Ohrdruf and his wife saw the dead bodies of starved slave labourers at Ohrdruf Nord camp, they hanged themselves. Ike cabled Marshall suggesting that leaders of Congress and

---

[29] Life magazine, 30 April 1952, p 70
[30] When Patton lost a company in a vain attempt to rescue his son-in-law from Hugenberg prison camp, he censored the operation and then "forgot" to lift the censorship (Ike message to Marshall, 15 April 1945)
[31] The Eisenhower Museum has "almost no readily-identifiable manuscript regarding the persecution of Jews during World War II"

a dozen prominent editors and publishers should come and see the camps. On 17 April, Kay and Ike took a flying trip to London where he told Churchill at dinner that British MPs and editors would be welcome too.

The following day, Ike invited Kay's mother to lunch at Telegraph Cottage and then went to 10 Downing Street where the Prime Minister said he wanted him to take Berlin. Ike saw no military sense in it. Hitler – by this stage an "outright madman", according to Ike – celebrated his last birthday in the bunker in Berlin on Friday 20 April 1945. The same day, Patton almost died. A "plane which looked like a Spitfire" with RAF markings made three attempts to shoot down his light aircraft, but crashed on the third attempt.[32]

Ike spent the next day at SHAEF Main at Versailles and then flew back to Reims in the afternoon. He decided that SHAEF Main and Forward were to be moved to Frankfurt. In his order of the day, Ike said that the "ragged remnants of Hitler's armies in the west" were "tottering on the threshold of defeat", and the number of dead and wounded German soldiers would "never be accurately known".[33] He wrote again to Kay's mother from Reims, expressing relief that there had been no recent reports of Germany "trying to launch any fly-bombs against London".

As the attack through the Siegfried Line progressed, Patton crossed the Moselle west of the Rhine, seized the plateau at the junction with the Rhine and attacked the German rear. Beetle Smith told journalists at a press conference: "That was the second critical point in the campaign. Ike then rolled the bridgehead down toward the Frankfurt area so that the Seventh Army would not have to cross against opposition. The Ruhr pocket, when it was finally reduced two days ago, contained over 300,000 troops. The German forces which might have opposed our further advance were eliminated."

---

[32] Patton diary
[33] Daily Mirror, 21 April 1945

Beetle said that Berlin had a psychological value, but nothing like it had when it was the centre of German communications and government. "Germany had two hearts – one, Berlin; the other, the Ruhr. We had selected as our target the Ruhr, which was the industrial heart of Germany...Any time we go into Berlin, it will be on an Allied basis, I will assure you of that.[34]

"One thing to remember – as long as Hitler or any of his representatives are standing on a rock around Salzburg, proclaiming they are free Germans and broadcasting to all isolated fortress areas holding out that everything is going to come out all right, they are going to hold out. Our target now, if we are going to bring this war to an end and bring it to an end in a hell of a hurry, is this national redoubt."[35] Beetle said Hitler was "probably at Berchtesgaden", but he wasn't sure. (In fact Hitler stayed in Berlin where he and his wife, Eva Braun, committed suicide in the bunker beneath the Reich Chancellery.)

The Americans now seemed to be preoccupied with the threat of German secret rays and gas attacks (though the Germans never used gas warfare in World War Two). Kay's typed diary notes said: "We have had littlebits [sic] of evidence that the German may be gaoing [sic] to use gaas [sic]. It was suggested that we bring over gas shell [sic] to enable the 9th air force to use them if necessary. There are indications that the German has invented a new kind of 'Ray' that would stop the motors of our bombers. Spaatz suggests that perhaps we could take couter [sic] measures." Beetle told press correspondents: "Our artillery and air preponderance is so great that, within a few hours after the Germans would fire a gas shell or drop a gas bomb, we could rely on a ratio of about, I should say, 20 to one. If they were going to use gas, the time would have been when we were concentrating in the Normandy beachhead." Ike had

---

34 78,000 Soviet soldiers were killed in the battle for Berlin
35 The Allies believed this Goebbels myth

previously discussed the possible use of gas before D-Day, on 13 March 1944.

Beetle was asked: "Has there been any change in policy in handling German prisoners since we have picked up some of our own?" He replied: "There is going to be. We have got a lot of mines to be cleared up all through France and Belgium and places like that.[36] An awful lot of work to be done pretty soon when we've got all our prisoners back. General Eisenhower is having all these poor wretched people who were killed buried by civilians. As a matter of fact, we always intended having a lot of this work done by German prisoners. We have been very circumspect because, as you know, they are perfectly ruthless with ours. We shall stay within the limits of the Geneva Convention."[37]

The British Prime Minister also maintained that German prisoners-of-war should clear mines. "Let the Germans find all the mines they have buried, and dig them up," he said. "Why should they not?"[38] (The reason was because it was in breach of Article 32 of the 1929 Geneva Convention: "It is forbidden to employ prisoners of war on unhealthy or dangerous work.")

The war was now accelerating towards its end. The Russians entered Berlin on Monday 23 April. Ike visited hospitals in Paris the following day. He spent the night at the Raphael and the next morning called in Com Z staff to discuss black market activities in Paris after spotting Com Z officers in "very fine" vehicles at the front. On 25 April, the US First Army linked up with the Russians near Torgau, on the Elbe. Moscow announced that Himmler had offered to surrender unconditionally to the United States and Britain, but his proposal was rejected because it did not include Russia. Directive JCS 1067 from the Joint Chiefs of Staff on 26 April 1945 ordered Eisenhower to "impose controls to the full

---

[36] Allied mine-clearing equipment was said to be "totally inadequate"

[37] One German propaganda leaflet denied that Allied POWs were forced to do dangerous work, such as clear mines

[38] Alan Brooke war diaries, 16 May 1945

extent necessary to achieve the industrial disarmament of Germany" and "take no steps looking toward the economic rehabilitation" of the country. But Ike denied that he was merely facilitating the Morgenthau Plan to reduce post-war Germany to a pastoral economy.

On 28 April, Italian communists captured and shot Mussolini and his mistress, Claretta Petacci, and hung their corpses upside down at a Milanese petrol station.[39] Hitler committed suicide in the Berlin bunker on 30 April. Ike issued a statement to the German people four days later assuring them that Hitler had not died a hero. But in neutral Portugal, flags were flown at half mast, while in the Irish Free State, Prime Minister Eamonn de Valera expressed his condolences to the German ambassador.[40]

GIs who had fought in Africa, Italy and the European campaign were told they wouldn't have to fight any more. But transport was badly needed for displaced persons,[41] prisoners of war and the distribution of food. (A year after the German surrender, official rations in the US zone were still no more than 1,275 calories a day, while the Germans' winter ration was only 1,000 calories – half that required by an adult male for proper nutrition.[42]) In Holland, where the Germans were still holding out, the people were starving. Ike told the German commander there that the Allies planned to drop food supplies and any German who tried to interfere would be treated as a violator of the laws of war.[43] The Germans designated the dropping grounds and agreed to meet SHAEF's representatives to arrange for more relief.

---

[39] "A typically Italian stunt to murder him" said Patton in May 1945
[40] Daily Express, 3 May 1945
[41] "Like animals, or worse" according to General Gay (Journal, 10 April 1945)
[42] At Buchenwald concentration camp, political prisoners were fed only 800 calories a day; an average of 100 a day died (Patton diary, 15 April 1945)
[43] CHAR 20/215/46-49

At Reims, Ike had to make some recordings and movies for the "grand finale". He redrafted his broadcast and newsreel speech for VE Day three times. (He didn't have to learn it for the recording, but he had to recite a few paragraphs from memory for the movie.) But he took time out to present Kay with the Bronze Star "for meritorious service" on 4 May.[44]

The US Seventh Army took Munich and Dachau concentration camp on Sunday 29 April. At Reims a couple of days earlier, Ike had talked to editors and publishers who had seen Buchenwald concentration camp and had interviewed liberated American prisoners-of-war. Ike said he hoped every American newspaper would print detailed stories of German cruelty. However, when he learned later that day that men of the 15th US Regiment, 45th Infantry Division, had machine gunned to death 520 German soldiers – including a doctor carrying a Red Cross flag – at Dachau, after the soldiers took over from fleeing guards pending the American arrival, he hushed up the killings.

---

[44] New York Times, 5 May 1945

UNCONDITIONAL SURRENDER

On Friday 4 May, in Monty's tent at Lüneburg Heath outside Hamburg, Field Marshal Wilhelm Keitel signed [1] the unconditional surrender of the German forces in Holland, northwest Germany including the Friesian Islands, Schleswig-Holstein and Denmark. The Germans undertook to carry out any Allied orders "without argument or comment". Representatives of the Allies' naval, military and air forces were at the surrender, though Monty would not allow representatives of other services to be present. Ike was waiting for a phone call from Monty, but instead received a call from Winston Churchill to say he was very disturbed to hear that the Russians were landing in Denmark, where there were already many communists. [2]

When Monty's call had not come by five to seven in the evening, Ike said he might as well go home, but Kay suggested that he wait "just another five minutes". At 7 o'clock, the call came. [3] As Kay eavesdropped, Ike told Monty that, if the Germans had the authority of the new German Führer, Admiral Karl Dönitz, to stop all the fighting, they should be sent to his HQ at Reims. It was still unclear whether the Germans had authority to surrender all land, sea and air forces, but they were being flown to Reims anyway and would arrive about 11am on Saturday. The main Allied signatories were to be Beetle and Ken Strong, who had negotiated with General Castellano in Lisbon. Beetle had signed the Italian surrender in Sicily, after Ike had declined to sign it himself. Ike said he wouldn't even meet the Germans until after they had signed the final unconditional surrender. Late on 4 May, Ike issued a proclamation: "Any further losses the Germans incur are due to their failure

---

[1] Using "an ordinary pen you could buy in a shop for tuppence" (Montgomery memoirs)
[2] Original diary 4 May 1945
[3] Original diary 4 May 1945

instantly to quit. They know they are beaten. Any further hesitation is due to their own stupidity or that of the German government. On land, sea and in the air, the Germans have been thoroughly whipped. Their only recourse is to surrender."[4]

While he waited for the Germans to arrive, Ike met the US soldiers who had linked up with the Soviet soldiers at Torgau and accepted a presentation of the makeshift flag which the Americans had used to identify themselves to the Russians. Ike promoted all the Americans one grade.[5] About noon on 5 May, the secretariat confirmed that the plane carrying the Germans had landed near Brussels, and that they would drive to Reims after lunch because the weather wasn't suitable for flying. The German signatories were to be Admiral Hans Georg von Friedeburg, Commander-in-Chief of the German Navy,[6] and Colonel Fritz Poleck, of the Oberkommando Wehrmacht, the German equivalent of the US War Department or the British War Office. So certain were the British that the Germans were about to give up that a notice appeared in the British newspapers saying that air raid warnings and shelters were to be abolished.[7]

The two Russian representatives were to be Major-General Ivan Susloparov, an artillery officer who was head of the Russian mission to France, and his interpreter, Colonel Ivan Zenkovitch. Ike worried what would happen if the Russians refused to accept the surrender. The Chief-of-Staff of the Red Army had seemed to grant him authority, but the messages were unclear. The French did not have a representative at the signing. Ike said this was an oversight and someone from the de Gaulle group should be on hand to sign as a witness, though not as a participant. De Gaulle sent Major-General François Sevez as a representative of General Juin.

---

4 News Chronicle, 5 May 1945
5 Original diary 5 May 1945
6 Friedeburg subsequently took poison on 23 May 1945
7 Original diary 5 May 1945

Room 119, the war room of the *Collège Moderne et Technique*, where Ike met his commanders and staff most mornings, was designated as the place for the signing. The walls were covered with battle maps showing the disposition of the Allied forces, and charts showed air operations, casualty lists, supplies, railway and communications systems and three-day weather charts. On one wall a 'thermometer' marked with swastikas recorded the number of German prisoners taken.[8] Ike wandered through the war room which was full of "cameras, arc lights, movie cameras etc" and commented: "The damned war room looks like a Hollywood setting."[9] Beetle immediately announced that whoever was responsible for the cameras and lights in the war room should remove them. "This isn't going to be a show," he barked. "There's going to be a surrender. Get it out immediately." Preliminary discussions were to take place in Beetle's office but Ike said that, unless the Germans were authorised to sign, they would not be taken to the war room. Photographs could be taken as they entered the room and again as they left. Ike said Beetle could clear out the war room if he liked, then went for a nap.

Shortly after 5 o'clock, the Germans arrived. They were met by two British officers who saluted, the two Germans responding without the 'Heil Hitler' salute. They were taken to an office where von Friedeburg hummed to himself as he washed and changed his collar. Poleck seemed more nervous. After a 20-minute conversation, von Friedeburg said he wasn't authorised to surrender to the Russians, but only to parley with the Allies and then communicate with Dönitz. But a radio link had still not been set up between Reims and Flensburg, the new German capital.

Beetle insisted that the German signatories had to agree to unconditional surrender. All German forces, aircraft, and surface ships were to remain where they were, and not to be damaged or scuttled. The OKW must enforce all orders

---

[8] Ludington Daily News, 6 May 1995
[9] Original diary 5 May 1945

issued by the Allied command, and the surrender terms also had to apply to the Russians. But von Friedeburg said the German High Command could not inform outlying forces because communications had been disrupted by Allied bombing. He insisted that he would need at least 48 hours before he could sign, and tearfully referred to the hardships of German civilians. Beetle retorted that the Germans were still enemies and would remain so until the surrender. But after they capitulated, they would be treated in accordance with the normal dictates of humanity. However, if the new German government did not promptly agree to surrender, it would be charged with continuing the hostilities. The admiral took the terms back to the office and asked for whisky. He sent a message in SHAEF code to the Second British Army Headquarters, the nearest to Flensburg, which was to courier the deciphered message to Dönitz.

Dönitz told von Friedeburg that the Chief-of-Staff of the German Army, Generaloberst Gustav Jodl, who had succeeded General Heinz Guderian in March, was flying to Reims and would have authority to sign. "It is very obvious that the Germans are scared to death of the Russians," said Kay, and that the two Germans who had been sent to sign the surrender were "playing for time". [10] Even after the surrender, the Germans continued to try and surrender to the western Allies "so that the Russians wont (sic) get them". [11] During the day, three more German armies surrendered to the US 6th Army Group.

"We've all been hanging around the office," said Kay. "It's now 8 o'clock. Bedell has just told E [Ike] that nothing is going to happen tonight so we are all going home." [12] Before he left, Beetle asked Butch to superintend the two fountain pens used to sign the surrender, and to make sure that no

---

[10] Original diary 5 May 1945
[11] Patton letter to wife, 9 May 1945
[12] Original diary 5 May 1945

one stole them afterwards.[13] The pens – one solid gold and the other gold-plated – had been sent to Ike many years before by Kenneth Parker, a friend who had asked that they be used to sign the surrender and that one pen then be returned to him. Afterwards, Ike gave the gold-plated pen back to Parker, and the solid-gold one to President Harry Truman.

Ike had been invited to a reception at the WAC house but accepted only when he was assured that the French and Russians were going. He decided to stay at the women's house for a few minutes and then go home. Later, at dinner at home, Ike said that German wives and children had been sent to Czechoslovakia to avoid the bombing of German cities. The Germans were now stalling for time as Czechoslovakia was being overrun by the Russians. But once Ike had German representatives with authority to act, he did not propose to let them dilly-dally. He wanted the German Army to accept that it had been decisively beaten so there would be no repeat of the World War I claim that it was the German home front that had lost the war, not the Army.

Beetle phoned Ike to say that the Germans had again asked for another 48 hours. Ike replied: "You tell them that 48 hours from midnight tonight, I will close my lines on the western front so no more Germans can get through, whether they sign or not and no matter how much time they take." During that 48-hour period, a further 700,000 German troops streamed across the Elbe to surrender to the Americans – who, contrary to the Geneva Convention,[14] took many of their personal possessions. American officers and men displayed trophies such as German cameras and glasses.[15] In one pile of confiscated belongings was a sword engraved with the name "Eisenhauer" which was given to Ike as a souvenir.

---

[13] "Someone nicked the pen" used to sign the surrender at Luneberg Heath, Monty complained
[14] Articles 5 and 6
[15] Rommel, The Desert Fox, p 163

Von Friedeburg and Poleck spent the night under guard in the seven-room villa for officers visiting SHAEF at 3 Rue Godenot. They dined at 11pm on tomato juice, pork chops, mashed potatoes, peas and carrots, fruit, coffee and red wine. Von Friedeburg commented on the fine linen and remarked that the owner of the house must be rich. The Germans listened to the radio in the sitting room until after midnight, then went to bed.

On 6 May 1945, Hermann Göering was taken into custody by the US 36th Infantry Division. Ike promised to take care of his wife, Emmy, and seven-year-old daughter Edda. (A British newspaper wrongly reported that Göering had been forced to shoot his wife and daughter, and then himself.[16]) In fact, Göering's wife and daughter were later interned together in Camp Ashcan, an Allied prisoner-of-war camp in Luxembourg. Göering took poison after being sentenced to death at Nuremberg.

When Jodl arrived in Reims on 6 May, the expressionless grey-coated general and his aide walked from their car into the headquarters building. They had been brought by car because the weather was still "too bad for flying".[17] An Allied officer saluted and the German Chief-of-Staff returned the salute and was taken to meet von Friedeburg. When the admiral opened the door to Jodl, there was no salute, but Jodl said "Aha". Soon afterwards, von Friedeburg came out and asked for coffee and a map of Europe. Shortly after 6, Jodl and von Friedeburg were taken to Beetle's office, where they stayed nearly an hour and a half. Then Beetle talked to Ike for about 20 minutes. He said there would be at least three hours' delay while Jodl sought the authority of Dönitz using a code that he had brought.[18]

---

[16] Daily Express, 28 April 1945
[17] Original diary 5 May 1945
[18] A telegram from Churchill marked "Urgent but not to be delivered till he wakes" sought details of Ike's "act of military surrender" (CHAR 20/217/108)

About 1.30am on Monday 7 May, Ruth Briggs phoned Butch to say that Ike had arrived at the headquarters building and "The big party is on." The end of the war in Europe was to be announced simultaneously by the governments in Washington, London and Moscow. In the war room, General Strong placed the documents for signature in front of Beetle Smith, before whom Butch put the solid-gold fountain pen. Beetle spoke briefly to the Germans, with Strong interpreting. Were they prepared to sign? Jodl gave a slight nod. At 2.41am British Double Summer Time on 7 May, Jodl (later hanged at Nuremberg[19]) signed the surrender, watched by von Friedeburg. Kay was one of only three western women to witness Germany's formal surrender.

Jodl signed the first document with the gold-plated pen and the second with a Sheaffer pen given to Butch in Algiers, surrendering "all forces on land, sea, and in the air who are at this date under German control" to the Supreme Commander of SHAEF and simultaneously to the Soviet High Command, from 23.01 hours on 8 May 1945. Generals Smith and Susloparov (earlier approved by the Russians[20]) then signed both documents on the other side of the table, with Sevez as witness. But the Russians later said that Susloparov was not authorised to sign the surrender document, which they insisted be signed in Berlin. [21]

Jodl then stood with his fingers resting on the table, his eyes brimming with tears,[22] and said to Beetle in English: "I want to say a word." Reverting to German, he said: "General, with this signature the German people and German armed forces[23] are, for better or worse, delivered into the victor's hands. In this war, which has lasted more than five years, both have achieved and suffered more than perhaps any

---

[19] Eisenhower later described this execution as "a mistake"
[20] Original diary 5 May 1945
[21] Original diary 7 May 1945
[22] Ludington Daily News, 6 May 1995
[23] Churchill wrote: "Alexander has taken a million prisoners; Monty took over 500,000 yesterday and far more than a million today" – Churchill, pp 330-331

other people in the world. In this hour, I can only express the hope that the victor will treat them with generosity."

The Germans were then taken to Ike's office and stood in front of the seated general. "Do you understand the terms of the document of surrender you have just signed?" he asked. The Germans said yes. "You will get details of instructions at a later date, and you will be expected to carry them out faithfully." They clicked their heels, bowed and left.

After the surrender had been signed, Ike called in Kay[24] and held up the fountain pens in a "V for Victory" sign for the photographers. Movie and still films afterwards show her, the only woman, standing behind Beetle for the official photos. At one point, Ike turns to her and speaks directly to her. But Kay was later excised from the official photographs. Technical Sergeant Al Meserlin, Ike's personal photographer, did not know why the photo was altered after he sent the film to the Army Pictorial Service laboratory in Paris.[25] "All our stuff went through the wartime censors. Usually they just cropped out identifying terrain details so as not to reveal Eisenhower's whereabouts, like when he went to Bastogne," he said later. Meserlin said he had taken Kay's picture a number of times, though "we don't know what went on at night".[26]

After the surrender, Ike recorded a short newsreel and radio message in the war room, but had to do a second take after using the word "armistice" instead of "surrender". Ike then dictated a brief cable to the Combined Chiefs saying: "The mission of this Allied Force was fulfilled at 0241, local time, May 7th 1945. Eisenhower." About 3am, Ike, Kay, Ruth Briggs and Air Marshal Tedder drove back to Ike's chateau and drank Champagne till dawn. After almost three years, Ike had achieved victory in Europe, wrote Kay. "No man deserves greater praise for the part he played...He is the only

---

[24] Original diary 6 May 1945
[25] http://articles.latimes.com/1995-05-28/news/mn-6970_1_germans-gen-dwight-d-eisenhower-official-photo
[26] LA Times, 28 May 1995

person in the whole Allied command who wanted nothing for himself." [27] Ike finally went to bed at nearly 5am. He stayed up only long enough to phone General Bradley and tell him to "get the word around" about the ceasefire. Kay and Ruth stayed up until 6am and then slept for only two hours. [28]

However, a tired Beetle had not realised that the European Advisory Commission had approved the wording of a final surrender agreement, and the instrument of surrender signed at Reims was not as agreed by the Soviets. After the mistake was noticed, SHAEF announced early on Monday morning that the documents signed in the early hours only "formalised the surrender" and that the "official surrender" would be signed in Berlin on Tuesday. Orders were sent to all Allied forces telling them that hostilities would end at one minute after midnight, Tuesday-Wednesday 8/9 May Double British Summer Time. The orders were to go out in the clear, without being coded, but Ike noted the Combined Chiefs' order that news of the surrender was to come simultaneously from the Allied capitals, so the dispatches were sent in code. The other correspondents were "put on their honour" not to publish the story "until told to do so". Ike would boast that he could take correspondents into his confidence, "asking them to say or write nothing until the need for secrecy had ended". [29] But the Germans had already broadcast an announcement on Radio Flensburg informing their own forces. A cable received in the Pentagon's War Message Room at 14.31 on 7 May 1945 said German Radio was broadcasting that Admiral Dönitz had declared the unconditional surrender of all fighting German troops, as to continue the war would mean only "senseless bloodshed and futile disintegration". News of the surrender was also announced by Radio Luxembourg. The news was then relayed by Edward Kennedy, Associated Press's Paris bureau chief, "in defiance of all the rules of secrecy and censor-

---

[27] Original diary 6 May 1945
[28] Ike later wrote that "my group went to bed to sleep the clock around"
[29] at ease, p 321

ship".[30] Ike was extremely annoyed, but there was little he could do until the Allied governments announced the news. But as a result of his despatch, Kennedy was sacked by Associated Press in November 1945. It took AP until 2012 to apologise.

[30] Original diary 6 May 1945

SURRENDER IN BERLIN

The phone in Ike's office rang all day after the Reims surrender. Winston Churchill rang eight times about the announcement of VE Day, interrupting Ike reading his latest Western, Cartridge Carnival.[1] Eventually, about noon, with the backing of the Prime Minister and Beetle, Ike told the Russians he would not attend the signing in Berlin on Tuesday 8 May, as the main Russian figure, Marshal Georgi Zhukov, was not senior enough. Instead, he would send his deputy, Air Marshal Tedder.

Kay arrived at Ike's office about 10.30 on Monday morning. "I said that I would love to go to the signing of the surrender because that was *the* great thing," said Kay in 1972. "The one in France [Reims] was only very small and very informal, and I was fortunate. He gave me permission to go."[2] A message had just come in from the Russians saying that the Germans in Czechoslovakia were refusing to surrender to the Russians, but were going over to the American lines – one of the main reasons why the Germans in Reims had been playing for time. "They are just scared to death of the Russians," said Kay.[3] The Germans had good reason to be fearful of the Soviets; as soon as the Red Army crossed the border into East Prussia on 21 October 1944, Russian soldiers raped or crucified up to 70 German civilians and Belgian and French prisoners-of-war at Nemmersdorf.[4] [5]

---

[1] By William Colt MacDonald, published 8 March 1945
[2] Kay was the first Irishwoman to enter the German capital (p 3, Cork Examiner, 13 June 1945)
[3] Original diary, Monday 7 May 1945
[4] "All women who ran [in Berlin] were shot and those who did not were raped." (Patton letter to wife, 21 July 1945)
[5] A German propaganda leaflet condemned "bestial Godless Bolsheviks" with pictures of German victims of Soviet troops in Schirwindt (AI-172-12-44) and 148 raped and murdered women at Lauban

While Jodl was signing the surrender agreement in Reims, German radio was broadcasting that Germany had made a separate peace agreement with the western Allies, but was still going to continue fighting against the Russians. "Up to the very last moment, the Germans were doing their very best trying to split [ourselves⁶] and the Russians," said Kay.⁷

The four C-47s carrying the Allied and German parties left from the airfield near Reims at 8.15am on Tuesday (de Lattre de Tassigny missed the flights and had to catch up). They landed at 11.30am in Stendal, 65 miles from Berlin, but there were no Russians to meet them. Tedder debated whether to proceed without an escort, but "An American pilot told us that the Russians had shot down a pilot the day previous," said Kay.⁸ The Russian escort eventually turned up about 45 minutes later and the group – with the Germans now joined by Field Marshal Keitel – flew on to Berlin's Tempelhof airfield. "I shall never forget the sight as we flew over the city," said Kay. "We were flying at about 2,000 feet but as we gradually came down, one could see that the whole place was gutted."⁹

The group was met by General Susloparov, the three national anthems were played and Tedder inspected the guard of honour then made a short speech. The Russians had provided a fleet of 30 cars. "Everybody had to run to get a seat," said Kay, as the Russians had not reserved seats for anyone. Most of the cars had been confiscated from the Germans, and had identification plates written in Russian numerals. The Russian drivers "drove like the French, hand on the horn most of the time," said Kay.¹⁰

---

⁶ Writing undecipherable in original diary
⁷ Original diary, 7 May 1945
⁸ Original diary, 8 May 1945
⁹ Original diary 8 May 1945
¹⁰ Ike's orderly had commented that "all the French need on any motor vehicle is an accelerator and maybe a horn" (Sgt Mickey and General Ike, p 145)

Kay became the first Irishwoman to enter the ruins of Berlin. About every six blocks, the cars passed through a German road block – two trams side by side with the spaces between them and the buildings on either side filled with rubble from bombed buildings. No German citizens were allowed on the route. The city was cloaked in haze, with many buildings still smouldering. "What I saw today is something I've never seen before," said Kay. "There is not one building left standing in Berlin."

The cavalcade was directed by traffic police, uniformed Russian girls in three-quarter-length tunics, straight skirts and short black boots. After driving for about half an hour, Kay and her friends arrived at an army engineering school at Karlshorst on the eastern side of the city. Tedder, Spaatz, Butch and Ramsay's successor, Admiral Harold Burrough, were assigned to a cottage with electricity and running water. Kay's group was shown to a small "not very nice" room for which the Russians apologised. "We said it was fine for a few minutes," said Kay. The Russians then told their guests that the group would probably be in Berlin for a week. "That shook us," said Kay. "We didn't even have a tooth-brush with us."

About 1.30pm, Kay was taken to Tedder's house. At first there did not appear to be anything to eat, but an hour later – "after a bit of agitation on someone's part" – a Russian girl appeared with caviar on white bread, ham, fish, red wine, a sweet white wine "like Passover wine" and cognac. On a German radio in the living room, Kay and the Allied officers listened as Churchill from London, Truman from Washington and de Gaulle from Paris all proclaimed VE Day. The national anthems were then played. "It was an amazing thing to be in Berlin and hear the speeches," said Kay. "Of course there was not a single GI there." But the Russians wouldn't believe the war was over until they heard it officially on Moscow radio.

At about 4pm, everyone followed Tedder to Zhukov's HQ where the Russian marshal was presented with a SHAEF flag and then had 90 minutes of talks with the Allied generals. Afterwards they all went back to Tedder's villa until 6pm when they were told that they would have to spend the night in Berlin. Some of the plane crews had to go back to Tempelhof, but it took an hour for them to get permission from the Soviets. On the way back to the airfield to pick up overnight luggage, Kay saw her first Berlin civilians. They passed women, children and baggage and a few horse-drawn vehicles. Hundreds of shabby and scantily-clad Germans, many without shoes, trudged along the street, carrying baggage or pushing handcarts. Queues of German civilians with anything that would hold water queued at the public water pumps.

Back at the cottage, the Russians said there would be a further delay before the signing. This time they were unhappy about some of the translations. "There is nothing certain," said Kay. "You cannot possibly hurry a Russian." In the meantime, the hosts brought out cheese and "very mild" German beer. Eventually, the group went to the huge two-storey room in the concrete building half a block away where the signing was to take place. More talking, waiting and drinking followed until, after a wait of more than three hours, the "great moment" finally came. Under a balcony on one side was a ten-foot table for the Germans. Across one end of the room, there was a long table from which extended three similar tables, one for the press and two for the official party. The Russian army seemed to have "a lot of generals, some of them quite young". Everyone stood up as Marshal Georgi Zhukov came in. Zhukov sat in the middle of the head table, Tedder on his right, Spaatz on Zhukov's left and General 'Roi Jean' de Lattre de Tassigny on Tooey's left. On Tedder's right was the Russian deputy Minister of Foreign Affairs, Andrey Vyshinsky, in civilian clothes. There were about 100 Russian reporters and photographers. Zhukov, whose chest was covered with medals, stood at the two microphones and called the assembly to order.

The Russian guard brought in the "bunch of Nazis".[11] Field Marshal Wilhelm Keitel, dressed in a pale blue uniform, looked "most military".[12] He raised his silver-tipped baton in salute, and sat down. Keitel looked "absolutely magnify-icent,"[13] said Kay, "medals and decorations everywhere. He wore one particular medal which he was given by Hitler personally and [it] is known as the Blood Bath".[14] Luftwaffe Colonel General Hans-Jürgen Stumpf, the highest-ranking Luftwaffe officer that the Germans could find, was on Keitel's right and Admiral von Friedeburg on his left. "All kept up a most military appearance during the whole ceremony," said Kay.

At about 11.30pm, Tedder stood up with the surrender document, and asked if the Germans accepted the surrender terms. His question was translated into Russian and then into German. Keitel replied that he accepted the terms on the paper. He was told to come forward (wearing his monocle and taking off the glove on his left hand) and sign several copies. He was still arguing that he wanted 24 hours' delay. "Naturally this was refused," said Kay. One Russian shouldered other photographers and reporters out of the way but was punched on the jaw, to which he responded in kind.

When Keitel returned to his seat, von Friedeburg and Stumpf walked up to the head table and signed. Zhukov and Tedder then signed as representatives of the Allies, with Spaatz and de Tassigny witnessing the signatures. When the Allies had finished signing, Zhukov stood up and ordered the Germans to leave. Keitel rose promptly, followed by the others, stood at attention, saluted with his baton, turned on his heel and strode from the room. The whole signing "took about 15 minutes," estimated Kay. "The next time I saw Field

---

[11] Original diary, 8 May 1945 contd
[12] Original diary, 8 May 1945 contd
[13] 1972 Thames Television interview
[14] Actually Blood Order, awarded to those who had taken part in the 1923 failed coup

Marshal Keitel was at the Nuremberg Trials," she added. "I was there for a couple of days. Göering was always acting up to the crowd."[15]

The 150 Allies then left the hall and, while they waited outside, uniformed waitresses set the tables for the ceremonial banquet which started at about 1.30 in the morning. "They had women doing everything, which surprised me," said Kay. At each place was a bottle of vodka, red wine and Russian champagne. Soon Zhukov arose and proposed a toast to Stalin, interpreted sentence by sentence by a Russian lieutenant standing beside him. As Zhukov raised his glass, everyone stood and the Russians drank the toast in vodka. Then Zhukov said: "General of the Army Eisenhower has given the most magnificent performance of any general of the current time. His great strides in the west helped me in the east. I raise my glass to the greatest military strategist of our time – General Eisenhower."

These were the first of 24 official toasts. The party thereafter continued with toasts to the "late and great" President Roosevelt, who had been such a friend to Russia, to the new US President, to Winston Churchill and to General de Gaulle. The English and Russian toasts were translated into Russian or English; the French toasts only into Russian. "If you didn't understand Russian, it was too bad!" said Kay.[16]

"All the Russians were very friendly," she said.[17] "A lot of them didn't speak English and yet there were a few that spoke *beautiful* English, that were educated, say, at Oxford and Cambridge. I remember speaking to one and I thought 'Oh I'll never forget your face as long as I live. If there's another war, I'll never forget you.' He was rather young, he was quite young. He was very pleasant but you always kept feeling that they really hated us, which I'm sure they did."

---

[15] 1972 Thames Television interview
[16] Original diary, 8 May 1945 contd
[17] The World at War 1973 (episode 25)

High-ranking officers of all nationalities carried on toasting the leaders until eventually they were so drunk that they had to be carried out. "It went on for hours and hours and hours," said Kay. "The Russians were very boisterous." [18] About 5am or 6am, Kay went back to the room, sat around for about 30 minutes then took a sightseeing drive round Berlin to the Chancery, Reichstag, Unter den Linden and the Opera House. "There was absolutely nothing standing" except the outside walls. Around 6.45am, Kay arrived back at Tempelhof airfield and flew back to Ike's office in Reims.

"Instead of the pressure easing for E [Ike], it seems to be almost worse," said Kay. [19] At the end of the week, the Germans were still fighting the Russians in Czechoslovakia, despite the surrender. Patton's army had stopped on the banks of the Moldau River at the Russians' demand, notwithstanding an uprising by the Czech resistance on 5 May. Thousands of Germans killed themselves after the surrender, including one in five of the 53 admirals, one in seven of the 98 Luftwaffe generals and one in ten Army generals. [20] On 10 May 1945, Sudeten leader Konrad Henlein slashed his wrists with his broken spectacles while in US custody. General Marshall cabled Ike: "No more suicides", but the suicides of leading Nazis continued. [21] Himmler and von Friedeburg took poison on their arrest by the British in May 1945, Robert Ley killed himself in October 1945 and Göering swallowed a poison capsule after his trial at Nuremberg in October 1946.

The day after the surrender, on 9 May 1945, Ike's HQ sent a letter to all German cities and towns under SHAEF's control warning that anyone caught gathering food for the DEF camps or taking food to the prisoners would be shot. SHAEF announced that German civilians were to be allowed 1,150

---

[18] 1972 Thames Television interview
[19] Original diary 11 May 1945
[20] Life magazine, 14 May 1945
[21] Bodyguard of Lies claimed 81 of the 2,500 Wehrmacht generals committed suicide, p 801

calories a day, compared to the 4,000 calories a day for US soldiers.[22] The same day, in a letter to Mamie, Ike said that Germany was "devastated. Whole cities are obliterated; and the German population, to say nothing of millions of former slave laborers, is largely homeless. There is certain to be unrest, privation and undoubtedly some starvation next winter. It is a bleak picture".

Ike also mentioned to Mamie that he was going to theatre in London – though he omitted to mention it was with Kay: "Some good friends of John's and mine have asked us to a theater and supper party [the following Tuesday 15 May]. So for the first time in this war I hope to go out - unless John doesn't want to do so. It would be fun, I think. Haven't seen a show and eaten in a restaurant in three years." Ike and Kay then flew back to Northolt with 18 bottles of Champagne "for General Eisenhower's private VE party". They drove straight to Telegraph Cottage and played a couple of holes of golf (Kay had played golf properly for the first time on 30 April 1944[23]), before sitting together on the garden bench where Ike told Kay he would "try my damnedest" to have a baby with her. After lunch, before they drove back to London, Ike held out his arms and invited Kay to give him a "victory kiss".

In London, Ike was overwhelmed with congratulatory messages and invitations to receive the freedom of a number of British cities, including London, where he was to make a speech at the Guildhall on June 12. He invited Kay's mother and his son John to join him, Kay and half a dozen others for a "private V-E Day celebration" at Omar Bradley's suite in the Dorchester hotel. The group of ten then drove in three cars to the Prince of Wales theatre to see Strike A New Note. Ike's secretary Sue Sarafian said later: "Kay went, but her mother went with her, and John. It was perfectly harmless."[24] Kay, who was in her WAC uniform, sat next to Ike in

---

[22] The Stars and Stripes, 30 April 1945
[23] Diary 30 April 1944

his box but the audience recognised him and began cheering him and calling for a speech. "I wonder if you people realise what it means to me to be back here among friends, among people whose language I can *almost* speak," Ike told theatregoers. After meeting star Sid Fields and the rest of the cast backstage, the party had dinner at "a big table against the wall" in Ciro's nightclub where the orchestra serenaded Ike with "For He's A Jolly Good Fellow". Ike asked Kay to dance first and, after dancing with the other women in the group, finally returned to Kay. [25]

On 17 May, Ike rejected proposals from German leader Admiral Dönitz for a combined Allied-German campaign against the Soviet Union. Such efforts "to cause dissension in the Allied camp" were "doomed to utter failure", said Stalin. [26] Ike recognised, however, that the western Allies' relationship with Russia was at about the same "arms-length stage" as that of the Americans and the British at the start of US involvement in the war. Any evasiveness by the western Allies made the Russians suspicious.

On Monday 21 May, US newspapers ran a story that 50,000 American prisoners-of-war, repatriated from German camps, were being held at an American camp in France under conditions worse than those they had experienced while prisoners of the Germans. Ike said he wanted to visit the camp immediately. He took four US Senators with him to the "Lucky Strike" tent camp near Le Havre. The Red Cross had organised clubs and recreation facilities at the airfield formerly used by the Germans. After joining a line with a mess tin, Ike walked a mile and a half back to his plane through throngs of former American prisoners, chatting to every fourth or fifth man.

Ike flew from Reims to Paris on 22 May, while his household and office equipment were moved to new headquarters in

---

[24] www.ibiblio.org/lia/president/EisenhowerLibrary/oral_histories/ Jehl_Sue-Sarafian.html
[25] The New York Times, 16 May 1945
[26] Order of the day, 1 May 1945

Frankfurt. He stayed in the ambassador's suite at the Hotel Raphael. Averell Harriman, whom Ike invited to lunch with his daughter Kathy, responded by inviting Ike and Kay to Moscow. Both later visited Moscow separately, and Ike went on to Leningrad with Zhukov after the Potsdam Conference.

DEALING WITH THE GERMANS

Ike was appointed military governor of the US-occupied zone based in Frankfurt, and moved to a villa in Bad Homburg just outside the city. SHAEF HQ moved to the six-storey *IG Farbenindustrie* building in the city before the end of May 1945. The building had been untouched by Allied bombing – in fact there was even a rumour that the Allies had deliberately not bombed it so that they could use it after the war. The building comprised six 'spokes' radiating from a main arc, with a continuous elevator. At the back of the building was a chrome fishpond with lilies and goldfish. Above this pool, near the snack bar and officers' club, there was a large bronze statue of a seated female nude. Many GIs posed for photographs with their arms around the statue or lying in its lap.

Ike's huge first-floor office was the former board room, Q3-130. On the desk at one end were a green plastic phone and matching green lamp, with two dogs at the base. Tall walnut columns framed the big windows, which overlooked the "utter devastation"[1] of Frankfurt. While his visitors talked, Ike took cigarettes from a plain wooden box and lit them with paper matches. In the office, he wore a short olive-drab 'Ike jacket' in the style of the British battle jacket. The jacket was part of the 'new-look' American uniforms which had started to arrive from Philadelphia shortly before D-Day. Kay had an anteroom adjoining Ike's office, with a window installed between them. Secretary Sue Sarafian said: "Every person who came to visit the general would always stop in and see Kay first. They all loved her, she was a very likable person."[2]

---

[1] Patton diary, 5 November 1945
[2] www.ibiblio.org/lia/president/EisenhowerLibrary/oral_histories/Jehl_Sue-Sarafian.html

Ike's Irish Lover

One of the problems Ike constantly had to contend with in Frankfurt was the breakdown in discipline among Allied soldiers, which could even involve rape, murder or theft. On one occasion the safe at IG Farben was used to store the crown jewels of Hesse which had been recovered from three US officers who had stolen them. The jewels and gold, then worth $2.5 million, had been hidden by their original owners in the cellars of Kronberg Castle, just outside Frankfurt. Air Force Colonel (and attorney) Jack Durant, his WAC girlfriend Captain Kathleen Nash and Major David Watson had removed the jewels from their settings and sold them in Switzerland. Some were buried in the grounds of a church in Virginia in the United States. Others were given by Watson to his girlfriend in Belfast, Northern Ireland. The three officers were eventually arrested and jailed after courts-martial in Frankfurt.

Occasionally Ike would give an interview to a news correspondent. He explained to a reporter for Yank newspaper that there were two reasons for the occupation: military and political. On the military side, there were uprisings to put down, people and property to guard, labour gangs to supervise. On the political side, Germany had to be got back into shape. "We are working towards a government of Germany by the Germans under the supervision of the Allied General Control Council," he said. "At first we'll have to look down the Germans' necks in everything they do. Finally we've got to see to it that the terms of a continuing peace are agreed upon and that there can be no effective opposition to such a peace. If the Germans show a liberal attitude and a desire to live peacefully, then the necessity for an occupation force starts dying out." But Ike admitted that, "without a framework, anarchy beyond precedent would engulf many of the liberated and conquered lands".[3]

Ike was "very sympathetic" to the idea of bringing soldiers' wives over from America, but pointed out that there was a shortage of shipping, food and accommodation. "Proper

---

[3] at ease, p 317

housing" was a serious problem, not just for the troops but for the Germans and displaced persons (DPs).[4] "I'm just as badly off as any GI today. I don't want to be here. I'm 54 years old and I lead a kind of lonely life," he said. In a letter to Mamie, Ike said he hoped to work out a policy to allow Allied families to come to Germany, but the "lowest private" must have the same rights as "the highest general", and that would be problematic because of the "lack of suitable quarters".[5]

One of the immediate issues faced by the victorious Allies was who to trust and work with. Most German officials had been supportive of the National Socialists, even if they now claimed to have been anti-Nazi. The Potsdam Four-Power Declaration stated that "...Nazi leaders, influential Nazi supporters and high officials of Nazi organizations and institutions and any other persons dangerous to the occupation or its objectives shall be arrested and interned. All members of the Nazi Party who have been more than nominal participants in its activities and all other persona hostile to Allied purposes shall be removed from public and semi-public office, and from positions of responsibility in important private undertakings."

The denazification programme began when the first Allied troops occupied the border towns of Germany; the first Special Branch office was set up in Aachen following its capture in October 1944. SHAEF established the authority for these investigations even before the invasion of Normandy. On 9 November 1944, a SHAEF directive formally defined the categories of members of the National Socialist party since 1 January 1933[6] who were not to be employed after the war. The occupation forces also arrested and interned specified categories of German leaders, those in high government posts of the Third Reich and members

---

[4] On 22 August 1945, Ike said that "suitable accommodations" for Jewish DPs would be requisitioned from the owners "wherever necessary"
[5] Reims, 12 May 1945
[6] Later changed to 1 May 1937

of the 'criminal organisations' specified by the International Military Tribunal. By the end of 1945, US forces had arrested and interned more than 100,000 Germans. Everyone had to register, and all civilians had to stay indoors from 7pm to 6am.[7] Daily passes were issued to doctors, midwives and crucial tradesmen to enable them to move around more freely. Of 1,521,832 Germans who filled in questionnaires (*Fragebogen*) between 1 April 1947 and 30 April 1948, 247,193 were considered to be unemployable Nazis, 101,077 were given 'adverse recommendations' and only 6,148 were said to have taken part in anti-Nazi activities. Patton himself claimed that, as military governor of Bavaria, he had "removed from or deprived of office 49,088 Nazis".[8]

On 25 May 1945, Ike told US Judge Robert Jackson in the Hotel Raphael in Paris that, although he was not in favour of shooting people without trial, he hoped the Nuremberg trials would not take long. All those given the death sentence at Nuremberg should be hanged, rather than shot, he added. Members of the Gestapo should be held in common prisons. "Any bastard who belonged to that outfit" was guilty of war crimes, he said. (The Gestapo and SS were subsequently declared illegal organisations, which enabled the Allies to "get at members of these bodies against whom it may not be possible to prove specific crimes".[9]) But on 22 September, General Patton told a press conference that too much fuss was being made about the denazification programme. He had ignored the SHAEF order banning the Allies from using former Nazis to restore railways and public works. Patton suggested that the Nazis "were just another political party, like the Republicans and Democrats".[10] He had earlier said that being a member of the SS meant "no more in Germany than being a Democrat in America – that is not to be quoted".[11] When Beetle Smith and Eisenhower heard about

---

[7] Daily Mail, 3 October 1944
[8] Letter, 22 October 1945
[9] Daily Express, 15 June 1945
[10] Original diary, 26 September 1945, and at ease, p 308
[11] Regensburg, 8 May 1945

the remarks, Patton – insisting that he had been misquoted – nevertheless said he considered that the communists were as dangerous as the Nazis.[12]

The Soviets were not the only targets of General Patton's criticism. Though he had been horrified by the concentration camps, he viewed the Jews as the authors of communism and "lower than animals". He said US soldiers frequently had to use force to prevent Jews and others "defecating on the floor when ample facilities are provided outside".[13] He criticised the "sub-human characteristics of these people in that they do not understand toilets and refuse to use them except as repositories for tin cans, garbage, and refuse..."[14] And he condemned "the compilation of lies which the communist and semitic elements of our government have levelled against me".[15]

For Ike, Patton's remarks were a bridge too far. In "one of the stormiest sessions ever staged" at SHAEF headquarters, on 27 September, he lost his temper and told Patton that he would "very likely relieve him of his command of the Third Army". Instead, Patton would be put in charge of the 15th Army, which was charged with writing the history of the US involvement in the war. Ike said he would not give Patton "any definite decision until he had slept on it". Ike later admitted that "George's temper and my own capacity for something more than mild irritation"[16] meant the two men would inevitably clash. He warned Marshall that Patton was "mentally unbalanced" and, the following day, he relieved Patton of the military governorship of Bavaria and put General Truscott in command of the Third Army.[17] Patton

---

12 Churchill stated: "I fear increasingly that new struggles may arise out of those we are successfully ending" - February 1945 letter to his wife
13 Patton diary, 15 September 1945
14 Patton diary, 1 October 1945
15 Patton letter, 22 October 1945
16 at ease, p 173
17 Original diary 28 September 1945. General Giraud said France was "shocked to the heart at the treatment accorded the greatest soldier since Napoleon". (Patton letter 22 October 1945)

accepted the command of the nominal 15th Army because he did not want to be part of the destruction of Germany, which he believed should be a buffer against the "real danger which is Bolshevism from Russia".[18]

(Patton died of heart failure 12 days after a minor car accident on 9 December 1945, and was buried in Luxembourg alongside his men. His 30-year-old "niece" Jean Gordon, with whom he'd had a relationship since 1932, was found dead in her gas-filled Manhattan apartment shortly afterwards.)

Back in England, Telegraph Cottage was closed up permanently on 30 May 1945. At the beginning of June, Ike decided to spend another night on the Riviera, where he attended a reunion dinner of West Point classmates. The South of France had become a rest camp for thousands of GIs and officers, and Ike said that the GIs, who had the run of Nice, seemed much better behaved than some of the officers in Cannes. While flying back to Frankfurt from the Riviera, Ike outlined the text of the talk he was to give at London's Guildhall when he was to receive the freedom of the City. He drafted and redrafted his speech again and again, and even read it out loud to try and improve it.

On 5 June 1945, Ike flew to Berlin to sign the quadripartite agreements with the Russians, British and French under which Germany was to be ruled by the Allied Control Council.[19] Ike and Monty went together to pay their respects to Field Marshal Zhukov. Ike presented Zhukov with the highest decoration America gave to foreigners, the Legion of Merit. Zhukov said that he wanted to give Ike the Order of Victory but had to await approval from the Supreme Soviet in Moscow. Ike declined an invitation to that evening's banquet, notwithstanding Zhukov's persistence, but he called in for 15 minutes to toast President Truman, Prime Minister Churchill and Stalin. Ike flew back to Frankfurt and

---

[18] Patton: A Genius for War, p 771
[19] Daily Mail, 6 June 1945

Kay the same day. Five days later, Zhukov arrived in Frankfurt to present Monty and Ike with the Order of Victory. The square platinum decoration was covered with diamonds and rubies. One magazine[20] said it was worth $100,000 but Ike reckoned the true value was nearer $18,000. After a private conference in Ike's office, he and Zhukov had lunch in the nearby recreation centre. From the mess hall veranda, they watched a fly-past by 1,700 American and British military aircraft. (Many heavy bombers had already returned to the United States.) Numerous toasts were then drunk to the Allied victory.

Ike said: "Speaking for the Allied forces, we are going to have peace if we have to fight for it...I believe that there is not a single man around this table that would not give back all the honours, all the publicity and everything else that this war has brought to him if he could have avoided the misery and suffering and debt that have been brought to the populations by reason of this war."

---

[20] Reader's Digest

HONOURS GALORE

Two days after the Zhukov visit, Ike received the freedom of the City of London. Kay typed up his speech, but rejected his offer of the manuscript. Ike's speech brought tears to the eyes of many, including the Prime Minister. Even his critics said it was "a wonderful speech".[1] Before the ceremony, Ike slipped out of the back door of the Dorchester for a walk in Hyde Park, but he was recognised and a crowd gathered round him when he stopped to sign an autograph for a taxi driver. A policemen advised him to move on, but Ike continued to sign pound notes, ten-shilling notes and all sorts of pieces of paper. Within 15 minutes, admirers were coming from everywhere. Finally Ike insisted: "Listen, folks, I've got to get back and make a speech."

Thirty years to the day after he graduated from West Point, Ike rode with Air Marshal Tedder in an open landau from the Dorchester to the bomb-scarred Guildhall. After being presented with the sword of the Duke of Wellington – a "curved, oriental scimitar, encrusted with jewels"[2] – as a symbol of the (not yet completed) Sword of Honour, Ike told the Lord Mayor that he probably couldn't have made the speech unless he knew he was among friends. "Humility must always be the portion of any man who receives acclaim earned in the blood of his followers and the sacrifices of his friends," he said.

Kay also attended the ceremony and was at the Mansion House afterwards for lunch. A crowd of 30,000 gathered beneath the Mansion House balcony as Ike, with the Prime Minister and Clemmie Churchill in the background, said: "Whether or not you know it, I am now a Londoner myself. I've got just as much right to be down in that crowd, yelling, as you have." At lunch, the Prime Minister said Ike would

---

[1] Alan Brooke war diaries, 12 June 1945
[2] at ease, p 299

"always bring our countries together" in peace the same way he brought them together in the "grim and awful cataclysm of war". He said Ike had taken a "terrible decision" to go through with the invasion of France despite adverse weather. "Not only did he take the risk and arrive at the fence, but he cleared it in magnificent style," said Churchill.

After lunch, Ike called on the Queen Mother and then King George VI, Queen Mary and Princess Elizabeth at Buckingham Palace. King George presented him with the Order of Merit (OM), the first American to receive the only British military decoration the sovereign can bestow without government approval. The King also gave Ike a handwritten letter of gratitude. Ike had already received the highest military honour of the British government, the Order of the Bath, presented by the King in Algiers. Ike and Kay then dined at 10 Downing Street, where Ike showed off his OM. He flew back to Frankfurt with Kay for a day, then on to Orly on June 14. Ike's plane was due to arrive at the French airport first, but the newly-promoted Air Chief Marshal Tedder's plane arrived beforehand. When Tedder disembarked, the French band mistook him for the Supreme Commander and started playing The Star-Spangled Banner and the Marseillaise, but not God Save the King. (Ike arrived a few minutes later, and the band played the same tunes all over again.)

At the *Arc de Triomphe*, General de Gaulle made Ike a *Compagnon de la Libération*, stooping to kiss him on both cheeks. Ike placed a wreath on the Tomb of the Unknown Soldier, signed the guest book and then stood at attention next to de Gaulle to review the French troops. Ike then drove through streets lined with cheering Parisians to pay his respects at the tomb of Napoleon and at the mausoleum of Marshal Foch. In a speech at the *Hotel de Ville*, Ike praised the French contribution to the war. The audience cheered and clapped but, not speaking French, Ike didn't understand enough to know which part of his statement the French were applauding. De Gaulle gave a state dinner that night in honour of the Americans (with the sole exception of Ike's

ADC, British Brigadier Jimmy Gault). The senior British officers attended a French cocktail party beforehand, and Tedder was then invited to witness the presentation to Ike before dinner of the sword Napoleon had worn as First Consul – but not to attend the dinner. The snub to the British led to frantic telephone calls between Paris, Frankfurt and England until Tedder finally "remembered" that he had a prior dinner engagement.

That summer of 1945, Ike was feted in many European cities, including Brussels, Amsterdam, Warsaw, Prague and Belfast. He was awarded university degrees by Oxford, Louvain and Queen's, swords in London, Paris and Brussels and an ashtray containing coils of the first cable laid across the Rhine at Remagen, which he kept on his desk.

On June 16, Ike left Frankfurt without Kay to fly to the United States in a plane specially sent by President Harry Truman. A 24-hour stopover in Bermuda allowed him to rest before his arrival in Washington on 19 June. Ike was greeted by Mamie and up to 30,000 others, with thousands more lining the road. The idea of standing in an open car to acknowledge the cheers hadn't even occurred to Ike, but he managed not to fall over in the moving vehicle. After receiving the keys to the city, Ike addressed a joint session of Congress on Capitol Hill (wearing his glasses and dreaming of "our return to our loved ones"). He said he spoke as the commander of the three million American citizens who, "at your behest, have faced resolutely every terror the ruthless Nazi could devise".[3] The headlines in the US papers the next day said: "Oh God, It's Swell to Be Home", "Nearly a Million Welcome Ike", "Eisenhower Calls for End of Germans' General Staff" and "Congress Pays Ike Its Greatest Ovation in 25 Years".

After lunch at the Statler Hotel, Mamie and Ike went to the White House, where President Truman presented him with another oak-leaf cluster to his Distinguished Service Medal.

---

[3] 18 June 1945, speech to joint session of Congress

Following a brief rest at the Wardman Park hotel, Ike was driven again to the White House, where President Truman had arranged a dinner for 53 officers and men. There were no speeches, and Ike left the White House by 9.30pm. There were then ceremonies in Washington, New York, West Point, Kansas City and Abilene. In Topeka, Ike injured his leg again getting off the train to greet a group of soldiers. The train started off without him and, when he ran to jump on the steps, he missed and banged his knee.

While Ike was away, Kay flew to the Riviera in Ike's C-47 and stayed at the *Hotel du Cap d'Antibes* for a couple of weeks. "Beautiful weather at Antibes – we just lazed all day," wrote Kay in her diary. But Ike and Clark then turned up and, due to a misunderstanding, had to wait 30 minutes at the airport for transport. "I have never seen [Ike] so mad," wrote Kay. "We all caught hell...Such a shame all this happened...Every time E gets away, something always seems to happen."[4] The next day, Ike seemed to have forgotten his bad mood. "We all went swimming and ran around the bay in a lovely speed boat – Wayne Clarke [sic] left after lunch. Didn't do much all day but everyone had a good time. Early to bed."[5]

Kay also got into trouble for mislaying a vital letter from the RAF for three days. The incidents were the first storm clouds in the couple's relationship. The next day, Ike left for Frankfurt where he again wrote to Kul, describing his holiday in White Sulphur Springs with Mamie, and promising to stay in touch.[6] After a few hours in the office, with the weather unsuitable for flying, Ike was driven to Munich – a journey of more than seven hours – to visit displaced person camps. He found conditions reasonable in most of them.[7] However, he insisted that Jews be cared for in special centres and that, if necessary, German families should be

---

[4] Original diary 13 September 1945
[5] Original diary 14 September 1945
[6] 18 July 1945
[7] Original diary 16 September 1945. A US report on Lansberg Camp in December 1945 said there was "not the slightest evidence of malnutrition in the camp" and inspecting officers were "shocked at the waste of food"

expelled from their homes so the houses could be taken over by Jewish Displaced Persons. He also handed over several hundred thousand prisoners-of-war to France to use as slave labour.[8]

Back in Germany, Ike hosted two parties for junior SHAEF staff at Kay's suggestion. He would still go riding with Kay or come to the WAC house and stay for supper and bridge, sometimes till 4am. He was also still interested in the possibility of Kay becoming a US citizen, discussing the matter with President Truman at the 1945 Potsdam Conference.

Ike was now enjoying the peace. He and Kay went to *Sous le Vent* again, and this time Ike went swimming, drove a speedboat, visited nightclubs and restaurants and sunbathed with Kay on the terrace. But he worried about the difference in their ages. "Twenty years is a big difference. It's all right now, but what about ten years from now?" he asked. After the South of France, they took a fishing trip to Bavaria with Beetle Smith, and then visited General Clark in Salzburg on the Austrian border. Clark took them to see Hitler's holiday home at Berchtesgaden, and Ike made sure Kay was in the photographs. Although the Eagle's Nest had not been hit by bombs, Hitler's house, Göering's adjoining chalet, a large greenhouse and the SS barracks were bombed by the RAF just weeks before. At the entrance to the Eagle's Nest, a paratrooper guard said soldiers[9] had collected so many souvenirs that it was now guarded to prevent further pilfering. The Americans used the Eagle's Nest as a "military command post" until it was handed back to Bavaria in 1960. But when Ike spotted a sign saying "Officers Only", he ordered that the sign be removed immediately. A group of sightseeing GIs cheered.

---

[8] Patton diary, 29 August 1945
[9] 40,000 had already seen it, said Patton protesting at an order to destroy it (Diary 31 August 1945)

DIVORCING MAMIE

As Ike became even more well known in the United States and Britain, his "personal life" was coming under increasing scrutiny, not least by FDR's successor, President Harry S Truman. Kay said she later learned that Eisenhower had cabled General Marshall saying that he wanted to divorce his wife Mamie and marry "this Englishwoman", as Truman referred to Kay.[1]

Marshall responded that if Ike "ever came close to doing such a thing, he'd not only bust him out of the Army, he'd see to it that he never for the rest of his life would be able to draw a peaceful breath" and that "if he ever again even mentioned a thing like that, he'd see it to it that the rest of his life was a living hell". Ike was ordered to get straight back to the US. It wasn't the first time that the famously humourless Marshall had intervened when a senior officer's divorce appeared to be imminent. In October 1944, Patton had jokingly told him that General Fred Walker's wife planned to divorce him because she "thought he was a slacker". Marshall, not realising he was being ribbed, insisted: "No she won't, I'll talk to her."[2]

Marshall recognised that Ike's relationship with Kay "was hazardous for Eisenhower's future, both personally with respect to his marital relationship and politically with regard to any potential political career to which he might aspire".[3] Truman later told his biographer Merle Miller that he took the Eisenhower-Marshall exchanges from Ike's file in the Pentagon "and I destroyed them". The details were published in Miller's book[4] and later confirmed in an interview with the President's second cousin, General Louis W

---

[1] William Safire, New York Times, 6 June 1991
[2] Patton letter to his wife, 26 October 1944
[3] Eden-Eisenhower Correspondence 1955-1957, University of North Carolina Press, ed Peter Boyle
[4] Plain Speaking: An Oral Biography of Harry S Truman

Truman. The general said "Cousin Harry" had shown him the letter that he had written to Eisenhower. "He had written that certain things would have to happen about his driver friend [Kay Summersby], or he was going to kick him [General Eisenhower] out." General Truman said the President had "very definitely" made an issue of the relationship between Ike and Kay, and had told General Marshall about it.[5]

The story was also confirmed by retired Major-General Harry Vaughan, President Truman's White House aide. "In 1952, before the Republican National Convention was held, Senator Robert Taft of Ohio and Eisenhower were jockeying for position to get the presidential nomination," he said. "The Taft boys heard about Ike's letters to Marshall and wanted to get copies. Truman heard about that. He ordered the Pentagon to send him the letters. He didn't want the Taft gang spreading them all over the country. But I don't think he destroyed them. I think he sent them to General Marshall with a covering note which said 'These belong in your personal files. I don't think they should be used for dirty politics'."[6]

President Truman's assistant, Dr David R Steelman, saw the cable from Ike, as he confirmed in a 1996 interview.[7] According to Steelman, General Marshall phoned him one day in late 1945 and said he wanted Steelman to go with him to see President Truman. He brought the cable from Ike. "Marshall said he wanted me to be a witness," said Steelman. "Eisenhower had said he was going to divorce Mamie and marry Kay, and Marshall told him 'If you do that, I'll bust you out of the Army, so help me. Don't you dare do that'...Truman said 'Take the letters over and burn them'. And so on the way out, Marshall said to me 'This is one time I'm going to defy the President. I ain't going to burn them; I'm going to file them. I'm going to leave them in

---

5 www.trumanlibrary.org/oralhist/trumanl.htm
6 The Bakersfield Californian, 10 February 1974
7 Interview with Niel Johnson in Florida on 29 February 1996

the record'. And then he did...Those letters came up missing...somebody stole them out of the files, and nobody knows what became of them. They've never been found." It wouldn't be the first time Marshall's files had gone missing. A report on the Katyn massacre by the Soviet Union, written in 1945 by US Colonel John van Vliet, was destroyed by Marshall's assistant Chief-of-Staff for intelligence, Major General Clayton Bissell.[8]

Professor Garrett Mattingly, who used to censor sensitive cables from Washington during the war, also corroborated the story in the early 1950s to history faculty colleagues at Columbia University, where Ike was President.

The exchange between Ike and Marshall was also cited by leading British journalist Malcolm Muggeridge in his 1981 autobiography. He said that, in late November 1948 at the Garrick Club in London, the Secretary of State for War, Sir James Grigg (a man of "unflinching straightness"[9]) "talked very indiscreetly as usual. [He] said that at the end of the war Eisenhower had told [Field Marshal] Alan Brooke that he proposed to get a divorce and marry Kay Summersby, and devote the rest of his life to promoting Anglo-American relations".[10] As David Williams, secretary of the Malcolm Muggeridge Society, said: "The diary was contemporaneous and hand-written and Muggeridge would have had no cause to misreport."[11]

The number of witnesses of the exchange between Ike and Marshall, their seniority and the fact that they would no reason to lie would seem to suggest that the story recounted by President Truman was accurate. But Kay didn't know about the exchange at the time. She was visiting Copenhagen where Ike's C-54 was to take part in an aerial display. She also accompanied Averell Harriman and his daughter Kathy

---

[8] Select Committee on the Katyn Forest Massacre, US Government Printing Office, 1952
[9] Alan Brooke war diary notes, 27 July 1945
[10] Like It Was, Malcolm Muggeridge, p 310
[11] Email to author, 11 February 2015

to *Sous Le Vent* again. She then took a trip with the Harrimans to Vienna, Budapest and Moscow, where she was invited to a cocktail party and reception at the Chinese embassy, attended the ballet, visited the Kremlin and listened to 100 men of the Red Army choir sing It's A Long Way To Tipperary in Russian.

Ike had been a guest at receptions in Amsterdam and Prague, and Kay returned on his 55th birthday, Sunday 14 October. Ike came to Kay's house for his birthday dinner and they had steak (his second favourite, after oysters), a birthday cake and Champagne and then played bridge until 4am.[12] The next day they went riding, then back to Ike's house to shower and relax with a drink in the library.

Ike closed the door and then sat near her on the leather davenport. "Come here, I've got a surprise for you," he said, kissing her. He told her she was going to Washington to take out her US citizenship papers. What exactly happened that night at Kay's house has never been confirmed but Kay said they dressed slowly afterwards, kissing occasionally. He told her to comb her hair, and then ordered a chicken salad and white wine for them in the library. But whatever did happen, it didn't mean Ike was growing soft on the question of women joining their menfolk in Germany. Two weeks afterwards, Ike refused to allow the wives of Mr Justice Lawrence and Mr Justice Birkett to join them in Nuremberg. If he'd allowed this request, he'd have had to allow Mamie to come over to Europe too!

Kay said Ike later offered her the cigarette case de Gaulle had given him – platinum and gold with five sapphire stars, a sapphire clip and de Gaulle's signature – but she turned down the gift. As Ike had promised, Kay then flew from Frankfurt to Washington in Ike's Skymaster[13] arriving on 1 November 1945 to finalise her US citizenship. (She made sure that her application for a certificate of arrival

---

[12] Original diary 14 October 1945
[13] Number 9146

mentioned that she had travelled with "General Lucius Clay and Ambassador Robert Murphy. No relationship.")[14]

---

[14] US Dept of Justice naturalisation application, 23 November 1945

THE END OF THE AFFAIR

When Kay got back to Germany, Ike was packing to go via Paris to Washington on 10 November 1945 to take over from Marshall as chief-of-staff in the Pentagon.[1] "It's just for a few weeks," he told her, promising to return and take her to Washington at the start of 1946. They dined together and, at 6am the next day, kissed each other goodbye in the office before Ike left. He had told his personal staff – including Kay – to be ready to leave in 10 days. Then a cable arrived from Washington to say 'Lt Summersby' had been dropped from the list of those due to leave. No explanation was given.

"Nothing was ever the same again," said Kay. She left the office, went back to her apartment, lay on her bed and stared at the ceiling, finally accepting that Ike had put his political career before their relationship. She cried until midnight. The next day she could not face the office so went riding, then returned to work the following day. She "smiled a lot", behaved normally and went to lunch with friends at the officers' club. The Deputy Military Governor, General Lucius Clay (who spoke no German) told her he wanted her to run his VIP guesthouse in Berlin.

Nine days after leaving Germany, Eisenhower succeeded General Marshall as chief-of-staff of the US Army, an appointment he said he greeted with "no personal enthusiasm". Three days later, in a typed note[2] addressed to "Dear Kay" in Frankfurt, Ike said: "I am terribly distressed, first because it has become impossible longer to keep you as a member of my personal official family and secondly because I cannot come back to give you a detailed account of the reasons." He said there would be opposition to anyone who was not a "completely naturalized American citizen" working in the War Department and that, as she would be discharged

---

[1] Original diary 10 November 1945
[2] 22 November 1945

from the WACs immediately on reaching the US, she would be a civilian again so it was impossible to employ her in the War Department. (That didn't happen.) As the US newspapers said at the time: "It would be an unlikely situation that would find a British subject [Ireland was not yet a republic] holding a post as administrative assistant in Washington to an American Chief-of-Staff."[3]

Ike said that there was "no question" that Kay had the right to return to the US indefinitely, once the WACs were disbanded in Europe, even if she chose to work for Clay as a civilian, though Kay's new employer had promised to promote her "as soon as you are well-established in your new job". Ike said he would not try to express "the depth of my appreciation for the unexcelled loyalty and faithfulness with which you have worked for the past three and a half years under my personal direction". He was going to hospital that night and would try to send a more formal letter when he got out. He repeated that he was "personally much distressed" at the end of such a "valuable" association "in this particular fashion, but it is by reasons over which I have no control". He said that if he could be of any help to Kay, she should let him know "instantly either by a letter or by cable". After she came to the United States, he would do his best to help her find a suitable job. After settling details concerning Telek and his pups, Ike finished by asking Kay to "drop me a note from time to time – I will always be interested to know how you are getting along. With lasting and warm regard, Sincerely, DDE". A handwritten postscript said Ike was in bed with a bad cold and taking medicine constantly. "Take care of yourself – and retain your optimism," he wrote.

Patton, who had been told that Ike was not coming back from the US because of his cold, said that Prince Bernhard of the Netherlands arrived to decorate several Allies, including Kay, but she was "in a high state of nerves as a

---

3 Washington Evening Star, 6 November 1945

result of hearing that General Eisenhower is not returning".[4] A month later, in a more formal War Department memo from Washington (which Ike asked to be passed on to "Lieutenant Summersby"),[5] he wrote: "Many thanks for the present which I shall open on Christmas. My sincerest wishes to you for happiness and all good luck in the new year. (sgd) Dwight D Eisenhower." In a handwritten note, he added: "The break-up of my wartime personal staff has saddened me immeasurably." On Christmas Eve, Ike had his new ADC, Lieutenant-Colonel James Stack, send a routine cable to his successor[6] confirming that First Lieutenant Summersby's performance of her duty from 1 July 1945 to 20 November 1945 had been superior. "She was in charge of all personal correspondence and office appointments," he wrote. "Outstanding in reliability, tact and devotion to duty."

A broken-hearted Kay stayed (with Telek) in Berlin for almost a year, looking after VIPs for General Clay.[7] At the start of 1946, Ike sent General Clay a typed "to whom it may concern" letter[8] saying Kay had been employed by the American forces in Europe since the summer of 1941. She first worked as a civilian driver, then as "personal assistant" in Ike's office and finally as his secretary in charge of all mail. Ike said Kay's "outstanding characteristic" was her reliability, "a trait that was particularly important during the war when her position made it impossible to keep from her knowledge operational secrets of the gravest type". He said that Kay had "an engaging personality" and was "particularly capable as a receptionist and in managing appointments". After inviting prospective employers to contact him, Ike concluded: "Lt Summersby is definitely a superior type."

In a separate handwritten note to Kay, Ike said: "I've asked Gen Clay to allow you time to type your diary so that I might

---

4 Patton diary, 23 November 1945
5 21 December 1945, routine message to General Clay
6 24 December 1945, service message to General Joseph T McNarney
7 She was ordered to report to General Clay within two weeks of 27 November 1945
8 15 January 1946

have a copy. I do hope you can do it so that I may have the paper in my records...I promise I'll never publish it, if there is ever anything to make out of it, that is certainly yours. (Possibly a poor joke, but I mean to say I recognize that you have a better claim to that diary than anyone else ever had for another)." Kay typed up a transcript of some of the journal she had kept from June 1944 to April 1945.[9] (She did not record either of the German surrenders in the typed notes.) Kay sent the typed diary notes[10] to Eisenhower's new US secretary with a letter[11] saying: "I have typed the diary up very quickly. As you know I am no typist. Nevertheless I hope you will be able to retype it for the Boss."

On 11 March 1946, a typed letter from Ike thanked Kay "for the trouble you are taking in typing up your diary and to assure you that it will be of the most tremendous help to me if I ever need to refresh my memory concerning those years when we were serving together". However, it was a further two years before he started to write his memoirs of the war, Crusade in Europe – in which he mentioned Kay just once in passing, as a member of his staff.[12] Another letter from Ike in Washington in about March 1946, with staff and personal news, referred to the recent publication of Harry Butcher's diary, My Three Years with Eisenhower. "Haven't seen Butch for weeks – about half the people seem to think he has published a masterpiece – the other half thinks he is a skunk. Curious," wrote Ike. He urged Kay to stay optimistic: "Easy to say! I know, but it's all one can do."

In a handwritten letter on 26 April 1946,[13] Ike told Kay: "I'm dreadfully sorry you are so miserable at Berlin. If you should

---

[9] Typed up by Kay in Berlin, but the transcript for Crusade in Europe is not a verbatim copy of Kay's diary
[10] The notes at the Eisenhower Library in Abilene, Kansas, show that she switched typewriters from the start of 1945
[11] 30 September 1945
[12] 8 February 1948
[13] Auctioned by Sothebys in New York on 11 December 2008 as part of a larger lot including a beach photo of Ike and Kay for $43,750.

like me to do so I'll be glad to write to Gen Ridgway[14] asking him if he has a place for you...Any letter or recommendation that I can send will be gladly, very gladly, written." Kay was promoted to WAC captain in the spring of 1946. In a letter five days after Easter Sunday,[15] Ike thanked "Captain Kay Summersby" for her Easter card and told her he had made three speeches in New York. "You know how I hate these things," he added. Ike sympathised again with Kay's desire to leave General Clay's staff and offered to help her find a position at the United Nations. "I just dictated a brief note for you...This scrawl is just to say that whatever I can do for you will be done – I don't know whether the citizenship thing will enter the picture, but all we can do is try to get you a job. I believe the organization will be stationed near NY City.[16] In any event, don't get downhearted."

Kay was becoming keener to leave Germany as events there were becoming increasingly uncomfortable. The US Senate proposed to investigate "black market activities and sensational sex stories" in the German capital. The allegations that US soldiers were making huge profits from the flourishing black market in Germany were investigated by the Senate's Special Committee to Investigate the National Defense Program. One US officer in Berlin said that Russian soldiers would pay $200 for a $1 carton of American cigarettes, $150 for a bottle of whisky and $1,000 for an army wristwatch. Another way of making "hundreds of pounds a day" was by juggling with Belgian and French francs or with French francs and US dollars.[17] "These men are not thinking of the national interest and the American way of life, but of padding their own pockets," the committee was told. The amount of money being sent home by American soldiers could amount to three times their pay. (There were even reports that the defeated Germans were

---

[14] Deputy Supreme Allied Commander in the Mediterranean
[15] 26 April 1946
[16] Despite having its first meeting in San Francisco, the UN's headquarters were eventually in New York
[17] Evening Standard, 10 November 1944

forced to use separate toilets on all US military government installations, because they would otherwise steal the Americans' toilet paper![18])

On 14 August 1946, Colonel Francis P Miller told a Senate Special Committee that German occupation troops in France "had a better record in their personal contact with the population than the American troops occupying Germany". Colonel Miller also raised the race issue. He said white US officers were afraid to control negro troops, and soaring rates of venereal disease among negro personnel showed the extent of the breakdown of discipline. Almost two thirds of those convicted of murder were black, while blacks also accounted for more than half of all rapes. In 1946, a quarter of US troops sent to the stockade were blacks, even though they comprised less than 10 per cent of the US Army. The report eventually concluded that the denazification programme was "a glaring failure", the widespread fraterni-sation with German women was undermining the effective-ness of military government, US demands for "luxurious accommodations" had created a "desperate housing sit-uation" and a number of high-ranking US Army officers were involved in "gross black-marketing". (General Lee had earlier reported 140 cases of black-marketeering to Ike.[19])

Kay's boss, General Clay, was opposed to the investigation, which made Kay even more determined to leave. General Everett Hughes saw her "looking downcast" in the office of Colonel 'Tex' Lee, who said there was "no solution evident in her case". The only possible solution was to go to the United States, which Kay did. She sailed aboard the US army transport ship SS General SD Sturgis to New York, arriving on 10 October 1946 and declaring her intention to become a

---

[18] Ike had made the point that three things were necessary on any trip in war areas: "water, rations, and toilet paper" – Sgt Mickey and General Ike, p 57
[19] Diary 15 December 1944

US citizen in Washington District Court six weeks later, on 18 November 1946.[20]

Back in America, she caught up with old friends and went to "dozens of parties". She met many married US officers who'd had girlfriends in Europe during the war, so were very wary of her. However, she was sympathetic to the natural needs of servicemen who were based thousands of miles away from their spouses, often for years. Having a sexual relationship while overseas was "off the hometown score-board," she said.

Kay's mother wrote to Ike at Christmas 1946, and referred to a meeting between Kay and Ike.[21] She visited the Pentagon while she was in Washington and, while there, called on Ike. Ike stood to greet her and they chatted about her future plans. When she said she might look for a job in NY, he repeated: "If there's anything I can do..."

---

[20] US Dept of Justice form 16 January 1951, question 13, and statement of facts, question 12
[21] Letter of 20 December 1946

RAPE!

When Kay returned to the United States as a captain in the US Women's Army Corps, she was posted to Hamilton Field in California as assistant public relations officer in the air force. Although the 1,600-acre United States Air Force base was situated on the idyllic shores of San Pablo Bay, it was still 3,000 miles from Ike – about as far away from Washington as possible on the continental United States. Kay didn't know whether Ike had anything to do with her posting, but by November 1946, he'd been the army's Chief-of-Staff for a year. She had also made some powerful enemies when Ike ignored officials' advice and commissioned her in November 1944 as the only non-American WAC officer in Europe.

California was sunny – sunnier than drab, depressing wartime Europe, London or even west Cork and, even though Kay earned the princely sum of $2,400 a year and could live well, life on the base could be "terribly dull", she said. As a vivacious Irishwoman, who'd been deeply involved in the most significant parts of the war in Europe and Africa, the daily drudgery of PR work was more than Kay could stand. She was fed up with reading in the WAC training manual how to apply her make-up or do her hair – though life at Hamilton Field wasn't without its exciting moments. Six months earlier, a Flying Fortress aircraft had crashed into a hill near the base, killing two of the crew. According to one surviving crewman, the B-17 was carrying secret nuclear equipment for the Operation Crossroads tests in the Bikini islands. But that was just a blip. Kay wanted a little excitement in her life. She was soon to get her wish.

On the night of Tuesday 11 February 1947, former janitor Marion Bryant tried to strangle her while she was asleep in the WAC officers' quarters. The 22-year-old, powerfully-built ex-serviceman from Marin City said afterwards[1] that he just wanted to rape a woman – any woman.

"I didn't have any particular woman in mind," Bryant told FBI Special Agent James Neel.[2] "I thought I would have a better chance to rape a woman there as I didn't think there would be any men around." Bryant knew his way around Hamilton Field, as his wife, Ruth, used to work as a maid at the base. No passes were needed to enter the base, and the perimeter fence was not carefully guarded which made it an easy target.

About 9pm on 11 February, Bryant had met his friend 'Fat' Williams at the cafeteria in Marin City. Both men were at a loose end that night and Williams suggested hanging out with a few of his friends based at the Squadron C area of Hamilton Field. The two men drove in Williams' brown Chevrolet sedan to the base. After about a quarter of an hour chatting to his friends, Williams decided to leave, but Bryant had other ideas. "Just drop me off at the top of the hill," Bryant told his friend. Bryant offered to pay for the ride, but Williams wouldn't take any money.

As Williams drove off, Bryant looked around, considering where he'd find the most likely victim. Many of the lights were still on, so he couldn't do anything yet, he decided. Every time he heard cars approaching, he'd hide behind trees or bushes and, after a wait, he crept up to the WAC officers' quarters on San Pablo Avenue. "I approached the WAC officers' quarters as carefully as I could, so I wouldn't be seen," said Bryant. He thought he'd pass for a soldier from a distance in his khaki shirt, olive-drab battle jacket and green army cap – despite his brown shoes.

Outside Building T-575, a lone light bulb was blazing on the porch, so Bryant unscrewed it. The darkness closed in again. Bryant found an open screen door with another door ajar

---

[1] In a seven-page confession after six hours' questioning
[2] FBI statement made 15 February 1947 (because Hamilton Field was a government reservation)

just inside. He went into the day room, turning out lights in the day room and the hall as he went and using his flashlight to see his way. He ignored the sign in the hall which read "No men allowed in this building". "I was looking for a woman to rape. I wasn't looking for something to steal," he said later.

He had just entered the darkened laundry room when a woman dressed in a pink housecoat came in and switched on the light. Bryant quickly hid himself but the woman looked behind the door and spotted him. "What are you doing here?" she screamed. "Get out, and get out fast!" Bryant half arose and mumbled that his wife used to work at Hamilton Field, but he said he didn't try to rape the woman "because she scared me". He started walking out of the building but began to run when he saw the woman pick up the telephone. A military policeman was on the scene within 10 minutes. The woman described the intruder to the MP, who went out to his jeep to report the intruder.

Outside, Bryant waited in the drizzling rain at the top of the hill until eventually he heard a bugle blow and the lights all over the base went out. "I decided to go back to the WAC officers' quarters to get a woman to rape," he said. The door he had used before was now locked, so Bryant climbed onto a chair and used a small knife to cut out the corners of a window screen. He unlatched the screen and put it on the ground, but then found that the window was locked. While trying to remove the putty from the window frame, he broke the glass and snapped the knife blade. Police officers later found fragmentary latent fingerprints on the glass, and were able to find seven points of similarity with Bryant's fingerprints.

After waiting until he was sure nobody had heard the glass breaking, Bryant crawled in through the window. It was just after half past two in the morning and everyone in the building was sound asleep. He unlocked the front door to make sure he had an escape route, and turned out two hall lights, one by the phone. He waited until everything was quiet, then he noticed that the door to Room 3 – Kay's bedroom – was partly open and crept in.

"I saw a woman asleep in the bed in the room," Bryant told police. "I waited in the room for about ten minutes before I did anything. It was my intention to rape this woman. I put both of my hands on this woman's neck, and started to choke her. While choking her, I received sexual gratify-cation.[3] This woman kicked the wall when I was choking her."

After a few moments, Kay played dead. Bryant thought she was unconscious, but as he relaxed his grip on Kay's neck, she managed to scream "Cynthia". Red Cross assistant field director Cynthia Balmer, the only other person living on the ground floor of the officers' quarters, ran into Kay's room and turned on the light. Bryant pushed past her and raced out of the unlocked front door. After throwing away the broken knife and hiding for a while, he casually dried his clothes in the unlocked boiler room "as they were very wet from the rain", then took a cab home from outside the main gate.

Balmer immediately tried to ring the front gate to report the break-in and attempted rape. But she couldn't find the number, so started yelling for the sentry from the door at the end of the hall. A sentry appeared after about 10 minutes, and the Military Police arrived shortly afterwards. They interviewed Kay and anyone else who could help identify the assailant – particularly First Lieutenant Gladys McManimie, the woman dressed in the pink housecoat who'd had a good view of Bryant in the laundry room.

The MPs called in civilian police from the sheriff's office in San Rafael, who were particularly interested in the fact that the intruder said his wife used to work as a maid at the base. The housekeeper recalled Bryant's pregnant wife, Ruth, and

---

[3] Bryant claimed he choked Kay because it gave him a "sexual thrill"

the culprit was arrested later that day. A local newspaper[4] said the "hunt for a young negro man dressed in GI clothes who had been terrorizing some of the women in Marin City" had ended when Bryant confessed to several rapes and attempted rapes.

Two weeks earlier, for instance, a "negro soldier" had climbed through a window in a Marin City apartment, the paper reported, and throttled a woman. She woke up and screamed so loudly that he was frightened away. Bryant admitted that he'd also climbed through the window of another apartment in Marin City the previous December, threatened the woman there with a knife, and then raped her. Four weeks later he entered another apartment through an open window and raped another woman.

McManimie, who was Hamilton Field's assistant commercial transportation officer, identified Bryant to police. She was "sure beyond any question of a doubt" that Bryant was the man she had seen, she told them. Because at first the police thought the would-be rapist might be a black serviceman, McManimie had spent seven hours checking out 475 black troops in the overseas negro squadron, Squadron TC1, and Squadron C. McManimie and Balmer then attended an identity parade with "some colored men" and viewed pictures of convicted black and white sex criminals in the San Rafael sheriff's office. When she saw Bryant, who was casually chewing gum, "cold chills ran over her".[5] "I know that is the man," she said.

Balmer, whose bedroom was directly opposite Kay's, told police that she'd gone to bed about midnight after locking up. About ten to three in the morning, she thought she'd heard voices from Kay's room and got up. "I looked into Captain Summersby's room and saw a negro man standing by the head of her bed...Captain Summersby was calling 'Cynthia'. I said 'Oh my God, get out'...At this time she was

---

[4] Sausalito News, 20 February 1947, Marion Bryant Arrested On Rape Charge
[5] FBI report 70-843 of 21 August 1947

making noises that sounded like strangling noises." Balmer immediately ran for the telephone in the hall and Bryant raced past her out of the building. Kay followed her friend but "collapsed on the floor outside her room".

In her statement,[6] Kay – a "recent transferee" to Hamilton Field [7] – told the FBI that she'd gone to bed alone about mid-night on 11 February. A few hours later, "I awoke and felt someone choking me. My room was dark. I felt two hands on my throat. I couldn't see who was choking me. The person choking me was holding my throat very tightly and I was losing consciousness very fast. I tried to move but I couldn't. I don't know if the person choking me was on or off the bed. I pretended that I had lost consciousness and relaxed. The person choking me relaxed their grip. I was then able to scream. I called 'Cynthia'." When Balmer switched on the light, Kay "saw a negro standing in the doorway to my room". She then lapsed into unconsciousness.

McManimie, whose room was upstairs, heard someone screaming and ran downstairs. She saw Kay lying near the stairs, "blood dripping on the front of her pyjamas, and she was having a hard time trying to talk and she kept trying to get up".[8] Immediately after the assault, Kay's mouth was bleeding because she had bitten her tongue during the attack.[9] "As a result of this choking, my tongue was bitten and bruised, and bothered me for a week," said Kay. "My eyes were bloodshot for three weeks and the right side of my face was bruised. My throat was also bruised for some time. In fact, there still is a mark from this on the left side of my neck."

Bryant was charged with entering a building on a military base with intent to commit rape, and bail was set at $10,000. Initially he told police that Williams had gone to

---

[6] 21 April 1947
[7] FBI teletype, 13 February 1947
[8] FBI report, 21 August 1947
[9] FBI report 70-843 of 21 August 1947

the base with the intention of murdering a WAC officer, but before long he withdrew that claim. Following an unsuccessful attempt to escape from San Rafael county jail, Bryant was handed over to the federal authorities on 23 April for trial. He was indicted by a federal grand jury on 7 May.

Bryant's first trial, in May and June 1947, was held before federal judge Michael J Roche. The Waterford-born lawyer was chief judge of the Northern District of California from 1948 to 1958, during which he presided over the trial of 'Tokyo Rose'. When the FBI decided not to produce the details of the latent fingerprints at Bryant's trial, defence attorney George Anderson argued that the Government was suppressing evidence. He asked why the prosecution had not introduced Kay's original statement in which she said that she'd "scratched and clawed" [10] at her attacker's face – though no scratches were found on Bryant's body.

Anderson also brought up the racial question and even referred to the southern accent of Assistant US Attorney Joseph Karesh. (Karesh, a former rabbi, was later appointed a Superior Court judge in San Francisco and was the judge in the 1978 trial of Black Panther Huey Newton.) Bryant also claimed that his confession had been beaten out of him, and the Daily People's World [11] newspaper showed an "antagonistic attitude" in its reports of the trial. [12] Bryant's trial went on for eight days but, in the end, despite deliberating for seven hours, the jury of eight men and four women could not agree on a verdict. Judge Roche refused to acquit Bryant and ordered a retrial. FBI director J Edgar Hoover later assured a concerned woman from Louisiana that any ideas she might have about the FBI disregarding Bryant's civil rights were "completely without foundation". [13]

---

[10] Daily People's World report
[11] Allegedly a Communist paper
[12] US Dept of Justice memo, 23 August 1947
[13] Letter 8 December 1947

In Bryant's second trial, which began in San Francisco on 26 August, the prosecution introduced the fingerprint evidence, producing an expert who claimed that the latent fingerprint was made by Bryant's left index finger. Later, Bryant's defence counsel applied to withdraw from the case because of an unspecified "disagreement" with his client. The motion was denied and, on 8 September, after retiring for three hours, the jury found Bryant guilty. Judge Louis E Goodman [14] sentenced him to 15 years' imprisonment in McNeil Island, Washington State for the "particularly brutal" [15] attempted rape. [16] He was given five years each on two charges of burgling the WAC quarters with intent to commit rape, all sentences to run concurrently.

At first, the army "was desirous of keeping the case confidential, as Captain Kathleen Summersby, a WAC officer, was the victim of this assault. This individual was formerly the driver for General Eisenhower over seas". [17] But Kay's name leaked out when the trial began and, because of her previous assignments, the trials eventually received "considerable publicity", adding even further to Kay's woes.

---

[14] Chief judge of the Northern District of California from 1958 until his death in 1961
[15] US Attorney letter, 9 September 1947
[16] Sausalito News, 11 September 1947
[17] USG office memo, 14 June 1947

LAST WORDS

Three months after the attempted rape, Kay wrote to Ike[1] and told him: "If ever you have a moment, I should love to hear from you." Ike's reply referred to an April visit by Kay's mother, whom he had met in Washington. "I know that your mother's visit must be a real treat for you both," he said. Ike also mentioned that 'Tex' Lee had called his new son 'Dwight David Eisenhower Lee'. "Laugh that off," he added.

But after her shocking experience, Kay wasn't in a laughing mood. She decided to leave the US army. On 30 July 1947, she was discharged as a WAC[2] and, after a six-week holiday with her mother in Los Angeles, she flew back to NY to relax as an American civilian. She slept late, lunched with friends, shopped for clothes, had her hair done, went to cocktail and dinner parties and then danced all night. At one party, she met Wall Street broker Reginald Heber Morgan, her future husband. He asked her to marry him, but he was already married so the wedding had to be postponed until he could get a divorce.

Ike wrote to Kay at the Commodore Hotel in New York[3] thanking her for advising him of the change in her wedding plans but he was "most sorry to say that it is absolutely impossible for me to come to New York at any time during that particular period. Actually, I am to go into the hospital at that time for my annual check-up and will be there several days. This will further complicate my schedule and already it is so congested that I have had to break a number of engagements for late November and early December, two of which involved a New York trip". Ike wished Kay and her new husband "every possible happiness", and said he would "never lose the intense desire to see everything work out for

---

[1] From the HQ of the 4th Air Force, Hamilton Field, 9 May 1947
[2] US Dept of Justice naturalisation form, 16 January 1951
[3] Letter 12 November 1947

the best for you and those close to you". He signed the letter "Cordially, DE". In a PS at the end of the letter, Ike asked: "Why don't you get married on your birthday?[4] That would make both dates easy for your husband to remember!!! D".

By now, however, Kay was having second thoughts about leaving the WACs. In a letter from the Hotel Webster on West 45th Street, New York,[5] she told Air Force Secretary W Stuart Symington Jr that she "would very much like to get back into the Army and wonder if there is some way that you could suggest that I could be recalled to active duty in the armed forces". Kay said she had dropped by Symington's office the previous day to apologise for not writing to thank him for bringing her up to New York (from Washington). She said that, the day after Symington left, she had suffered a "nasty accident in New York, cut my leg very badly" and was confined to her hotel room. The stitches had now been removed so she could get around again. In an accompanying document, she said she was commissioned as a WAC lieutenant on 21 November 1944.[6] She had returned to the United States in November 1946, transferred to the Air Forces and been assigned to Hamilton Field in January 1947 as assistant public relations officer. After the attempted rape, she had requested to be declared surplus to requirements in May 1947 "on compassionate grounds" (about the time she wrote to Ike), and was finally discharged from the Army in July 1947.

In response, Symington wrote back[7] thanking Kay for her note. "You surely seem to have your share of troubles. I hope that cut did not destroy the excellent contour," he said. The Air Force Secretary said he was "looking into that matter" and assured Kay that "it would be good to have you back with us". The same day, Symington wrote to Ike enclosing the letter from Kay and his reply, which he said spoke for

---

[4] 23 November
[5] 12 December 1947
[6] Her US naturalisation form said she was commissioned a day earlier
[7] Letter 26 December 1947

themselves.[8] "I met this girl in the summer of 1946 in Berlin when some of us went through and think she is great," he said. "I am sending all this data to our General Counsel as she [Kay] said she had about the roughest time I have heard of lately and if there is any thought you have about how we could get her back, I would appreciate it. It isn't any fun seeing somebody in trouble." However, if the new Chief-of-Staff did anything about Symington's letter, Kay did not rejoin the WACs.

On 27 December 1947, Ike sent another letter to Kay's mother, signed "Ike Eisenhower", with typewritten New Year's greetings, adding in a handwritten postscript, "Heard you were ill – hope you're better now." Kay herself started working for Tex McCreary at the end of 1947, but her circumstances were to change again in 1948, as her youngest sister Sheila, who was working for the Geological Survey, died suddenly in England[9] resulting in her 68-year-old mother having a nervous breakdown.

On 31 May 1948, Kay wrote again to Ike[10] saying: "I have been meaning to write to you for months, but I have had so much worry and trouble lately that it has been difficult to get down to letter writing. My youngest sister passed away very suddenly a few weeks ago in London. She had been ill, but we all thought she would pull through. Her death has been a great shock to me. Now Kul has had a complete break-down, so naturally I am worried to death. Then again I have had a lot of trouble with my book, the guy who was helping me turned out to be useless, so I had to get rid of him, have got somebody now who is really good." Kay said she had never found out what exactly happened about the Army. "When I think how stupid I have been over everything." Kay said she had got "most of my things from the West coast", adding: "When you have some spare time I should love to see you,

---

[8] Letter 26 December 1947 signed 'Stuart'
[9] She was buried in Kensal Green cemetery in London (Cork Examiner, 6 May 1948)
[10] Typed letter from c/o ES Travers, 22 East 69th Street, New York

also want to ask your advice regarding a number of things."
After some personal news, Kay signed off: "Kindest regards.
Affectionately, Kay".

Ike replied the next day in a typed letter signed "With
kindest regards and the very best of wishes",[11] saying how
distressing it was to learn of the tragedies in Kay's family. He
"deeply" sympathised on the death of her sister and added
that her mother's breakdown "must add immeasurably to
your burdens". But he added that he was "somewhat
astonished to learn that you were in New York working on a
book". He thought she had rejoined the WACs "some
months ago", but she had a "fine adviser" in George Bye,
whom he had met only briefly. (Bye was also the agent for
Henry Morgenthau.) In what seemed to be a snub, Ike said
there was little possibility of meeting Kay: "I can scarcely
estimate when there might arise an opportunity for you to
come past the office. The days are an unending series of
conferences and work, and within a very few days I must
take over direct responsibility for administration.[12] My time
is practically solidly booked through June and July, and in
August I hope to take a trip to the west. It has been a fight to
keep at least one afternoon a week free for golf." Six days
later, Ike took over from Nicholas Murray Butler as
president of Columbia University, a college with 30,000
students in New York City.

Kay continued to work on her first book, Eisenhower was my
Boss (in which she made no mention of their affair),
recalling her work for Ike from 1942 to 1945.[13] The
publishers were initially unsure about the title of the book.
One of the suggestions was: I was Eisenhower's Girl Friday.
But when the suggestion was put to Ike, he vehemently

---

[11] 1 June 1948
[12] Of Columbia University in New York
[13] Her friend Kathy Harriman said: "As peace returned many underlings
of the war leaders sprang into print, I felt they abused their wartime
privilege (& luck) of being on hand as history was made" (10 December
2001)

disagreed. In a letter to Bye,[14] Ike said: "I had never heard of such an expression as 'Eisenhower's Girl Friday' until I saw it in your original letter. It has struck me unfavourably and I still believe that some other title would be more accurate and more descriptive. I do not understand, for example, why my name has to appear in the title." Ike suggested calling the book 'A Wac in SHAEF'.

Two days later, following letters from George Bye and Kay's publisher about the title of her book, Ike wrote again to Kay.[15] "The suggestion they made seemed a bit out of line and I informed them to this effect. You know, of course, I wish you the best of luck in this publishing venture; but since these people asked me for my honest opinion, I had to give it to them." He signed off: "With best of luck, Cordially, DE". When the book was eventually published in the autumn of 1948, Kay's mother insisted that Ike had approved it and there was "nothing cheap at all about it...Thank goodness, the English is good".[16] Others disagreed. "If American generals were in the habit of confiding in women car drivers and secretaries...then their characters must slump in the eyes of the world," said the military correspondent of The Sunday Times. "One can only hope that much of the book is untrue."[17] As well as having her first book ghost written, Kay began hanging around Columbia University in New York, in the hopes of meeting Ike. Eventually she bumped into him. Flustered, she lied that she'd come to see the sister of an English friend, but Ike replied: "Kay, it's impossible. There's nothing I can do."

When the book was finally published, Kay sent Ike a copy. In a letter acknowledging receipt,[18] he said: "Dear Kay: I have just got around to opening the package that contained your book. Thank you very much for your thoughtfulness. Leisure

---

[14] Letter to George T Bye, 535 Fifth Avenue, New York, 26 July 1948
[15] 28 July 1948
[16] Chicago Tribune, 20 December 1948, p 25
[17] The Times of India, 12 December 1948
[18] 30 September 1948

time is no [sic] nearly non-existent that I scarcely ever get to read but will seek an early opportunity to go through your account of the war. I have never gotten to read, completely, any book of the war except the one by General DeGuingand [sic],[19] but possibly it will be different after I get through this hectic winter." The letter was signed "Cordially, DE". However, he later told Harry Butcher that he "never got to read Kay Summersby's book except for the first and last chapters". He said that a serialisation of the book by Look magazine led to a "hew [sic] and cry" and "the result was not pleasant for me".

After publication of the book, Kay travelled around the United States with the Tynan Travel Bureau lecturing[20] on her experiences during the war. [21] The book was also serialised in a number of US newspapers. Despite their disagreement over the book title, Kay wrote a letter to Ike at Christmas[22] wishing him "a happy Christmas and lots of good wishes for the new year". Months later, Kay attended a talk Ike gave in New York to the Fellowship of United States-British Comrades. Though she sat far back in the audience, the New York Times reported that she was there and that she hadn't spoken to Ike afterwards. That summer, she spent two months in Ireland, Scotland and England with her mother[23] and seeing her cousins in Inish Beg.[24] She left New York on 7 July 1949 on an American Overseas Airways plane to London and cruised back from Southampton aboard the SS America on 20 October, arriving in New York six days later. On her eventual return to the US, she went clubbing almost every night (with Telek) to the Stork, 21, El Morocco

---

[19] Operation Victory, C Scribner's Sons, 1947
[20] She charged £100 per lecture (Eisenhower's driver was Irishman (sic), Irish Times, 3 August 1956)
[21] US Dept of Justice file 7 775 322, 10 March 1950
[22] 17 December 1948
[23] At 26 Gledstanes Road, Baron's Court, London W14
[24] Irish Independent, 20 July 1949

and the Copacabana. The dog "got her in places where she couldn't have gone alone".[25]

That summer, Ike was very sick.[26] Sent by his doctors from Washington to Key West, he spent 10 days without solid food or even cigarettes. Afterwards, he decided to give up smoking completely. "If I had lived for ten days without a cigarette, I could get along without them for another ten days, ten years, or ten decades," he said. Later, when Ike visited London with Mamie, Kay wrote to them at the Dorchester inviting them to drinks at her mother's, but received no reply. A few days later, a young major came to her mother's house on the pretext that Ike had asked him to take Kay out for a drink. "Kay, it's impossible," he said. "The general really is on a tight leash. He is not his own master."

Back in the United States in 1950, Kay started a "very good job" with Bergdorf-Goodman, a luxury department store based on Fifth Avenue in Manhattan. But there was continued interest in her relationship with Eisenhower. Ike realised that "everyone phone call I made or received was monitored from beginning to end", but he was sceptical about Harry Butcher's report in a personal letter on 16 October 1950 that 15 businessmen were putting up $1,000 each to tap Kay's phone to check whether she and Ike were still seeing one another. There had been a suggestion that Kay and Ike met in a friend's New York apartment and "trysted for the final time".[27]

At the end of 1950, on 16 December, Ike was named Supreme Allied Commander of the North Atlantic Treaty Organisation and given operational command of US forces in Europe. This involved travel all around Europe, but Mamie was determined that they should have roots in the US, so they bought a 190-acre farm in Gettysburg, the site of

---

[25] Chicago Tribune, 27 October 1948
[26] Chicago Tribune, 19 April 1953
[27] New York magazine, 7 May 1979, p 69. The chief telephonist at the White House was sacked "because she had been a confidante of Mamie's over the Kay Summersby affair" (Sunday Independent, 9 February 1975)

a major battle during the American Civil War. Kay sent Ike a Christmas card from her home at 155 East 49th Street, New York, and Ike responded the day after his arrival in Paris: "I should have replied earlier to your Season's greetings card but work and travel intervened."[28] Kay finally acquired US citizenship on 19 February 1951.[29]

Meanwhile, Ike rejected requests from Republicans and Democrats (including President Truman[30]) to run for president in 1948. As an all-American hero with no political baggage, Eisenhower could run for either party. "Cosy, not austere or full of airs",[31] he was "not a true liberal," according to his brother Milton, though he thought "along progressive lines".[32] Ike told VC Dickinson of California that he had "always felt that I should completely abstain from partisan politics".[33] But, surprised by the strength of the 'Draft Eisenhower' movement and moved by the film Serenade to Ike in Paris, Ike allowed his name to go forward as a Republican candidate in the first presidential primary of 1952.

On 11 March, Eisenhower won the New Hampshire primary against "Mr Republican" Robert Taft by 50 per cent to 38 per cent, taking all of the Republican delegates. Despite Ike's oft-repeated assertion – "Christ on the mountain, I'm a military man, not a politician" – he retired from active service on 31 May 1952 and formally accepted the Republican Party nomination for US President five days later. He comfortably beat the Democratic candidate, Adlai Stevenson, being elected the 34th President of the United States in 1952 with votes which included that of then-US

---

[28] He arrived on 1 January 1952
[29] Petition 593786, certificate 6916964
[30] "General Eisenhower is the best legacy Harry Truman could leave": Life magazine, 12 April 1948
[31] 2004 interview with Fanny Hughill
[32] Life magazine, 9 November 1942
[33] Letter 13 September 1950

citizen Kay Summersby (despite her insistence that she didn't "know anything about politics"[34]).

In the meantime, magistrate Hyman Bushel married Kay to 47-year-old stockbroker Reginald TH Morgan in the apartment of their friend, Joseph T Parsons, on 20 November 1952.[35] In his last recorded letter to Kay almost four weeks after the wedding, congratulating her on her marriage to Morgan, Ike said: "It was good to hear from you, particularly such happy tidings! Congratulations to the lucky groom, and to both of you my very best wishes for your continuing happiness."

Morgan had already been married twice and had divorced his second wife only in early 1952. He and Kay had an "extended honeymoon" in St Croix in the US Virgin Islands – but less than six years later, she obtained a divorce in Alabama on the grounds of Morgan's "cruelty".[36] After the divorce, Kay returned to costume designing, working for CBS-TV's Calucci's Department[37] and was subsequently the "fashion co-ordinator for the Columbia Broadcasting Corporation".[38]

Ike was elected US President for a second term in 1956, despite suffering a mild heart attack in September 1955 after playing golf in Denver. Kay called to see him at the White House but was later told "Don't contact him again." Ike referred to Kay's difficulties in his personal diary. "'I heard today that my valued secretary is in dire straits,' Eisenhower wrote one day in his dairy [sic]. 'I trust she pulls herself together...She is Irish and tragic'."[39]

In 1956, Ike was diagnosed with bowel obstruction (Crohn's disease) and had to have an operation. In November 1957,

---

[34] Chicago Tribune, 23 September 1952, p 10

[35] Morgan already had four children (Irish Times, 3 August 1956)

[36] 12 March 1958, certificate 2274

[37] James Coco played the supervisor of a New York office infatuated with his secretary

[38] p 6, Cork Examiner, 24 May 1961

[39] Tulsa World, 28 May 1995

he suffered a slight stroke. He returned to work after just three days, even though his speech had not fully recovered. Kay wrote to him when her mother died, but he did not respond. Telek eventually died in 1959 at the age of 17. In 1966, Ike was in hospital for 15 days having gallstones removed. Between April and August 1968, he had four heart attacks and 14 cardiac arrests. Ike's heart deteriorated rapidly from 26 March and he died at 12.25pm on 28 March 1969 in the Walter Reed Army Hospital in Washington. [40]

"I felt relieved when he died. He had suffered too long," said Kay. She said that it would be "indelicate and inappropriate" to say more about Ike than she had already said in Eisenhower Was My Boss. "Weren't you in love with Ike?" asked reporters. "Yes, I was in love with him," said Kay, "and so was everybody else who had anything to do with him. He had a quick temper, but he was a forgiving man and a fair man."[41] But one of Kay's ghost writers, Sigrid Hedin, insisted that Kay's affair with Eisenhower had lasted for several years. "Everybody knew that Ike was crazy about Kay. I said, 'Kay, were you in love with Ike?' She wouldn't answer, she just said, 'He was the catch of the world.' Hedin said the couple were "living in a goldfish bowl" but "I think Kay probably felt she was going to marry him," said Hedin.[42]

After being diagnosed with liver cancer, Kay started work on her ghost-written autobiography "Past Forgetting: My Love Affair with Dwight D Eisenhower".[43] "I feel free to talk about it now," declared Kay in her second book. Ike had been dead for seven years at that stage. "The general is dead. I am dying. When I wrote 'Eisenhower was my boss'[44] in 1948, I omitted many things, changed some details, glossed over others to disguise as best I could the intimacy that had grown between General Eisenhower and me. It was better

---

[40] A Review of the Late General Eisenhower's Operations
[41] The Bakersfield Californian, 10 February 1974
[42] People magazine, 11 July 1977, Vol. 8 No. 2
[43] Express Newspapers bought the right to pre-publication extracts (Sunday Independent, 13 February 1977)
[44] Dedicated to "Kul and one other"

that way," she said. "But times have changed. I do not believe that anyone today will construe our relationship as shameful."

Hospitalised in New York in 1973, she moved to a cottage in Southampton in Long Island two weeks before her death.[45] She died at the age of 66 just before her second book was published, leaving quarter of a million dollars and the continuing mystery of her relationship with Ike.

After Kay's book was published, Ike's son John published a selection of edited letters from Ike to his wife. *Letters to Mamie*[46] was intended "to demolish stories of [Ike's] alleged unfaithfulness with another woman [Kay]."[47] The commentary was written by John, who by then had been appointed US ambassador to Belgium. "[Kay] was perky and she was cute," said John.[48] "Whether she had any designs on the old man and the extent to which he succumbed, I just don't know." He accepted that nobody could be certain that something did not happen.[49]

Mamie died in Washington nearly five years after Kay, on 1 November 1979. She and Ike are buried together with their first son, Icky, at the Eisenhower Centre in Abilene.

As Ike himself once said: "Human relations are governed by neither fixed rules nor logic." But Kay no longer cared about rules or logic. She was finally at peace. Her ashes were sent back to her native West Cork to be scattered by her younger brother Seamus on the family grave outside the church of Rath and the Islands, a mile and a half from Inish Beg.[50] The MacCarthy Morrogh family grave – originally the grave of Kay's father and grandfather – is today marked by a large

---

45 On 20 January 1975
46 319 letters written between 1942 and 1945, Doubleday & Co, February 1978
47 Star-News, 29 January 1978
48 LA Times, 28 May 1995
49 Kentucky New Era, 15 December 1977
50 Her ashes were not "spread over Inish Beg", as the Cork Examiner reported (p 5, 21 January 1977)

Celtic cross and surrounded by a low concrete plinth topped by a decorative iron double railing. The original inscription reads:

In loving memory

James MacCarthy Morrogh

Born 29th April 1834

Died 11th May 1916

And his son

Lt Col DF MacCarthy Morrogh CMG

Late of the Royal Munster Fusiliers

(The date of birth has been erased)

Died 15th May 1932

Requiescat in pace

A second stone was added at the foot of the cross after Kay's death. It says:

Kathleen MacCarthy Morrogh

Born 23rd November 1908

Died 20th January 1975

Later, Kay's brother was buried in the same grave, as the stone testifies:

James MacCarthy Morrogh

Born 19th January 1912

Died 1st February 1994.

And so the story ended where it began, in west Cork.

DID THEY OR DIDN'T THEY?

As this book said right at the start, only Kay and Ike know how far their relationship went. Certainly it is true that the relationship between the pair was much more intense than the usual relationship between a general and his driver, but that is not to say that it was consummated. But many of the couple's colleagues, and most of the soldiers, thought that they were lovers. The alleged cable to Marshall, which has since disappeared, would show beyond all doubt that Ike intended to divorce Mamie and marry Kay.

Ever since the war, the controversy has raged, though most observers take the view that the relationship was consummated. In the 1976 book Bodyguard of Lies, author Anthony Cave-Brown wrote that, in 1942, when Ike first arrived in London, he "met and formed a relationship with his driver, Kay Summersby, an Irishwoman in her early thirties who had been a model and a film extra before joining the British Auxiliary Territorial Service (ATS) as a private. Mrs Summersby was divorced from her first husband and had met and was engaged to an American colonel when Eisenhower appeared on the scene. The colonel was later killed in action in Tunisia, where Mrs Summersby was sent when Eisenhower established his headquarters in Algiers. She became his confidential secretary, chauffeuse, hostess and companion, remaining a member of his 'official family' throughout the North African campaigns."[1]

[Although that paragraph contains the essence of the relationship, Kay did not join the ATS, but the MTC. She was not divorced or engaged when she met Ike. Dick Arnold was then only a major and he was killed while clearing mines in North Africa.]

---

[1] pp 536-537

Cave-Brown said that Kay followed Ike from Africa to London when he became Supreme Commander for Neptune and Overlord and, although she was a British citizen, "he arranged that she be given a commission" in the WACs. "She spent much time at Eisenhower's quarters at Telegraph Lodge, was seen frequently at his side on important social occasions and in due course Eisenhower wrote to Marshall asking his advice about whether he might divorce his wife Mamie and marry Mrs Summersby."

The closeness of the relationship made Kay a security hazard, as author Nigel Cawthorne wrote: "General Eisenhower himself was considered a security risk because, with his wife back in America, he was having an affair with the ATS driver Kate Summersby, an Irish divorcee. This could have left him open to blackmail" (though she wasn't in the ATS and she wasn't known as 'Kate'!)[2]

Cave-Brown related: "Despite official disapproval and embarrassment, Eisenhower did persist in the relationship, and because Churchill especially feared the consequences if it became known to the Germans – particularly Goebbels – that Eisenhower had taken a mistress, the affair was one of the most closely-guarded secrets of the pre-invasion period."

Cave-Brown wrote that the senior staff at SHAEF "discussed most secret matters quite openly" in front of Kay and she used to visit the American Bar at the Savoy and dine occasionally with US journalist Frank McGee, who became infatuated with her. The author said that McGee "disapproved of the relationship with Eisenhower". General Beetle Smith, who knew of the "triangle", as Cave-Brown called it, begged Ike to be cautious, but Kay nevertheless remained by Ike's side until July 1945 – or even later. It's clear that Ike, as Chief-of-Staff of the US Army in Washington, had considered his future and had decided to ditch Kay in 1945, maybe after contacting colleagues like General Marshall. Maybe he was more concerned about his

---

[2] p 73, Fighting Them on the Beaches

future political career. In any case, he had Kay posted as far away from him as possible, to California (where she was almost strangled and raped).

But their friendship (or relationship) survived the geographic separation, as the subsequent correspondence shows. Whether Ike continued the physical relationship, as suggested by Butch's 1950 letter, is a matter of conjecture.

Only Ike and Kay knew the truth.

REFERENCES

The Eisenhower Library, Abilene, Kansas, USA

The Imperial War Museum, Kennington, London SE1 6HZ, England

King's College library, The Strand, London WC2R 2LS, England

The British Library, Euston, London NW1 2DB, England

The George C Marshall Foundation, Lexington, Virginia, USA

Harry S Truman Library and Museum, Independence, Missouri, USA

Past Forgetting: My Love Affair With Dwight D Eisenhower by Kay Summersby Morgan (1977, Simon & Schuster)

Eisenhower Was My Boss by Kay Summersby (1948, Prentice-Hall)

My Three Years With Eisenhower by Harry C Butcher (1946, Simon & Schuster)

Sgt Mickey and General Ike by Michael James McKeogh and Richard Lockridge (1946, GP Putnam's Sons)

at ease: Stories I Tell To Friends by Dwight D Eisenhower (1967, Doubleday & Co)

The Patton Papers 1940-1945 by Martin Blumenson (1974, Houghton Mifflin)

Patton: A Genius for War by Carlo D'Este (HarperCollins, 1995)

War Diaries 1939-1945, Field Marshal Lord Alanbrooke (2001, Weidenfeld & Nicolson)

Bodyguard of Lies by Anthony Cave-Brown (1976, WH Allen & Co Ltd)

Siegfried, The Nazis' Last Stand by Charles Whiting (1982, Stein & Day)

Fighting Them on the Beaches by Nigel Cawthorne (2002, Arcturus Publishing)

Eisenhower by Steven J Zaloga (2011, Osprey Publishing)

Churchill by Ashley Jackson (2011, Quercus)

Eisenhower in War and Peace by Jean Edward Smith (2012, Random House)

The War Between the Generals by David Irving (1981, Allen Lane)

Rommel, The Desert Fox by Desmond Young (1950, Fontana/Collins)

Behind Enemy Lines: WWII Allied/Axis Propaganda by Edward Boehm (1989, The Wellfleet Press)

Burke's Irish Family Records (Buckingham: Burke's Peerage & Gentry, 2007)